Foreword

As one who has continually tried to search out useful materials in the relatively new field of intercultural and cross-cultural affairs, I have long been impressed by the Brigham Young University Culturgram series. I have both marvelled that they have been developed for so many countries and deplored the fact that they are available for so few.

When they were first produced little else was available. Now with more resources on the market, I still find that when I try to answer a wide range of questions about what to study and what to read about a particular country Culturgrams are still among the first good resource to be mentioned. And I am constantly amazed to learn that more people already know of Culturgrams than of any other single country-specific material on the market. In ten short years, Culturgrams have taken their rightful place on the still too sparse shelf of reliable area studies readings.

I like Lynn Tyler's term "people maps" to describe Culturgrams. Few other materials present a country's people—with their unique values, customs, and cultural assumptions—as well as Culturgrams do. Simple, direct, and brief, they pack a lot of valuable information into an amazingly small package.

The thing that first attracted me to Culturgrams was their obvious and unabashed modesty. They clearly had a very specific goal. They do not claim to present the definitive or final word on any culture. Yet, in a brief reading, they can increase almost anyone's knowledge of a country and its people many-fold.

The care with which Culturgrams are developed and field tested before they are released to the general public is unique. Dozens of country experts have checked them for accuracy and suggested changes, and they have gone through countless editings for precision in language and sensitivity to total impact. Such thoroughness should be the standard for all publications.

As an additional contribution to the field, I was impressed by Brigham Young University's willingness to share their methodology for developing culture-sensitive materials via its *How to Develop and Use Culturgrams*. This was a generous thing to do and its complexity demonstrated abundant proof that it is never a simple task to produce a simple product. I highly recommend this manual to all developers of cross-cultural materials if they are not already familiar with it.

The people behind the conceptualization and creation of Culturgrams have always made it very clear that they consider their work to represent only a minor contribution to the most basic and initial stage of the ever-changing intercultural field. The field itself is still in its initial stage—measured by their standards and mine. The Culturgram series has played and will continue to play a major part in its development.

The publication of this volume represents another stage in the use of Culturgrams. With the complete collection available in this two volume series, additional thousands should become more aware of the series and their important contribution in preparing Americans to make a better impression when they study about and interact with people from other cultures.

Robert Kohls, Executive Director
Washington International Center
Washington, DC

CULTURGRAMS:
The Nations Around Us

developed by the
David M. Kennedy Center
for International Studies
Brigham Young University

Ministry of Education, Ontario
Information Services & Resources Unit,
13th Floor, Mowat Block, Queen's Park,
Toronto   M7A 1L2

Volume II
Middle East, Asia, Africa, and Pacific Areas

About the Culturgram Series...

This book (volume II) includes the Culturgrams for the Middle East, Asia, Africa, and the Pacific Areas.

A related book (volume I) includes the Culturgrams for the nations of North and South America and Western and Eastern Europe.

These bound volumes of Culturgrams should be ordered from the Garrett Park Press, PO Box 190B, Garrett Park, MD 20896 (301/946-2553) at $14 prepaid or $15 if billed.

All Culturgrams currently available are also sold individual or in batches. To order individual or multiple copies of Culturgrams contact the Publications Services, David M. Kennedy Center for International Studies, Brigham Young University, 280 HRCB, Provo, UT 84602 (801/378-6528).

Do not call Brigham Young University regarding the bound volumes with Culturgrams, address those inquiries to the Garrett Park Press as specified above.

Copyright © 1988 Brigham Young University, David M. Kennedy Center for International Studies. V. Lynn Tyler, General Editor: Deborah L. Coon, Managing Editor and Marketing.

ISBN 0-912048-60-3

Library of Congress Catalog Card Number 88-080811

Table of Contents

Foreword
Introduction
Acknowledgements
Countries in order of their appearance

Algeria	New Zealand
Australia	Nigeria
China	Pakistan
Egypt	Philippines
Ethiopia	Samoa
Fiji	Saudi Arabia
Ghana	Singapore
Hong Kong	South Africa
India	Sri Lanka
Indonesia	Sudan
Iran	Syria
Israel, State of	Tahiti (French Polynesia)
Israel, and Occupied Territory	Taiwan, China
Japan	Tanzania
Jordan	Thailand
Kenya	Tonga
Korea, South	Turkey
Lebanon	Zaire
Lesotho	Zimbabwe
Malaysia	

Introduction

Since the first Culturgrams appeared 10 years ago, we have received thousands of inquiries about the set, its origin, and its usage. Perhaps the best way to introduce this book is to repeat the most commonly asked questions and respond to them.

How did the popular Culturgrams series develop?

In 1974, President Spencer W. Kimball of the Church of Jesus Christ of Latter-day Saints issued a challenge for members to take steps to build more effective bridges of understanding and friendship with people all over the world.

Brigham Young University was asked to contribute to this effort by inviting people from around 50 countries to "spend 15 minutes or so telling us what they think we most need to know about their country as a means of our better understanding each other." The reaction to these interviews and the widespread interest in the first published summaries of the research that followed provided the enthusiasm it took to sustain this series for the past ten years. This program, which has become more sophisticated and popular over the years, began in the BYU Language and Intercultural Research Center and was transferred in 1981 to the David M. Kennedy Center for International Studies.

What are Culturgrams?

Culturgrams have been called "people maps" as they summarize the unique customs, values, traditions, and lifestyles within a country. Written very simply, directly, and tightly they summarize in four pages such key elements of a nation and its culture as the following:

- Customary method of expressing greetings
- How to visit people in their homes
- Eating customs in the home and at restaurants
- Significance of gestures
- General attitudes of the people
- Population and its characteristics
- Language
- Religion
- Holidays, both religious and political
- Dating and marriage
- Normal business hours
- Diet and traditional foods
- Land and climate
- History and government
- Economy and its trends
- Education and literacy
- Transportation and communication
- Health
- Useful words and phrases
- Suggested readings
- Scale map of the country and its relationship to its continent

Culturgrams don't claim to produce experts on a country or its people. They can, and do, increase almost anyone's knowledge about a country and its people.

How many Culturgrams are there?

At present there are around 81 and the number grows each year. Existing Culturgrams are updated every two or three years. Volume I includes the Culturgrams for the countries of North and South America and Western and Eastern Europe. Volume II contains Culturgrams for countries of the Middle East, Asia, Africa, and Pacific Areas.

A writer's guide *How to Develop and Use Culturgrams* has helped this series more definitive and is available for the use of others developing materials sensitive to other cultures.

Who uses Culturgrams?

There are almost as many different types of users as there have been customers over the years. This list is illustrative, not exhaustive.

Teachers use Culturgrams to highlight cultural distinctions and to introduce the study of a country or region of the world.

Foreign student advisors and others working with international visitors use Culturgrams to gain their first insights into the cultures from which their visitors come.

Travelers use Culturgrams to develop an initial feel for the area and to learn recommended references for additional reading.

Teachers of English as a Foreign Language use Culturgrams in their classroom work to help students learn practical English while becoming more sensitive to things which distinguish one culture from another.

Business travelers use Culturgrams to become better prepared for business techniques and sensitive issues related to entertaining or being entertained.

Overseas development workers, Peace Corps Volunteers, missionaries, and community development specialists find Culturgrams helpful in training and orientation.

Libraries find Culturgrams a valuable addition to the relatively small body of easy to comprehend information on the cultures around us.

Acknowledgements

O. Leslie Stone and J. Thomas Fyans suggested that Brigham Young University ask visitors from abroad to describe their countries.

Justus Ernst, Ernest Wilkins, James Taylor, Max Rogers, John Carr, Irvin Neidegger, Spencer Palmer, Roger Dock, Stan Taylor, Joseph Stringham, Seymour Fersh, Robert Kaplan, Robert Kohls, Alice Smith, Beulah Rohlich, Robert Moran, David Hoopes, Diane Zeller, and many others helped to develop the concept of the Culturgrams and gather materials for the initial edition.

Lynn Jenson coordinated the Culturgram project aided by Gail Anderson Newbold and Pamela Jackson.

Jeffrey Marks, David Hatch, Paul Taylor, Marshall Witt, and Paula Knudsen Booth have worked on updating and revising Culturgrams over the years.

Michelle Moulton and Jeri Pace provided secretarial support.

Charles Bush and Melvin Smith of the BYU Humanities Research Center have assisted with computer technology.

Finally, the key to the Culturgrams has been the input from interviews, reports, and other direct contacts with international students, professors and returned Latter-Day Saints missionaries, visiting scholars, and those who used the early issues and made suggestions for their revision.

The process of revising and improving Culturgrams goes on daily. For this reason, suggestions from users are always welcome; see the address in the front of the book.

CULTURGRAM*

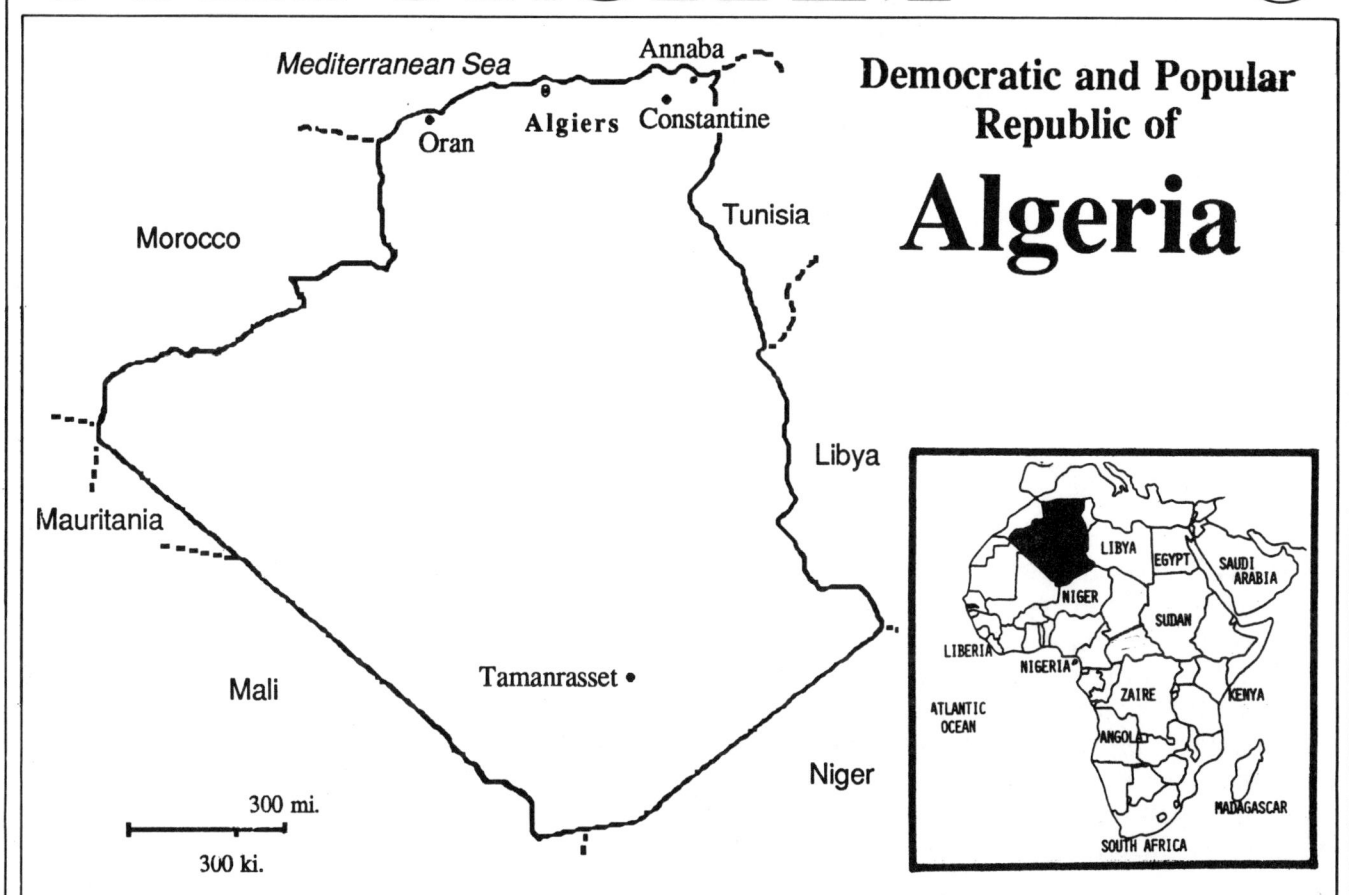

Democratic and Popular Republic of Algeria

CUSTOMS AND COURTESIES

Greetings: In Algeria, as throughout the Arab world, hospitality is a cultural keynote. This is especially true in Algerian cities, where Arabic custom is blended with equally warm Gallic (French) traditions. Greetings are genuinely cordial and open to friend and stranger alike; they are usually accompanied by a handshake, and frequently an embrace (between members of the same sex only). Anything less friendly in the way of a greeting is likely to be viewed as stand-offish, and first impressions are quite important in this part of the world.

Visiting: Visiting, whether for business or pleasure, is a social occasion in Algeria. During conversation, one should first spend considerable time discussing such things as the weather, health, or the latest news. When the formalities of small talk are over, the conversation should flow smoothly and logically to the topics at hand. One must always be careful not to discuss members of the opposite sex or the host's family, unless the host himself suggests the topic. One should never refuse refreshments, but may politely request a substitute if unable to eat or drink what is offered. If the visit is strictly for social purposes, it is customary to bring the host a small gift—food (but never alcohol) is appropriate under most circumstances.

*Culturgrams are briefings to aid understanding of, feeling for, and communication with other people. Culturgrams are condensations of the best information available. Your insights will be appreciated. If you have refining suggestions, please contact Brigham Young University David M. Kennedy Center for International Studies, Publication Services, 280 HRCB, Provo, Utah 84602 (801) 378-6528. Copyright © 1986. All rights reserved. Printed in the USA.

Eating: Although most Algerians now use western silverware, the visitor may still have occasion to eat a meal with the fingers in true Arabic style. As in all Moslem countries, only the fingers of the right hand should be used for eating. When seated with any group of people, take care that the soles of the feet or shoes do not show. Unlike many peoples, Algerians are complimented when you leave a little food on your plate, as this is a sign of the host's ability to more than adequately provide for his guests.

Gestures: Using the fingers to point at objects or people is generally considered impolite. As in all Moslem countries, separate use of the left hand should be avoided. When handing or receiving something from another person, use either both hands or the right hand only.

Personal Appearance: In the cities, western clothing is common for both men and women. Many Algerians (especially women), however, continue to wear traditional North African Moslem garb. The visitor should wear traditional and conservatively cut western clothing under all circumstances. Shorts, halter tops, or other abbreviated attire is definitely frowned on in Algeria and should not be worn publicly. Athletic clothing may be worn when participating in sports or recreation.

THE PEOPLE

General Attitudes: Algerians are a formal and traditional people, yet they are quite expressive and individualistic. One is expected to speak one's mind, yet do so in an inoffensive manner. Though Algerians greatly enjoy good conversation, being overly frank and direct in speech is considered very impolite. One never asks directly about another's private life or habits unless the other person brings up the topic. Expressiveness, courtesy, individualism, and formality are key attributes of the Algerian personality. In this strongly male-dominant society, sex roles are clearly and rigidly defined. While this may seem repressive to Westerners, it is not to the Algerians—male and female roles are simply different, and largely accepted by both sexes.

Population: Algeria's population of approximately 20.2 million is growing rapidly at a rate of 3.1% per year. Nearly 60% of the population is under the age of 20. About 66% of the people are city dwellers, and the population density is about 22 persons per square mile (58 in U.S.). About 84% of the population is Arab, while the Berbers, who mainly inhabit the mountainous and desert areas of the country, account for around 16%. Less than 1% is of French or European descent. Algiers, the capital, has a population of 2.2 million.

Language: Although Arabic is the official language, French is widely spoken in urban environments. Berber dialects are still spoken in many remote areas. Bi- or trilingualism is common.

Religion: Islam is the state religion and Algerians are 99% Sunni Moslem.

LIFESTYLE

The Family: The Algerian family is a very important, private, and male-dominated entity, often including 3 or more generations in the male line (grandparents, married sons and their wives, and unmarried children) under one roof. There is, however, a definite trend toward a smaller nuclear family unit. An Algerian's home is quite literally his castle, both in the city as well as in the county. An invitation to an Algerian home is an honor not to be taken lightly. One does not simply "visit" at will. Entertaining at home is highly formal and traditional.

Dating and Marriage: The western concept of dating is becoming increasingly common in urban areas. Traditionally, however, marriage represents the linking not just of individuals, but of families. Consequently, match-making is something of a family affair, and romantic love is seen as something that grows with time after marriage, not before.

Social and Economic Levels: While Algeria is a socialist nation, there is a small and wealthy elite, a large and growing business or middle class, and a very large lower class. Due largely to the egalitarian policies of the government concerning the distribution of national oil income, urban class distinctions are gradually becoming more a tradition and less an economic reality. The rural areas of the country, however, remain largely unaffected by socialist reform policies.

Diet: Urban cuisine can match the best in the world and has a strong Gallic flavor. Native Algerian cuisine is found in great variety in both city and rural environments. Popular are lamb and chicken dishes, stews, and pastas. *Couscous*, a pasta-like semolina cooked with lamb or chicken stew, is perhaps the most popular Algerian dish.

Recreation and Work: Recreation is largely a family activity and takes place primarily in the home. The workplace is totally distinct from recreational and family activities. Normal business hours are Saturday through Wednesday, 8:30 a.m. to noon, and 2:30 p.m. to 6:30 p.m.

Holidays: The Gregorian calendar is officially used in Algeria, but the everyday activities of the people are regulated by the lunar-based Islamic calendar. Thus, Friday (not Sunday) is the day of rest and worship, and Moslem Holy Days (which make up the bulk of observed holidays), vary in date from year to year. Ramadan, the fasting month, is ritually observed by most Algerians. National holidays are January 1, May 1, June 19, July 5, and November 1.

THE NATION

Land and Climate: Algeria, with an area of 919,595 square miles, is just over one-quarter the size of the continental United States, and is the world's tenth largest country. Approximately 90% of the population inhabits the northern coastal region called "the Tell." The central and southern parts of the country form part of the vast Sahara Desert, where only an occasional oasis can be found to support life. The Tell enjoys a mild Mediterranean climate and moderate rainfall, with a rainy season that extends from December to March. The Tell and the Sahara are separated by parallel ranges of the Atlas Mountains and the Haut Plateau.

History and Government: Algeria's earliest inhabitants were the Berbers, who still account for a significant minority of the population. The earliest important invaders were the Phoenicians, under whom the Carthaginian Empire in North Africa flourished (ca. 800 B.C. to 146 B.C.) until its destruction by the Romans. The region was held successively by the Romans and the Vandals until the Arab invasion of the middle 600s A.D. The present coastal cities of Algiers (2.2 million), Oran (633,000), Constantine (384,000), and Annaba (284,000) owe their development to the period of Arab conquest. From 1518 until 1830, Algeria was an integral part of the Ottoman Empire. In 1830 the country became a French-controlled territory, and ultimately, a department of the French Republic. Despite large-scale French colonization, a smoldering independence movement erupted into open warfare in 1954. After 8 years of bitter fighting, Algeria was granted independence on July 1, 1962. Fearing for their lives, nearly 1 million French and other European colonists were evacuated when the French Army withdrew. During the 1960s and 1970s, Algeria went through a trying period of adjustment and internal change, emerging as a firm socialist republic. Ultimate authority is vested in the National Assembly and local state assemblies (*wilayaat*). All citizens are members of local communes, which assume duties of political and economic control and direction at the local level.

Economy: Algeria's per capita income of $2,430 ($14,300 in U.S.) is relatively high for Africa, largely reflecting the national income from oil and petroleum products.

Agriculture employs approximately 31% of the labor force, but accounts for less than 10% of the gross national product. Once an exporter of food products, Algeria has been forced to import much of its food since becoming a socialist republic. Major exports include crude oil, petroleum products, natural gas, and wine, with the United States and Western Europe as major trading partners. Despite attempts at industrialization and major land reform, Algeria still faces wide-spread unemployment. Housing is one of Algeria's most pressing problems because of the high rate of population increase and the influx of people from rural areas to the cities.

Education: Algeria's educational system has grown remarkably in the last 20 years. Algeria's literacy rate is 46%. Schooling is free and compulsory to age 13. Education on all levels is still conducted mainly in French rather than Arabic, though a concerted effort is being made to alter this situation. The University of Algiers and newer universities in Oran and Constantine have managed to maintain a high level of instruction.

Health: Boiled water must be used even for brushing teeth, ice cubes, etc., and is supplied by major hotels. Food must be well cooked and served hot. Peel all fruit and vegetables before eating. Medical help is available in Algiers, but evacuation to Paris is recommended. For further medical information, contact International Health Consultants, PO Box 34582, Bethesda, MD 20817.

For Further Information

Because space is so limited in this *Culturgram* and needs are so varied, no suggested readings are included. We recommend a visit to your local library or bookstore. Check *Books in Print* and various cataloging systems for country-specific titles. Review *Encyclopedia Britannica* or similar comprehensive summaries. The U.S. government publishes *Country Profiles* which many libraries subscribe to. Computer searches (DIALOG, SDC, BRS, ISI) are now available at most major libraries. Contact the Embassy of Algeria, 2118 Kalorama Road, NW, Washington, D.C. 20008 or the Algerian National Tourist Office, 8 Rue du Docteur Saadane. The U.S. Embassy in Algeria is located at 4 Chemin Cherch Bachir Brahimi, Algiers.

How to Use This Culturgram

Quickly read the whole text as an overview. Then circle or give priority numbers to specific questions you have or ideas you want to pursue. Use the *Culturgram* as a guide to check on regional differences and current situations.

Maps

Culturgram maps are meant only as simple geographical orientations. Boundary representations are not necessarily authoritative. Different sources also vary spelling, transliterations, and accents.

Rev. 1/88

CULTURGRAM*

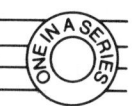

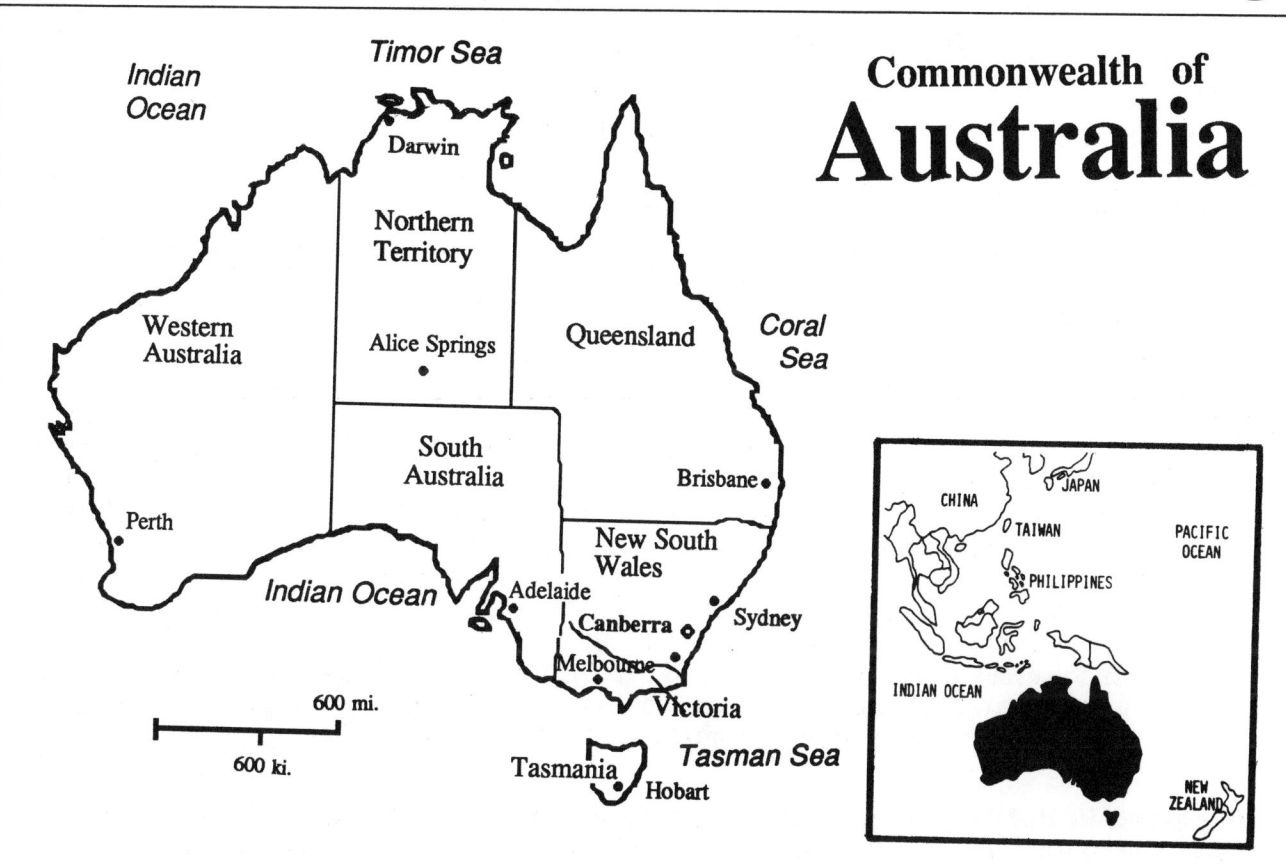

Commonwealth of Australia

CUSTOMS AND COURTESIES

Greetings: Australians will usually invite those they have just met to use their first names. They like to be called by their first names and greeted with a warm handshake. Men, however, should not shake hands with a woman unless she extends her hand first. A wave is an acceptable greeting from a distance. Men may use the term *mate* when referring to friends.

Visiting: When one visits a family, the host should be greeted in a warm and friendly manner at the door. A guest should not enter the home until invited to do so by the host. It is acceptable to take flowers for the hostess or a bottle of wine when invited for lunch or dinner. When departing, it is appropriate for the guest to shake hands with all the men present and thank the host or hostess for the hospitality and the meal.

Eating: The continental style of eating is common, with the fork in the left hand and the knife in the right. At a restaurant, a simple hand gesture will attract the waiter's attention. The bill is usually paid at the register after the meal. While tipping is not always necessary, it is often expected at fine restaurants, or if the service has been commendable. International credit cards are accepted at major restaurants and hotels.

Gestures: Rules of basic etiquette are strongly adhered to in Australia. Winking at women may be considered improper. Outward signs of familiarity, such as hugging, should be avoided. When yawning, one should to cover the mouth and excuse oneself. A clenched fist with raised thumb, as in the American hitchhiking sign, is a vulgar gesture.

---

*Culturgrams are briefings to aid understanding of, feeling for, and communication with other people. Culturgrams are condensations of the best information available. Your insights will be appreciated. If you have refining suggestions, please contact Brigham Young University David M. Kennedy Center for International Studies, Publication Services, 280 HRCB, Provo, Utah 84602 (801) 378-6528. Copyright © 1986. All rights reserved. Printed in the USA.

Traveling: The bus system is good in metropolitan areas. The driver notifies passengers of the fare to their destinations. Buses connect many outlying areas to shopping centers. Major cities have good suburban train systems; tickets are purchased at the station before departure. Taxis are rather scarce but can be hailed from the roadside or summoned by telephone. Sydney has a ferry system. Most Australian families have at least one car.

THE PEOPLE

General Attitudes: Australia is a very clean country and visitors are expected to meet Australian standards of cleanliness. There is a stiff fine for littering. Australians are easygoing and amiable, except perhaps, when religion or politics are discussed. Clubs and social groups are popular. Many men frequent the local pubs after work and on weekends. Men keep their emotions to themselves in public. Promptness is very important. Eye contact is important for showing real interest in a person. When conversing, Australians often gesture with their hands to emphasize and clarify.

Population: The population of Australia is approximately 15.7 million, and is growing at a rate of 1.3% annually (0.9% in U.S.). The population density rate is only 5 people per square mile (58 in U.S.). Approximately 75% of the people live in urban areas, one of the highest urbanization rates in the world. Over 40% of the people live in the 2 cities of Sydney and Melbourne. Over 98% of the people are Caucasian, having migrated from many parts of Europe. Before World War II, 95% of the people were of Anglo-Celtic stock. Since the war, however, heavy immigration from other countries has reduced this percentage to 60%. Today, Australia is a mosaic of many different nationalities, including Italian, Greek, Baltic, Yugoslavian, Dutch, German, Polynesian, and South American. Since 1975, more than 75,000 Indochinese refugees have migrated to Australia. Asians now account for about 1% of the population. The Aborigines are also a very small minority group. Approximately 50% of all Australians are under 30 years of age.

Language: English is the national language and is taught in all schools. Immigrant groups often continue to use their native languages, and radio programs are now broadcast in 52 different languages. Australians use many words and phrases uncommon to people from other English-speaking countries. Many also use a great deal of slang in conversation.

Religion: Approximately 76% of the people are nominal Christians, divided among the Anglican (36%), Roman Catholic (33%), and many other denominations. Immigrant religious groups account for about 5%.

LIFESTYLE

The Family: The average family has 2 to 3 children, although larger families are not uncommon. Average family size is 3.3 people, compared to 3.1 in the U.S. Although society is more family centered than it is in the U.S., Australian family life is similar to American family life. As in other parts of the world, there is an increasing number of single-parent families, and a large proportion of both fathers and mothers work. Teenagers are generally left on their own and become independent. Senior citizen communities, funded by church and community groups with government support, assist the elderly when they do not live at home. Service organizations also provide additional care. Day-to-day decisions are often made by the wife, with the husband and wife jointly making major financial and other family decisions.

Dating and Marriage: Western dating habits are also followed in Australia. Dating usually begins at age 15 or older. Dating in small groups is common. Movies, dancing, and socializing are the most popular activities. The average age for women to marry is 21, and for men just over 25. Church weddings are still common.

Social and Economic Levels: Although there are no major class distinctions, most people enjoy a relatively high standard of living. The average Australian home has 5 rooms. Australians have a life expectancy of 74 years.

Diet: Eating habits are similar to those in the United States. Fruits and vegetables are grown all year round. "Take-out" food establishments flourish. All varieties of fish, and other meat dishes are common. The main meal of the day is eaten in the evening.

Work Schedules: Most Australians work about 40 hours a week. Some work overtime in the evenings or on Saturdays. Businesses are open from 8:30 a.m. to 5:30 p.m. Monday through Friday, and from 9:00 a.m. to 12 noon on Saturday. One evening a week (usually Thursday) the shops are open until 9:00 p.m. in the cities. Some small shops and service stations stay open 7 days a week. Bank hours are generally shorter than they are in the U.S. (10:00 a.m. to 3:30 p.m.).

Recreation: Physical fitness and exercise are important to most Australians. Football (Australian rules), soccer, rugby, cricket, basketball, bicycling, tennis, lawn bowling, and swimming are all popular sports. People of every age spend much of their time in sports activities. Sportsmanship is very important and is often cheered, even in a losing team.

Holidays: Australia Day (January 26) commemorates the first European settlement in Australia. Other holidays are New Year's Day, Good Friday, Easter, Easter Monday, Anzac Day (or Veterans Memorial Day, April 25), Queen's Birthday (second Monday in June), Christmas, and Boxing Day (December 26). Labor Day, bank holidays, and holidays for local horse races vary from state to state.

THE NATION

Land and Climate: Australia is the sixth largest country in the world, approximately the same size as the continental U.S. It is the only country that occupies a complete continent. It is also the driest continent in the world. About one-third of the land is desert and another third is composed of poor-quality land. A long mountain range follows the east coast line with fertile farmland between the Pacific coast and the Great Dividing Range. The western slopes and plains are the location of the great wheat-producing areas of Australia, with cattle stations reaching to the edge of the barren interior desert. Summer is December through February—winter is June through August. The climate ranges from tropical in the north to temperate in the south.

History and Government: Aborigines were the only inhabitants when the Dutch discovered parts of the continent in 1623. Most of Australia was left largely undisturbed until 1770, when Captain James Cook took formal possession of the eastern coast for Britain. The British arrived in 1788 and penal colonies began in what has become modern-day Sydney, Hobart, and Brisbane. Many of the early settlers of Australia were prisoners or soldiers. Free settlements were founded in Melbourne, Adelaide, and Perth. With the discovery of gold in 1851, immigration of free men increased rapidly. In 1868, the practice of transporting convicts was curtailed. In 1901, the 6 colonies agreed to federate and became the Commonwealth of Australia. It is still a member of The Commonwealth, although a small yet strong anti-royalist feeling has developed in recent years. Independent and self-governing, Australia is composed of 6 federated states, the Australian Capital Territory, and the Northern Territory. The individual states enjoy much autonomy. The federal parliament consists of the senate (upper house) and the house of representatives (lower house). The party or coalition of parties commanding a majority in the lower house forms the government. The prime minister and his cabinet are responsible to the parliament. A governor-general formally represents the queen. The capital of Australia is Canberra. Robert (Bob) Hawke became prime minister in March 1983. The governor-general is Sir Ninian Stephen.

Economy: Australia has one of the strongest economies in the world. About 6% of the people are engaged in agriculture, while 33% of the labor force is employed in industry. Livestock is particularly important in Australia. The country is the world's leading producer of wool and the second largest producer of meat (large amounts of beef are exported to the U.S.). It also ranks third in sheep production and fourth in cattle. Australia is also a major producer of sugarcane, wheat, and oats. The country exports of a wide range of minerals. It ranks third in the production of uranium and iron ore (the leading export), and fourth in salt. Silver, coal, gold, and copper are other important minerals. Australia's manufacturing industry is geared largely to domestic demand, with small numbers of a wide range of goods exported, particularly to countries of Asia and the Pacific. Average annual gross national product (GNP) per capita is approximately $9,440 ($14,300 in U.S.) and is growing at a yearly rate of 2.2%. The unemployment and inflation rates are comparable to those in the U.S.

Education: There are 2 kinds of schools: public and private. Public education is administered by the state governments, and financed by federal funds. Schooling is compulsory from age 6 to age 15 (16 in Tasmania). Correspondence instruction, supplemented by radio, reaches children in remote areas. Approximately one-fourth of all Australian pupils attend private schools. All states have degree-conferring universities, tertiary colleges, and institutes. The school year begins in February and runs through the beginning of December, with holidays in May and August. The literacy rate is 98.5%.

Transportation and Communication: The transportation system includes taxis, rental cars, interstate bus lines, railways, and an extensive airlines system. Australia ranks fifth in the world in the number of automobiles per capita. Nearly all Australian households have a telephone. An independent national radio and television service is supplemented by a vigorous private enterprise commercial system of 3 major and a number of affiliated companies.

Health: Medical care of a high standard is paid for by a 1% levy on taxable income. For further medical information contact International Health Consultants, PO Box 34582, Bethesda, MD 20817.

For Further Information

Because space is so limited in this *Culturgram* and needs are so varied, no suggested readings are included. We recommend a visit to your local library or bookstore. Check *Books in Print* and various cataloging systems for country-specific titles. Review *Encyclopedia Britannica* or similar comprehensive summaries. The U.S. government publishes *Country Profiles* which many libraries subscribe to. Computer searches (DIALOG, SDC, BRS, ISI) are now available at most major libraries. Contact the Embassy of Australia 1601 Massachusetts Ave., N.W., Washington, D.C. 20036, or the Australian Tourist Commission, 489 Fifth Ave., 31st Floor, New York, NY 10017. The U.S. Embassy in Australia is located at Moonah Place, Canberra, A.C.T. 2600.

How to Use This Culturgram

Quickly read the whole text as an overview. Then circle or give priority numbers to specific questions you have or ideas you want to pursue. Use the *Culturgram* as a guide to check on regional differences and current situations.

Rev. 1/88

CULTURGRAM*

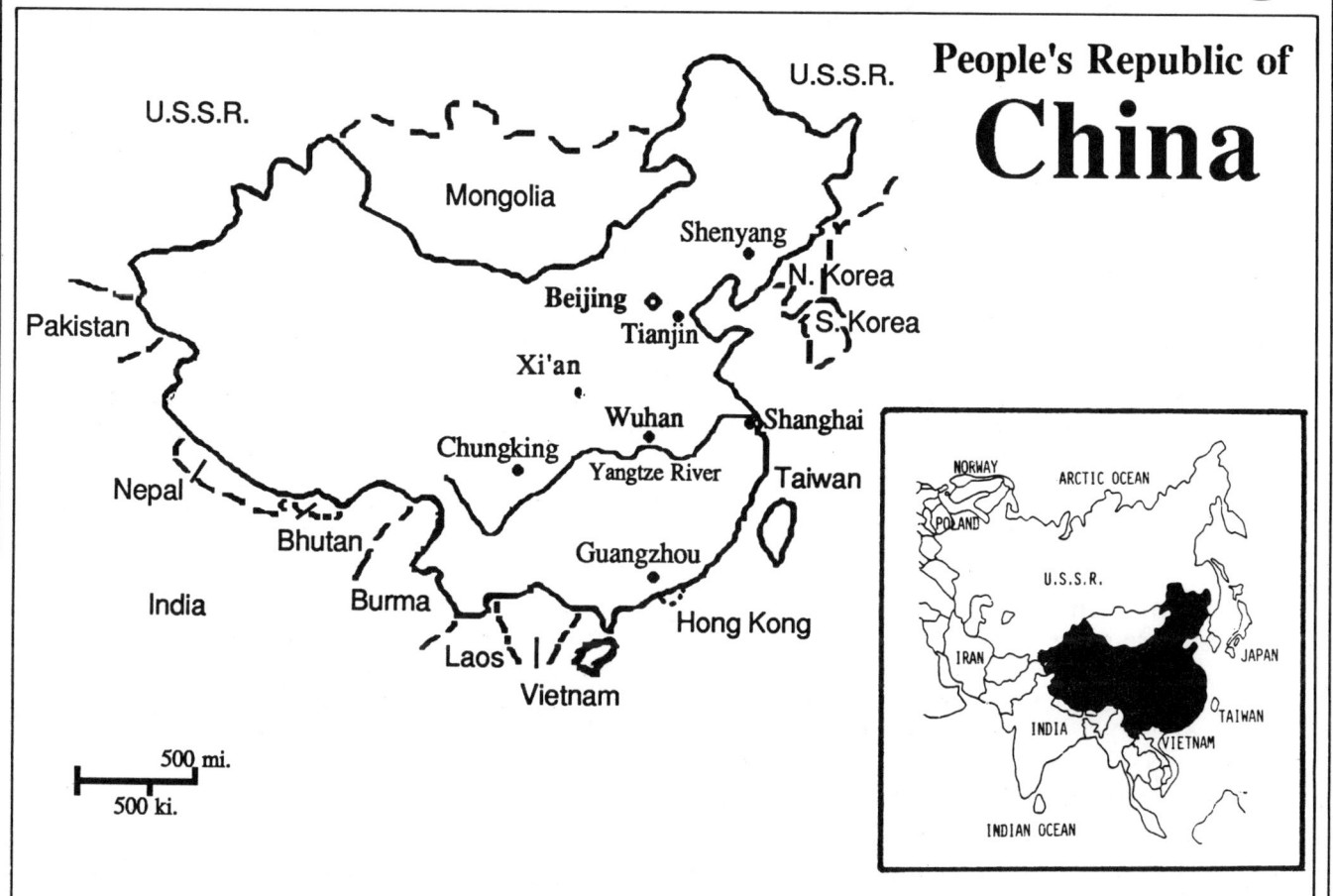

People's Republic of China

CUSTOMS AND COURTESIES

Greetings: A nod or a slight bow will usually suffice when greeting someone, but a handshake is also acceptable. The Chinese tend to be quite formal when introducing visitors and use the full title of their guests. Nonetheless, the Chinese often avoid identifying themselves precisely. Chinese names consist of a one syllable family name followed by a one-or-two-syllable given name. Addressing Chinese by their family name without a title is not polite; thus, Chen Yunpo should be addressed as Mr. Chen.

Visiting: Guests should be prompt, or even a little early. The guest should make the first move to leave. Guests are expected to conduct themselves with restraint, and to refrain from loud, boisterous speech and actions. Valuable gifts are usually not accepted from strangers. The Chinese enjoy discussing many interesting topics, including the differences between China and the West. In any situation, however, it is best to avoid belittling remarks about Chinese society or its leaders.

Eating: When invited to a home for dinner, it is polite to sample every dish served. Chopsticks are used for all meals and should be placed neatly on the table when one has finished eating. The food is placed in the center of the table. It is customary to hold the bowl close to the mouth when eating rice. Any bones, seeds, etc., should be placed on the table or in special dishes, not in the rice bowl. When dining at a restaurant, the host will pay the bill. Business is generally not discussed during meals. It is impolite to drink alone; therefore, toasts are usually offered to the people sitting

---

*Culturgrams are briefings to aid understanding of, feeling for, and communication with other people. Culturgrams are condensations of the best information available. Your insights will be appreciated. If you have refining suggestions, please contact Brigham Young University David M. Kennedy Center for International Studies, Publication Services, 280 HRCB, Provo, Utah 84602 (801) 378-6528. Copyright © 1986. All rights reserved. Printed in the USA.

nearby or to the whole table. At formal banquets, guests should have a short, friendly speech prepared to respond to what their host says. Nondrinkers may toast with water, juice, or soft drinks. Tipping is seen by some as something a superior does to an inferior, and, hence, is sometimes regarded as an insult.

Personal Appearance: Visitors to China can dress informally and comfortably for most occasions. Women should not wear shorts or halter tops. The Chinese wear little or no makeup or jewelry. Most of them—men and women alike—wear bulky jackets and trousers. Some women, however, are beginning to wear skirts, blouses, and dresses or brightly colored blouses under their tunics.

Gestures: The Chinese do not like to be touched by people they do not know. A smile is preferred over a pat on the back or similar gesture. It is especially inadvisable to exhibit physical familiarity with older people or people with important positions. The Chinese use their open hand to point rather than one finger, and they beckon to someone with the palm of the hand facing down.

THE PEOPLE

General Attitudes: The Chinese are noted for their good manners, hospitality, and reserve. The period of western domination and humiliation, however, is still a sore spot. They take pride in their nation, its long history, and its influence on other countries. Jokes about Chinese politics or leaders will not be appreciated. Confucianism, as a philosophy, still influences Chinese attitudes in a variety of ways.

Population: China is the most populous nation in the world with over 1,042,000,000 inhabitants—nearly one-quarter of the total world population. China's population is almost 4 times that of the United States. Ninety-four percent of the people are ethnic Han Chinese, with the remaining national minorities divided among 54 ethnic groups. Only 13% of the people live in urban areas, one of the lowest such percentages in the world. Although the average population density is 223 people per square mile (58 in U.S.), most of the population is concentrated in the eastern third of the country. In areas surrounding major agricultural sections, the population density may surpass 3,000 people per square mile.

Language: Standard Chinese, based on the Mandarin dialect, is the national language and is spoken by more than 70% of the people. Nearly all Chinese are bilingual, speaking the national language as well as a native dialect. The written language consists of *ideographs*, or characters, that represent an object or idea. There are approximately 40,000 of these ideographs and over 100,000 combined compounds (expressions containing 2 or more characters). A knowledge of 1,500 to 3,000 characters is adequate for everyday life and reading the newspaper. College graduates know about 6,000 characters. Other major languages spoken in China include Shanghainese, Sze chuanese, and Cantonese.

Religion: The official Communist ideology of the People's Republic of China encourages atheism. Citizens are guaranteed the right to religious beliefs. Religion does not hold a high place in society, especially in intellectual circles. Religious activity is usually discouraged by the government. Traditional religions such as Buddhism, Taoism, and folk religions, as well as Christianity, are still practiced by relatively few people. All churches and temples are open to the public.

LIFESTYLE

The Family: Historically, the Chinese were much more loyal to the family than to the nation. With the onset of Communism, however, the government has attempted to shift the people's loyalty away from the family and toward the state. Some family ties have been weakened as family members are sent to work in different parts of the country. Nonetheless, family ties as a whole are still intact. Limited living space often forces extended families to live together, even in urban areas.

Dating and Marriage: Chinese customs stress moral purity. Premarital sex and public displays of affection are discouraged. Due to the enormous population, effective family planning is a major goal of the government. Traditionally, the Chinese have had large families, but present law dictates that each couple may have only 1 child. Neighborhood authorities decide when each couple may have its child. Pressure is exerted on the young to marry late. The proper age for marriage in the cities is between 28 and 30 for men, and about 25 for women. In the country, it is about 25 for men and 23 for women. Weddings are simple. A couple first seeks permission from the local governing unit. If permission is granted, a legal contract is recorded without a wedding ceremony. The couple then joins family and friends in a marriage celebration. Wedding rings are becoming common in the elites.

Social and Economic Levels: Most rural families live in small, simple homes with 1 or 2 rooms, many having dirt floors and few windows. In the cities, families live in small apartments, often with communal bathroom facilities. Although there has been an increase in construction and an improvement in housing in recent years, modern housing projects are scarce and most people must wait about 2 years to get an apartment. Many boatmen and fishermen live on boats. In recent years, Radios and Televisions have become increasingly popular. China has the world's largest labor force (447 million). As a result of rapid population growth, unemployment has become an increasingly difficult challenge in China.

Business Hours: Office hours are generally from 8 a.m. to noon and from 1 to 5 p.m. Monday through Saturday. Shops are open from 9 am to 7 p.m. every day of the week.

Diet: Most Chinese cannot afford a wide variety of foods. Their diet varies depending on the part of the country in which they live. Rice, potatoes, barley soup, corn meal, steamed buns, and other grain dishes make up most basic family meals. Dishes made with pork, chicken, mutton, or fish are popular, but few Chinese can afford them regularly. There are few dairy products. Fruits and vegetables are eaten in season. Many regional styles of Chinese cuisine are famous throughout the world.

Recreation: In the cities there are many theaters, operas, ballets, and cultural-heritage monuments. Imported movies are especially popular and the average Chinese attends more than 10 per year. In the rural areas, however, the people provide their own entertainment, or are entertained by traveling cultural groups. Sports facilities are found in most cities. Popular sports in China include basketball, soccer, swimming, and table tennis. *Tai ji,* a stylized form of shadow boxing, is an exercise many enjoy. Chinese chess is also popular.

Holidays: The official public holidays are New Years (January 1), Labor Day (May 1), National Days (October 1-2), and the three-day Spring Festival (Chinese New Year), which occurs in January or February, varying from year to year according to the Chinese lunar calendar.

THE NATION

Land and Climate: China is the third largest country in the world, just larger than the United States. Most of western China is mountainous, arid, and isolated. The eastern third of the country has fertile agricultural land and river deltas. China, like the U.S., has a temperate climate, although summers are generally hotter and winters are colder than in North America. Monsoons affect the climate and lifestyle of southwestern China.

History and Government: The Chinese claim the world's oldest living civilization. China was ruled by a series of dynasties from the time its history was first recorded (ca.1500 B.C.) until early in the 20th century. In the 1920s, following the revolution led by Dr. Sun Yat-sen in 1911, Chiang Kai-shek established a Nationalist government in an effort to reunite a country fragmented by warlords. This government was finally defeated in 1949 by the Communist movement of Mao Tse-tung, who organized the peasants and drove Chiang and his army of 2 million to Taiwan. During the Mao era (1949-76) many economically crippling policies were implemented. Many feel that the *Great Leap*, as well as the *Cultural Revolution,* had disastrous effects. Policymakers after Mao have been more pragmatic. In 1971, the People's Republic of China was admitted to the United Nations in place of Taiwan. Currently the key organization in the government is the Chinese Communist Party, headed by Chairman Deng Xiao-ping. Recent cultural exchanges, trade agreements, and visits of Chinese leaders to the United States have greatly improved relations between the 2 countries.

Economy: China's gross national product is the sixth largest in the world (one-fifth that of the U.S.). Because of its large population, however, per capita income is only $300 per year ($14,300 in in U.S.). The Chinese economy is centrally planned and controlled, although limited-market economic policies have recently been introduced. Free markets are popular among the Chinese people. While only 11% of the land is arable, China produces a large amount of agricultural products. China is the world's leading producer of rice, tobacco, and pork, and the second largest producer of corn, barley, soy beans, peanuts, and eggs. It is the third largest producer of wheat, fish, and potatoes. Though predominantly an agricultural nation, China has many industries. It is the largest producer of tungsten, the third largest producer of coal, fourth in energy production, and fifth in steel. The government has launched the *Four Modernizations* program, which has the goal of creating a strong socialist economy by the year 2000. The currency is called *renminbi*, and the standard unit is the *yuan*. Currency cannot be taken out of China.

Education: Six years of schooling are mandatory in China. The majority of city children receive an education, but in rural areas some children receive none. Only a small percentage of the people graduate from high school and attend one of the approximately 450 universities and colleges. China's literacy rate is about 75%. This percentage is significantly higher in the urban areas, where it is becoming increasingly difficult to find work without having completed a high school education. The government is currently stressing the need for education.

Transportation and Communication: All major transportation facilities are state owned. Most travel in China is done by train and bicycle. Pedicabs can be found in some cities. Driving can be very confusing due to the large numbers of pedestrians, bicycles, slow-moving vehicles, and horse-drawn carts. All radio and television programming is handled directly by the government. Broadcasts are in Chinese and reflect state ideology.

Health: The country's medical care is considered by some to be the best in the third world. Water must be boiled before drinking. For further health information, contact International Health Consultants, PO Box 34582, Bethesda, MD 20817.

For Further Information

Because space is so limited in this *Culturgram* and needs are so varied, no suggested readings are included. We recommend a visit to your local library or bookstore. Check *Books in Print* and various cataloging systems for country-specific titles. Review *Encyclopedia Britannica* or similar comprehensive summaries. The U.S. government publishes *Country Profiles* which many libraries subscribe to. Computer searches (DIALOG, SDC, BRS, ISI) are now available at most major libraries. Contact the Embassy of the People's Republic of China, 2300 Connecticut Ave. NW, Washington, D.C. 20008, or China National Tourist Office, 60 E. 42nd Street, Room 465, New York, NY 10165. The U.S. Embassy in China is located at Xiu Shui Bei Jie 3, Beijing. (Ambassador Winston Lord)

How to Use This Culturgram

Quickly read the whole text as an overview. Then circle or give priority numbers to specific questions you have or ideas you want to pursue. Use the *Culturgram* as a guide to check on regional differences and current situations.

Maps

Culturgram maps are meant only as simple geographical orientations. Boundary representations are not necessarily authoritative. Different sources also vary spelling, transliterations, and accents.

Rev. 1/88

CULTURGRAM*

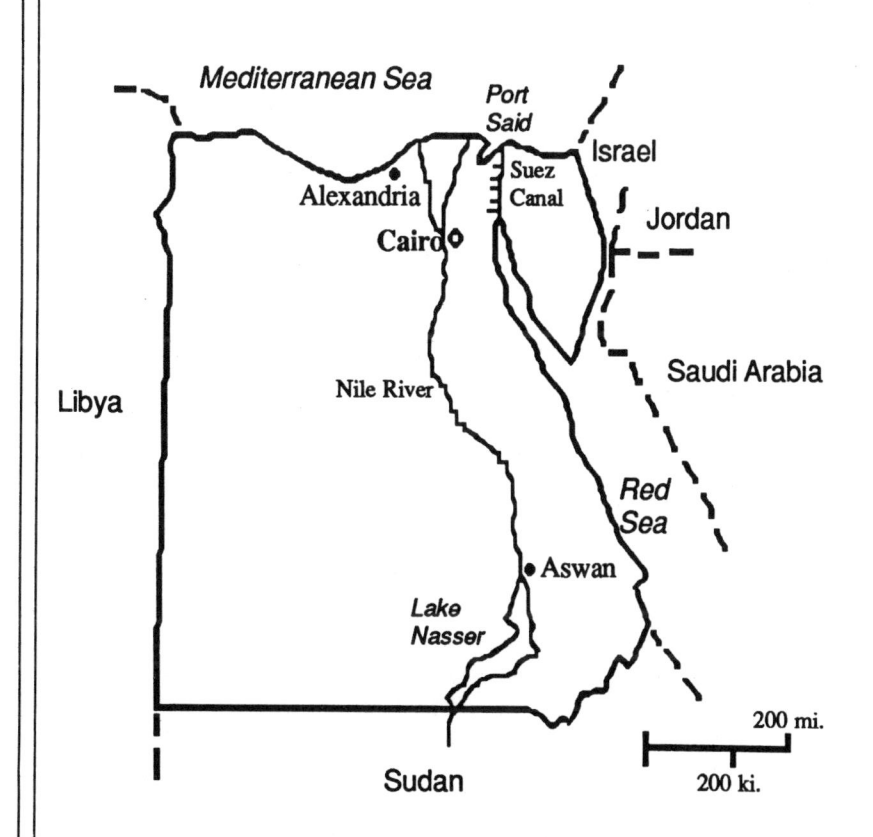

Arab Republic of Egypt

CUSTOMS AND COURTESIES

Greetings: Warmth in personal relations is very important to the Egyptians. Greetings are expressive and elaborate, with the host welcoming visitors several times and inquiring about family and friends. Egyptians like to establish a feeling of confidence and trust before proceeding with the business at hand; a cup of coffee and conversation usually precede any business dealings. Shyness or reluctance to socialize on the part of a visitor can easily be interpreted as giving a "cold shoulder." Address new acquaintances by their titles (i.e., Mr., President, Doctor, etc.), or by Mr., Mrs., or Miss, and their first names. French forms of address for women, such as *Madam*, are also used. Do not use first names without the appropriate title until invited to do so. Good friends exchange first names in informal settings, but may add the title to the first name in formal settings such as business meetings. Relating bad news on a social visit is considered impolite.

Visiting: Social engagements usually begin later than they do in the United States, and dinner may not be served until 10:30 p.m., or later. When invited to dine, it is customary to bring a gift of flowers or chocolates. Giving and receiving gifts should be done with both hands or the right hand, never with the left hand alone. Alcoholic beverages and smoking have become increasingly popular in some areas, and drinks are often served to foreign guests. Drunkeness, however, is not tolerated. Spatial distance between members of the same sex is much closer than in America, and much farther apart between members of the opposite sex. It is best to allow the Egyptians to establish the distance. In fact, good friends of the same sex may walk hand in hand in public areas. In conversation, Egyptians love to discuss issues on almost any topic. Foreigners should try to be sensitive to the Egyptians' point of view and make an effort to really understand it, even if they disagree with it.

*****Culturgrams** are briefings to aid understanding of, feeling for, and communication with other people. Culturgrams are condensations of the best information available. Your insights will be appreciated. If you have refining suggestions, please contact Brigham Young University David M. Kennedy Center for International Studies, Publication Services, 280 HRCB, Provo, Utah 84602 (801) 378-6528. Copyright © 1986. All rights reserved. Printed in the USA.

Eating: When entertaining, the Egyptians prepare elaborate and expensive meals. The amount of food may be overwhelming to a visitor. However, it is considered poor manners to eat everything on one's plate. Leftover food is a symbol of abundance and is a compliment to the host. Western dining etiquette is observed. However, tradition dictates that finger foods should be eaten with the right hand only.

Tipping: Tipping, or *Baksheesh*, is an institution in Egypt, and visitors would be wise to carry a large quantity of small change. *Baksheesh* is considered to be an act of "sharing the wealth." All public services, whether large or small, are normally rewarded. Taxi drivers, beauticians, and waiters should be tipped at least 10%. Other tips should be given according to the size and quality of the service.

Personal Appearance: Light clothing is suitable during the summer months, but warm clothing is a must in the winter. Business suits for men are required at both official and social gatherings. Women should dress conservatively. Low necklines, short skirts, sleeveless blouses, tight sweaters and pants, and shorts are considered to be in poor taste. Women dressed in this manner may be subject to misconceptions that could lead to harassment. Muslims who value fundamental Islamic beliefs dress modestly and traditionally. Women cover their hair and bodies totally (but not their faces). Men wear modest clothing, skullcaps, and often grow a short beard.

THE PEOPLE

General Attitudes: Egyptians seem to enjoy a relaxed, unpressured life, characterized by the phrase *Ma'aleesh*, which, roughly translated, means "don't worry" or "never mind." Both their business and leisure activities are governed by the philosophy of "*Inshallah*" (if God wills)—the concept of reliance on God which governs all aspects of Muslim life. They often have trouble responding favorably to the brisk, down-to-business attitude of many Americans. Egyptians are expressive and emotional. Because they identify with community groups, personal needs and desires often become secondary to those of the group. Egyptians are known throughout the Middle East for their marvelous sense of humor. They seem to endure difficult economic and living conditions with a great deal of composure.

Population: Egypt's population is approximately 48.3 million, and continues to grow at a rate of 2.6% annually (.9% in U.S.). About 90% of the people are of eastern Hamitic stock—native Egyptians. Small minorities include Nubians (a tribe located in southern Egypt), Bedouin nomads, Greeks, Italians, Syro-Lebanese, and Jews. The population-density rate is about 94 people per square mile (58 in U.S.). However, since 99% of the people live on the 3.5% of the land that is arable, the density rate along the Nile river is over 3,000 people per square mile, the 5th highest rate in the world. Cairo, the capital, has a population of over 5 million people, and the total metropolitan area contains nearly 10 million, making it one of the most populated cities in the world. It has attracted many migrants, as it is the major center for business and cultural activity in Egypt.

Language: Arabic is the official language, with English and French being widely spoken among the more educated and in places of business. The written "ancient" language differs greatly from the spoken Egyptian dialect used in everyday life.

Religion: About 90% of all Egyptians belong to the Sunni sect of Islam. Islamic philosophy is deeply rooted in the minds, hearts, and behavior of the people. The Islamic scripture, the Koran, is considered to be the final and complete word of God. They accept and revere all of the major prophets from Adam to Jesus, with Mohammed being "the last and greatest." There is also a significant minority of Coptic Christians, as well as some other minorities. Egyptian Muslims are generally tolerant of other religious minorities. However, there have been some recent problems between fundamentalist Muslims and Coptic Christians.

Holidays: The Western (Gregorian) calendar is used for all business and government purposes, but the Muslim calendar, based on the lunar month, is used to calculate the date of Muslim holidays. The year is 10 to 11 days shorter than on the Western calendar. For this reason, holidays vary from year to year. The 9th month, Ramadan, is a month of fasting wherein Muslims do not eat during the daylight hours. Friday is the Muslim day of rest and worship. The 2 major holidays take place at the end of Ramadan, and during the month of pilgrimage.

LIFESTYLE

The Family: Egypt is a male-dominated society and the family is a strong patriarchal unit. Traditionally, the Egyptians live as extended families, with 2 to 3 generations, including families of brothers and sisters, living under the same roof. However, increased urbanization is changing this tradition. The present trend is to smaller households of a man, his wife, and his unmarried children. Elders are generally respected for their wisdom and experience. The thought of putting aged parents in a rest home is repulsive to Egyptians. Children expect to support their parents in old age. Parents still play a key role in planning the future of their children, with influence ranging from the choice of university and profession to the selection of a mate. The Egyptians consider this support from their parents to be an important source of emotional security.

Dating and Marriage: Although attitudes toward dating are changing in more westernized circles, dating is not widespread. Public displays of affection are frowned upon. Moral purity is still highly valued in a woman, and is usually a key requirement in the marriage contract. Traditionally, marriages are arranged between heads of families, often with little input from the couple involved. However, this practice is not as prevalent now as it was in the past. Marriage is considered not only the joining of 2 individuals, but also of 2 families. Thus, both families are heavily involved in the wedding preparations. The wedding has great significance for all concerned. Housing is very expensive and hard to come by, given the large urban population and number of migrants. Therefore, in urban areas, engagements are often long while the couple collects money for an apartment of their own.

Work Schedule: On Friday (worship day), all government offices and public sector businesses are closed. Many nongovernment offices and businesses are closed Sunday instead of Friday. Most businesses are open from about 8:30 a.m. to 2:00 p.m. and usually open again from 5:30 p.m. to 9:00 p.m. In the summer, most workers take a long lunch break because of the heat, and then work later in the cool evening.

Recreation: Soccer is the national sport, but Egyptians enjoy sports of many kinds. Sports clubs are popular places for such activities as riding, tennis, and swimming, as well as soccer. The cinema is popular among urban dwellers and a wide variety of Egyptian and foreign films are shown. Other important centers of Egyptian leisure are the coffee house and the club, where men congregate to visit, discuss politics, play games, and enjoy each other's company.

Diet: Egyptians are fond of rice, bread, fish, lamb, chicken, turkey, and stuffed vegetables. *Tahina* (sesame seed paste), tomatoes, yogurt, and cucumbers are also usually found on the table. The Koran prohibits the consumption of pork and alcohol. Traditional foods include *fava* beans, chick peas with *tahina* and flat Egyptian bread.

THE NATION

Land and Climate: Egypt has a surface area of 386,662 square miles, approximately the same size as the state of Texas. Most of Egypt is dry and arid desert, spotted with several inhabited oases. The Nile River, the longest in the world, runs into the Mediterranean Sea north through Egypt, providing the life blood for the country. The Nile valley, a verdant strip of fertile land that flanks the Nile river, is the dwelling place for nearly all Egypt's citizens. Only 3% of the total land mass is arable. The summers are hot, with temperatures reaching up to 100° F., while the winter temperature seldom falls below 40° F. Rainfall ranges from none in the desert and the area south of Cairo to about 8 inches a year in the Nile delta.

History and Government: The earliest recorded Egyptian dynasty united the kingdoms of Upper and Lower Egypt about 3200 B.C. In 525 B.C., Egypt fell under Persian control. Alexander the Great's conquest in the 4th century B.C. brought Greek rule and culture to Egypt. Egypt was one of the first nations visited by Christian ministries (the apostle Mark) and was largely Christianized within 3 centuries following their own Coptic patriarch. Because of Byzantine religious persecution, Egyptians welcomed the Muslim invasion of 641 A.D., and since then Egypt has been largely Muslim. France and Britain exerted increasing influence on Egyptian affairs after completion of the Suez Canal in 1869. Britain made Egypt a protectorate in 1914. Although given official independence in 1922, the Egyptians regard 1953 as the year beginning real independence with the young officer coup that overthrew the British-supported monarchy. Gamal Abdel Nasser ousted the first president of Egypt in 1954, making himself dictator. Nasser led the government until his death in 1970. He was responsible for a number of reforms, including universal education, land reform, nationalization of major industries and banks, and Egyptian leadership of the Arab world. Also during this period, Egypt fought 2 wars with Israel, its northeastern neighbor. The Sinai Peninsula was taken by Israel in the 1967 war. Upon Nasser's death in 1970, former vice president Anwar al-Sadat succeeded him. Sadat liberalized economic policy, greatly reduced relations with the Soviet Union, and pursued peace with Israel. Through the efforts of President Sadat, great progress was made towards establishing a lasting peace with Israel. A peace treaty was signed in 1979, and the Sinai Peninsula was returned. On October 6, 1981, Sadat was assassinated by Muslim fundamentalists who were upset with his policies. Vice President Hosni Mubarak succeeded Sadat in 1982 and is currently the president of Egypt.

Economy: Between 45 and 50% of the people are employed in agriculture. Egypt produces many agricultural products, including cotton fiber, wheat, corn, and barley. Other important products include rice, onions, beans, and citrus fruit. Egypt is also the 10th largest cheese producer. Industry has played an increasingly important role in the economy in recent years. Textiles, food processing, chemicals, petroleum, construction, steel, and cement are all chief industrial products. Another important source of income is the Suez Canal. Tourism also plays an important role. Currently the average annual gross national product (GNP) per capita is approximately $437 ($14,300 in U.S.). A shortage of unskilled labor and a large foreign debt are sources of problems in the Egyptian economy. Inflation is relatively high, but the unemployment rate is only about 3%, one of the lowest rates in the world. The unit of currency is the Egyptian *pound*. Egyptian currency cannot be taken into or out of the country; it cannot be exchanged for hard currencies outside of Egypt.

Education: The government subsidizes free education through the university level, and thus boasts one of the highest literacy rates in the Middle East (40%). Egypt provides skilled and educated workers and professionals for many Arab nations. Universities are located in most urban centers, and about 40,000 students graduate each year. Almost 46% of university students are women.

Health: Water in most places is drinkable, but bottled water is recommended. Although milk in many places is pasteurized, it is advisable to be wary of all milk- or cream-based products. Fruit and vegetables must be washed before eating. Egypt has many excellent doctors, but medical facilities are limited. Hospitals usually require a substantial deposit before admitting a patient. Government hospitals are free. For further medical information contact International Health Consultants, PO Box 34582, Bethesda, MD 20817.

For Further Information

Because space is so limited in this *Culturgram* and needs are so varied, no suggested readings are included. We recommend a visit to your local library or bookstore. Check *Books in Print* and various cataloging systems for country-specific titles. Review *Encyclopedia Britannica* or similar comprehensive summaries. The U.S. government publishes *Country Profiles* which many libraries subscribe to. Computer searches (DIALOG, SDC, BRS, ISI) are now available at most major libraries. Contact the Egyptian Embassy, 2310 Decatur Pl., N.W., Wash., D.C. 20008, or the Egyptian Government Tourist Office, 630 Fifth Ave., New York, N.Y. 10111. The U.S. Embassy in Egypt is located at 5 Sharia Latin America, Cairo, Egypt.

How to Use This Culturgram

Quickly read the whole text as an overview. Then circle or give priority numbers to specific questions you have or ideas you want to pursue. Use the *Culturgram* as a guide to check on regional differences and current situations.

Rev. 1/88

CULTURGRAM*

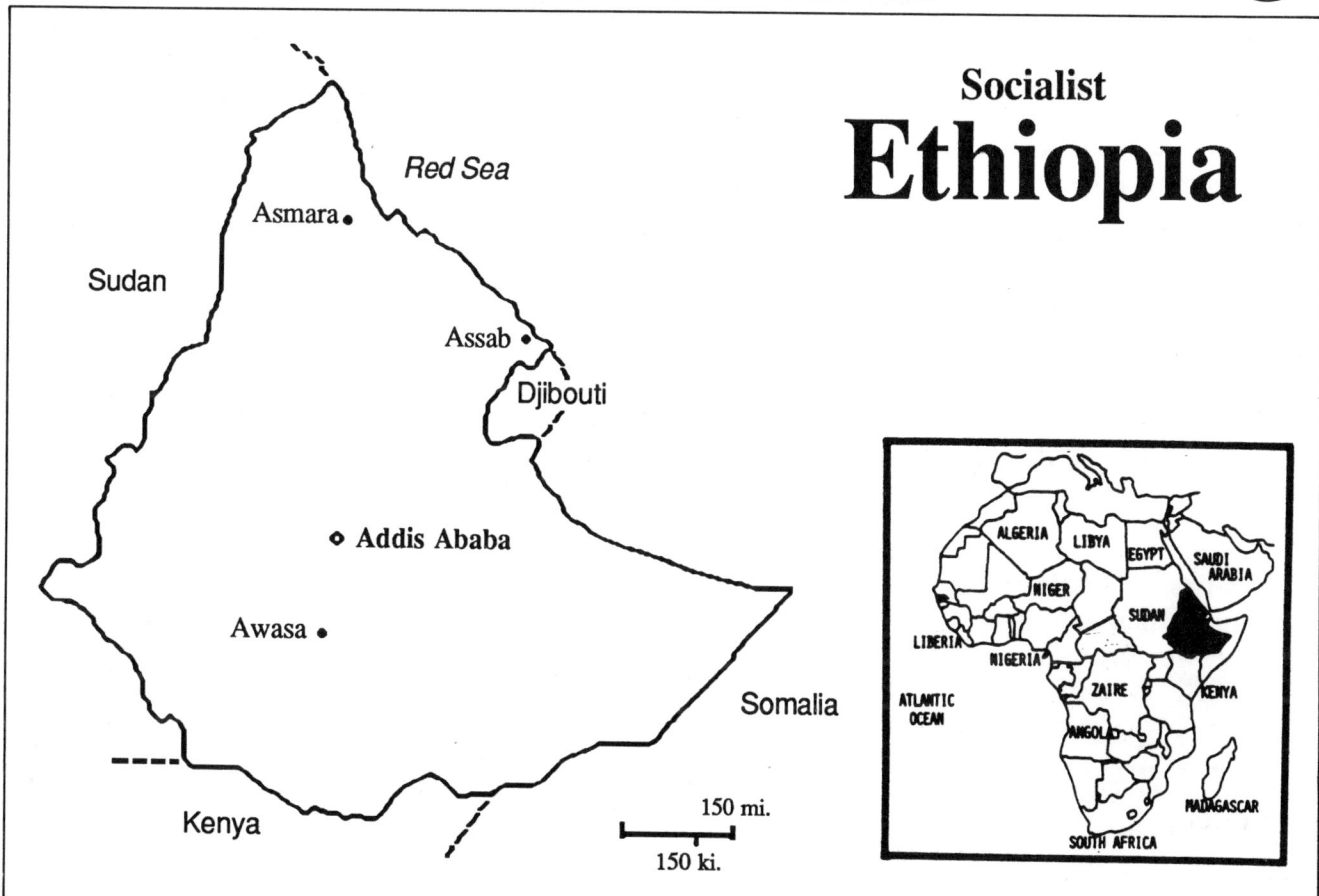

Socialist Ethiopia

CUSTOMS AND COURTESIES

Note: The population of Ethiopia is represented by over 100 different ethnic groups. Although the great majority belong to the Semitic and Cushitic groups, cultural mixing over many millenia has produced great diversity. This Culturgram will concentrate on the Amharic people, who have politically and culturally dominated Ethiopia for many centuries.

Greetings: Like most Semitic peoples, the Amhara place great emphasis on formal but very courteous greetings to both friends and strangers. Shaking hands with one or both hands, though more gentle than the western handshake, is common between members of the same sex. A formal but warm embrace is common between friends. Members of the opposite sex do not greet each other physically, but this rule does not usually apply to foreigners. Conversation should be positive and touch neither on highly personal topics nor on members of the opposite sex.

Visiting: The Amharic home is a highly private and personal domain. No visit should be made without an explicit invitation. A small gift is in order on one's first visit to a private home. Visitors are expected to partake of some form of food or refreshment, which should never be refused. Conversation should remain strictly social.

---

*Culturgrams are briefings to aid understanding of, feeling for, and communication with other people. Culturgrams are condensations of the best information available. Your insights will be appreciated. If you have refining suggestions, please contact Brigham Young University David M. Kennedy Center for International Studies, Publication Services, 280 HRCB, Provo, Utah 84602 (801) 378-6528. Copyright © 1986. All rights reserved. Printed in the USA.

Eating: The Amharic host takes pride in offering guests the best meal he is capable of providing, whether at a public restaurant or in his home. Visitors are often given more food than they are able to eat. Leaving a little food on the plate is perfectly proper, indicating the ability of the host to provide more than adequately for guests. As is customary throughout the Semitic world, one should not use the left hand for eating. While western-style eating utensils may be provided for foreign guests, most food is eaten with the fingers.

Personal Appearance: In the larger cities, most people wear western clothes under the traditional white *shamma* (toga). Full native dress is still worn by many, particularly on holidays. Visitors should dress neatly in conservative western clothing.

Gestures: Pointing is generally considered rude and should be avoided. Use of the left hand for giving or receiving objects should also be avoided. Because interaction space is closer than westerners are used to, one will sometimes notice another person's body odor. This is not usually a sign of uncleanliness; normal body odors do not have the negative connotation they do in other cultures.

THE PEOPLE

General Attitudes: All the peoples of Ethiopia, whether Christian or Moslem, tend to be somewhat complacent and passive, enduring present adversity with a stoicism unknown in the western world. They also tend to be quite formal in their dealings, not only with strangers, but with each other. In spite of these attitudes, a strong sense of individualism pervades the Ethiopian personality. Individuals are expected to stand up for their rights and desires, so long as they do not infringe on the rights of others. Genuine concern for one's fellowman and courtesy are noticeable underlying personality traits of the Ethiopian.

Population: The dominant Amharic people of central Ethiopia and the related Tigre people in the north and west account for approximately 32% of this country's 42 million inhabitants. The Galla, or Oromo (40%), and the Somali (6%), are important Cushitic peoples who inhabit the southern parts of the country. Addis Ababa, the capital, has a population of 1.2 million. Asmara is another major city. Population density averages 59 persons per square mile (58 in U.S.). Because of severe droughts, the annual population-growth rate has declined from 2.3% in 1982 to the present rate of 0.7%.

Language: Amharic, a Semitic language related to Hebrew and Arabic, is considered the official national language, and is the major medium of commerce, culture, and administration. Since the revolution of 1974, however, the government has stated that other Ethiopian languages have equal status. Most important of these are Tigrinya, and Gallinya (Orominya). Arabic is spoken in the northern province of Eritrea. The liturgical language of the Ethiopian Orthodox Church, Ge'ez, has produced a large and vibrant literature of considerable importance. English is taught in most schools and is the most widely spoken foreign language.

Religion: Approximately 40% of the population belongs to the Ethiopian Orthodox Church, which has been a mainstay of Ethiopian culture since the 4th century. An estimated 45%, located largely in the northwest and extreme southeast, is Moslem, while the remaining 15% follow tribal religions.

Holidays: Ethiopia uses the Coptic calendar. It is correlated with and similar to the old Julian calendar, such that the Ethiopian year 1978 began September 11, 1985. In addition, the Ethiopian 24-hour day begins at sunrise, so that 7:00 p.m. is popularly called one o'clock. Business is usually conducted using European time and calendar standards. Easter is by far the most important holiday, but other Christian Holy Days (particularly saints' days) are also commemorated. In addition, Islam in Ethiopia emphasizes the importance of saints. Moslem saints' days are equally important in the Islamic parts of the country. September 12th is the national holiday.

LIFESTYLE

The Family: The Amharic family is strongly patriarchal, a pattern typical of the Semitic and Cushitic peoples of Ethiopia. Sons usually bring their brides to live with or near their father's family, and 3 or more generations in the male line frequently live under one roof. Age is highly respected in Ethiopia, and grandparents are never shunned by family members. Women lead a more sheltered life than westerners are used to, and their duties and privileges are well defined both within the home and elsewhere. Families are very private, and invitations to a private home should be considered a special honor for the visitor.

Dating and Marriage: Western-style dating is not common in Ethiopia, but is becoming accepted in the urban centers. Since marriage represents the union of 2 families, the choice of spouse is most frequently arranged between the 2 families. The individual is allowed a certain freedom of choice, but usually abides by the traditional methods of finding a mate. Marriages in both the Christian and Moslem sections of the country are monogamous and tend to be lasting.

Social Levels: Ethiopian society has traditionally been highly stratified, with a small, largely Amharic nobility and upper class ruling the country. Though the revolution of 1974 forcibly and violently abolished class distinctions, many believe that a new governmental upper class has simply taken the place of the old one. There is a relatively large business middle class and an extremely large economic lower class. With the forcible break-up of large landholdings, class distinctions are beginning to blur, but most Ethiopians continue to be very much aware of the economic and social position they hold within their society.

Work and Recreation: Recreation tends to take place within the home and to be sharply separated from the workplace. Individual games of skill (board games, races) are the most popular kinds of recreational entertainment, although soccer has become quite popular in recent years. Work is highly bureaucratic.

Diet: The native Ethiopian diet is typically Semitic, with much use of lamb, goat, and fowl. Like Moslems and Jews, Ethiopians do not eat pork, turkey, or ham. The most common foods are *injera*, a fermented bread made of teff flour, and *wat*, a spicy stew made with beef or chicken. Strict religious dietary and fasting customs also affect the Ethiopian diet. European foods are found to a limited extent in the larger cities.

THE NATION

Land and Climate: Ethiopia has a land area of about 472,000 square miles (slightly smaller than Alaska), and is a land of extreme variation. The western section is extremely rugged and mountainous. It is separated from the high plains and semi-desert regions of the east by the Great Rift Valley, a zone of temperate climate with the greatest population density. Annual highland temperatures average 70° F., while lowland temperatures to the east may reach 95° F. during the warmest season. The rainy season is from mid-June to mid-September in the highlands, with the period from October to February being extremely dry. Rainfall varies widely from year to year, however, often causing extreme problems with both agriculture and animal husbandry.

History and Government: Ethiopia is one of the oldest countries in the world, and the oldest independent country in Africa. By far the most important period of consolidation was that of the Kingdom of Aksum (2nd to 9th centuries A.D.), during which the foundation of modern Ethiopia was laid. A strong monarchy was established, which lasted from those early centuries until its eventual violent overthrow in 1974. From the 4th century, the monarchy and the bulk of the Ethiopian peoples espoused Orthodox Christianity, which remains a major unifying cultural influence. Mussolini's Italian Army invaded and occupied Ethiopia from 1935 until 1941, when with the aid of British troops, control of Ethiopia was returned to Emperor Haile Selassie. Despite the Emperor's genuine interest in the welfare of his people, general economic and political unrest led to a revolution in 1974. In the following year, Emperor Haile Selassie died, the empire was abolished, and a socialist state was established. Since that time, Ethiopia has turned increasingly away from the west and toward alignment with other socialist and communist nations. The present government is a provisional military regime, which has stated as its goal the establishment of democratic and socialist principles of popular rule. These have not, as yet, been implemented.

Economy: Ethiopia's economy is almost entirely agricultural, and per capita income is only $119 ($14,300 in U.S.). Coffee, *teff* (a native grain), wheat, millet, pulses, and barley are the major crops. Over 90% of the labor force is devoted to agriculture and animal husbandry. Ethiopia's main exports are coffee, hides, and skins. Ethiopian agriculture has been plagued by periodic drought, soil erosion, and relocation of farmers to the cities. Although problems must be solved, the country has potential for self-sufficiency in grains, and for export development in livestock, grains, vegetables, and fruits.

Education: Education is not compulsory in Ethiopia. The literacy rate is approximately 15%. About 46% of school-age children are currently enrolled in schools.

Health: Some medical facilities are available in Addis Ababa and Asmara. Ethiopia has only 1 physician per 93,000 people, inadequate hospital space, and a life expectancy of under 40 years. Ethiopia is in extreme need of improved medical care. The primary problem is malnutrition, stemming from severe drought-related food shortages. For further medical information, contact International Health Consultants, PO Box 34582, Bethesda, MD 20817.

For Further Information

Because space is so limited in this *Culturgram* and needs are so varied, no suggested readings are included. We recommend a visit to your local library or bookstore. Check *Books in Print* and various cataloging systems for country-specific titles. Review *Encyclopedia Britannica* or similar comprehensive summaries. The U.S. government publishes *Country Profiles* which many libraries subscribe to. Computer searches (DIALOG, SDC, BRS, ISI) are now available at most major libraries. Contact the Embassy of Ethiopia, 2134 Kalorama Rd, N.W., Washington, D.C. 20008, or the Ethiopian Mission to the UN, 866 UN Plaza, Room 560, New York, NY 10017.

How to Use This Culturgram

Quickly read the whole text as an overview. Then circle or give priority numbers to specific questions you have or ideas you want to pursue. Use the *Culturgram* as a guide to check on regional differences and current situations.

Maps

Culturgram maps are meant only as simple geographical orientations. Boundary representations are not necessarily authoritative. Different sources also vary spelling, transliterations, and accents.

Rev. 1/88

CULTURGRAM*

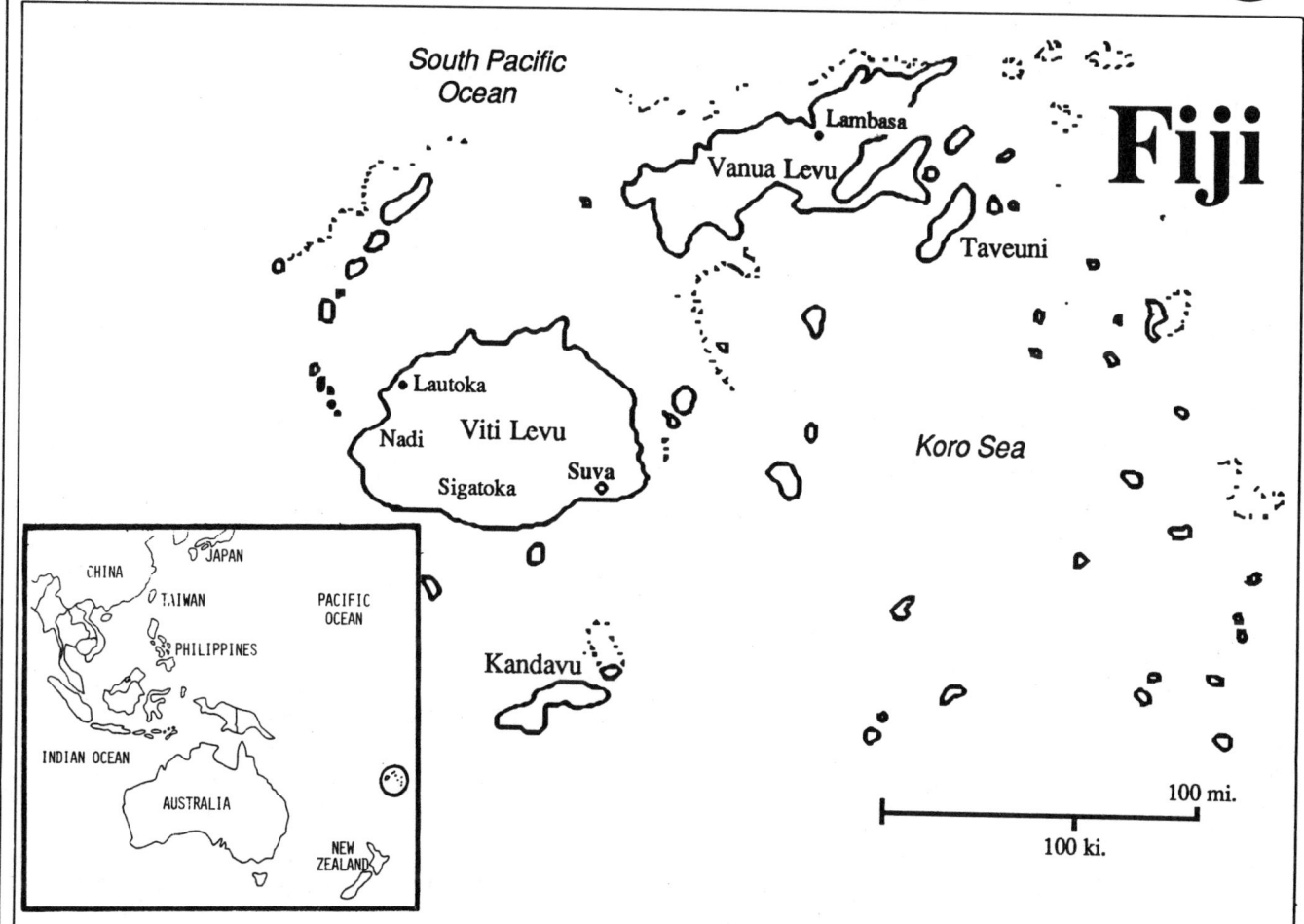

Fiji

CUSTOMS AND COURTESIES

Greetings: Fijians generally greet one another with a smile and an upward flick of the eyebrows. Handshakes are also appropriate, and the people often touch one another while talking. Different ethnic groups in Fiji (Asian, Melanesian, Polynesian, European, etc.) also have their own greeting gestures and phrases. Most people are called by their given names.

Visiting: It is customary to remove one's shoes when entering a house. Sitting cross-legged on a mat on the floor is common, but sometimes a guest may be offered a chair. The people of Fiji love to laugh, and visitors should feel free to laugh with them. Long visits by uninvited guests are not appropriate. Visitors should accept all gifts offered. Gifts are normally given at Christmas time and on birthdays. Fijians appreciate personal gifts.

Eating: Visitors should accept food offered them and eat as much as they desire. Customarily, the Fijians will serve a cup of *kava* or *yagona* (a somewhat bitter drink made from roots which may be numbing to the tongue) to their guests. Refusing to drink *kava* with the people is often taken as an insult. The Fijians are especially pleased if the visitor drinks the "*kava*" in one swallow, as only a small amount is served. Tipping is not necessary in hotels or restaurants.

*****Culturgrams** are briefings to aid understanding of, feeling for, and communication with other people. Culturgrams are condensations of the best information available. Your insights will be appreciated. If you have refining suggestions, please contact Brigham Young University David M. Kennedy Center for International Studies, Publication Services, 280 HRCB, Provo, Utah 84602 (801) 378-6528. Copyright © 1986. All rights reserved. Printed in the USA.

Public Meetings: It is best to talk about things closely related to the people. Fijians enjoy hearing about personal experiences in language that is understandable. They are more interested in knowing how much people care than how intelligent they are. As in most of the hot and humid South Pacific, the pace of day-to-day life in Fiji is much slower and more relaxed than in the West. Fijians usually arrive much later than scheduled meeting times. The Prime Minister has termed this lifestyle "The Pacific Way."

Personal Appearance: Conservative clothing is appropriate in all but very informal situations. Light clothing is worn year-round, although a light sweater may be needed during the cooler months from May to November. During the rainy season (November to April), raincoats and umbrellas are essential.

Gestures: Folding one's arms while talking to someone shows respect. In public it is generally considered discourteous to touch a person's head. People are called by waving the whole hand with the palm down. Eye contact is appropriate when speaking to someone, but staring is considered offensive. Nodding the head or flicking the eyebrows upward indicates agreement. If one is in doubt as to what to do, one may follow the lead of the host.

Shopping: Food or goods in local supermarkets have fixed prices, but tourist and open-market goods may be bargained for.

THE PEOPLE

General Attitudes: Fijians are known for their hospitality. They are generous, friendly, and easy going. Change is usually accepted readily by the Fijians.

Population: The population of Fiji is approximately 700,000 and is growing at an annual rate of 2.1% (0.9% in U.S.). The population-density rate is about 79 people per square mile (58 in U.S.). Less than one-fourth of the people live in urban areas. Approximately 50% of the people are descended from Asian Indians who came to Fiji as laborers in the 19th century. The Indians primarily live in the western and northern areas of Viti Levu, the main island. Forty-four percent of the people are native Fijians. The remaining 6% are of European, Polynesian, Chinese or other descent.

Language: English and Fijian are the official languages. Hindustani is spoken by the Indian majority. Other ethnic groups have their own languages and dialects. English spoken among the people may also include words and phrases from other languages spoken on the islands.

Religion: The Fijians belong to many different sects of Christianity, Catholic and Methodist being the most common. The Indians are mostly Hindu or Muslim, and the Chinese are either Christian or Buddhist.

LIFESTYLE

The Family: Traditionally, the Fijian people are family oriented and the father acts as head of the house. Fijian families are fifth largest in size in the world, averaging 6.3 people per family (3.1 in U.S.). The elderly are usually cared for by their children. Today, however, an increasing amount of individualism can be seen in Fiji, due largely to the pressures of modernization and industrialization.

Dating and Marriage: Dating is traditionally nonexistent in Fijian culture, but this practice is changing as western influence affects the society. Affection is generally not shown in public. The Fijian man chooses his own wife, and a grandiose wedding ceremony is held. Indian parents have customarily arranged their children's marriages, but this practice is also changing.

Social and Economic Levels: Fiji typically has a high crime rate. There is great disparity between the rich and the poor. Although most of the people have enough income to provide for the necessities of life, approximately 9% live in absolute poverty.

Diet: The typical Fijian diet consists of vegetables, beef, pork, fish, rice, fruit, bread, taro, cassava, and hot drinks. The Indians eat very spicy foods, often made with curry. *Roti*, much like tortillas, is also a common part of the diet.

Work Schedules: Businesses are open Monday through Friday, usually from 8 a.m. to 5 p.m., with a one-hour lunch break at noon. Restaurants and stores remain open during lunch and are closed on Saturday afternoon and Sunday, except the duty-free shops, which stay open when cruise ships are in.

Recreation: Fijians are very sports minded. Favorite sports include soccer, rugby, basketball, volleyball and boxing. Fijians like to swim and play golf. Tennis, cricket, and squash are also popular.

Holidays: The Hibiscus festival is held at Suva, the capital, in August. October 10th is celebrated as Fiji's independence day. The Indian Diwali festival (festival of light) is held on November 15. Some Christian holidays may also be celebrated.

THE NATION

Land and Climate: About 322 islands make up the country of Fiji, of which approximately 100 are inhabited. The total land area is about the same size as the state of Hawaii. There are 4 main island groups and 3 main islands. The largest of the islands, Viti Levu, constitutes more than half of the land area and is the seat of the capital, Suva. The larger Fijian islands are volcanic and mountainous and are surrounded by coral reefs. The windward sides of the islands are covered with dense tropical forests; the leeward sides consist of grassy plains. The climate is humid and tropical, with heavy rainfall. The cool or dry season is from May to November, and the hotter, rainy season is from November to April.

History and Government: The first Europeans to discover Fiji were the Dutch in 1643. Captain James Cook, a British explorer, visited the islands in 1774. Later, trading vessels came for sandalwood. For many years the islands were known as the "Cannibal Islands" because of the Fijians' reputation as fearsome man-eaters. After years of tribal warfare, Ratu Cakobau, of the Bau tribe, unified the rival tribes in 1855 with the help of neighboring Tonga. Tonga dominated Fijian affairs for the next 20 years. Cakobau was converted to Christianity in 1854 and became king of the Fiji Islands in 1871. After attempts to organize an effective government failed, Fiji offered cession to Britain, which was accepted in October of 1874. A local government was set up in 1876. Exactly 96 years after the cession of Fiji to Britain, on October 10, 1970, Fiji gained its independence from Britain. Sir Kamisese K.T. Mara became the nation's first prime minister in the parliamentary government. The country was governed by Prime minister Mara's Alliance party from 1967, one of the two major political parties in Fiji and consisting primarily of native Fijians. The opposition party was National Federation Party (NFP), made up largely of Indians. In May of 1987, two weeks after the election of the NFP, Sitiven Rahuka took over the country in a bloodless coup, restoring control to the native Fijians. The country is currently under his military rule. Fiji is a member of the British Commonwealth of Nations.

Economy: The economy is dependent largely on agriculture, which employs nearly 44% of the people. Sugar is the most important product, accounting for about 60% of the country's exports. Other important products include coconut and coconut products, bananas, ginger, and rice. Sugar milling and coconut oil production are the major industries. Tourism is becoming increasingly important to the Fijian economy. Average annual gross national product (GNP) per capita is approximately $1,852 ($14,300 in U.S.), which is relatively high for a small country. Unemployment is typically lower than in the U.S., and the economy is growing at a yearly rate of 0.5%. The monetary unit is the Fijian *dollar*.

Education: Fiji ranks fourth in the world in amount of educational expenditures per capita. The literacy rate is approximately 80%. Most schools in Fiji are owned and operated by religious groups such as the Catholics, Methodists, Latter-day Saints (Mormons), Hindus, and Moslems. There are also government-operated schools and schools run by a committee. Each school has its own uniform, and most schools accept both boys and girls. The University of the South Pacific in Suva, Fiji, attracts students from many Pacific areas.

Transportation and Communication: Most people travel by bus because they are regular and inexpensive. It is polite to offer seats to elderly women or mothers with babies. Taxis and private automobiles are also used but are more expensive. Few people own cars. Traffic travels on the left hand side of the road. There is one state-owned radio station, but there are no public television stations. The country is slowly introducing television into society, especially for education. Radio broadcasts are in English, Fijian, and Hindustani. There are 2 daily newspapers in English, and several in local dialects.

Health: The majority of the people are very clean, and there is little disease. The main cities have effective sanitation systems and tap water is clean and drinkable. For further medical information, contact International Health Consultants, PO Box 34582, Bethesda, MD 20817.

For Further Information

Because space is so limited in this *Culturgram* and needs are so varied, no suggested readings are included. We recommend a visit to your local library or bookstore. Check *Books in Print* and various cataloging systems for country-specific titles. Review *Encyclopedia Britannica* or similar comprehensive summaries. The U.S. government publishes *Country Profiles* which many libraries subscribe to. Computer searches (DIALOG, SDC, BRS, ISI) are now available at most major libraries. Contact the Embassy of Fiji, 2233 Wisconsin Ave., Suite 240, Washington, D.C. 20007, or the Fiji Visitors Bureau, 6151 W. Century Blvd., Los Angeles, CA 90045.

How to Use This Culturgram

Quickly read the whole text as an overview. Then circle or give priority numbers to specific questions you have or ideas you want to pursue. Use the *Culturgram* as a guide to check on regional differences and current situations.

Maps

Culturgram maps are meant only as simple geographical orientations. Boundary representations are not necessarily authoritative. Different sources also vary spelling, transliterations, and accents.

Rev. 1/88

CULTURGRAM

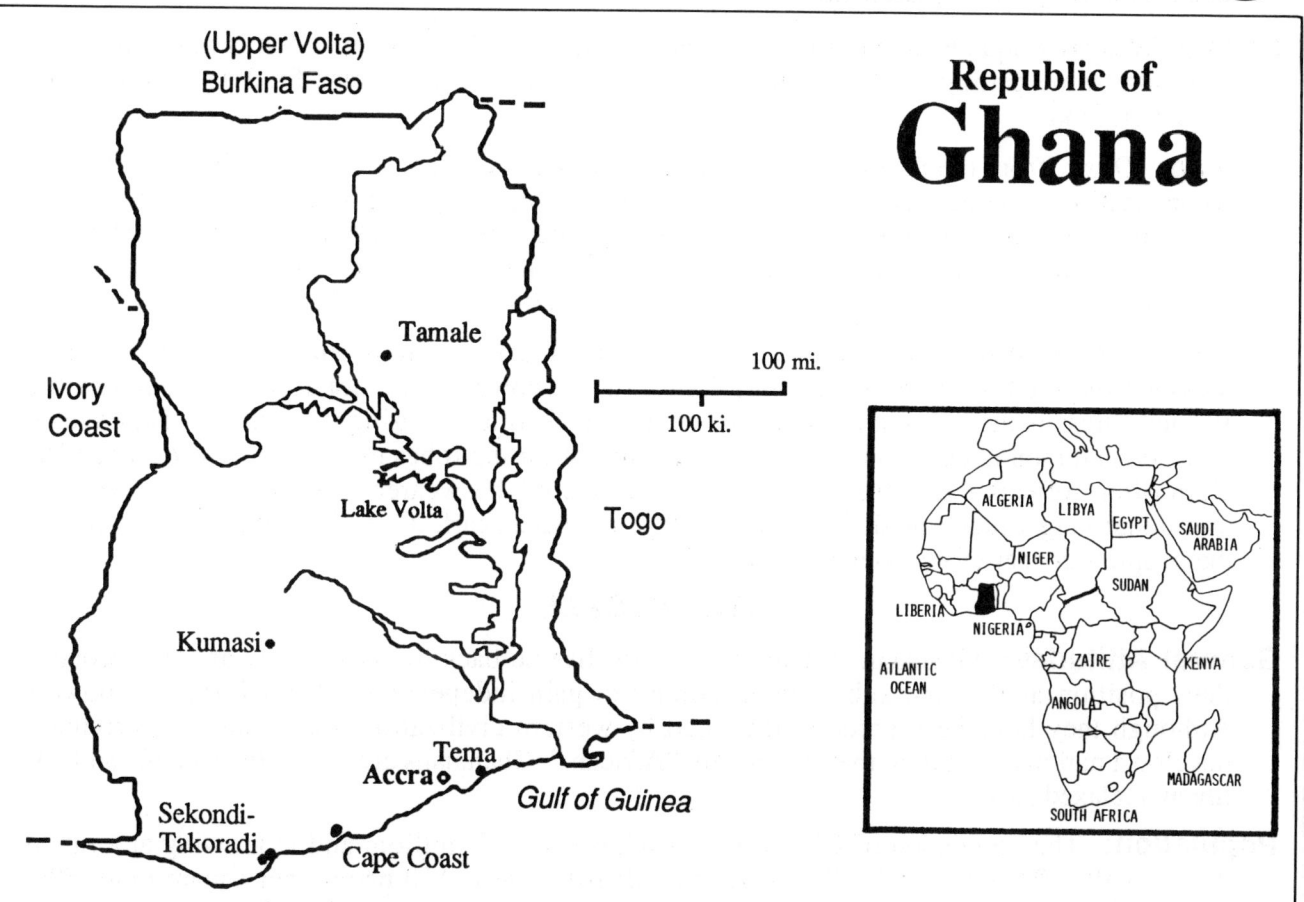

Republic of Ghana

CUSTOMS AND COURTESIES

Greetings: The population of Ghana is composed of many different ethnic groups, each with its own distinct language, customs, and culture. Because of the pronounced differences, it is difficult to describe any particular custom that is practiced all over the country. However, because of Ghana's long colonial affiliation with the British Empire, English greetings are common. Visitors should not use the word "tribe" when referring to a Ghanaian's ethnic background. This word has taken on a negative meaning and Ghanaians may be offended by its use or question the visitor's intentions. The term "ethnic group" is a suitable substitute, but questions about a person's "ethnic group" should be reserved until one is well acquainted. Asking people about where they are from can be an appropriate way to get to know a Ghanaian.

Visiting: Ghanaians try very hard to accommodate their guests. Although many Ghanaians are not time conscious, they are aware of western ideas regarding time and expect their western visitors to arrive on schedule. Children are taught to be quiet and respectful around adults, and may seem unfriendly at first. They are also trained to not look an adult in the eye, as such behavior is considered to be an act of defiance. Ghanaians are proud of their nation's efforts to create a

***Culturgrams** are briefings to aid understanding of, feeling for, and communication with other people. Culturgrams are condensations of the best information available. Your insights will be appreciated. If you have refining suggestions, please contact Brigham Young University David M. Kennedy Center for International Studies, Publication Services, 280 HRCB, Provo, Utah 84602 (801) 378-6528. Copyright © 1986. All rights reserved. Printed in the USA.

uniquely African society and may resent an attitude of superiority by Americans. Visitors should avoid gesturing with the left hand.

Eating: Western etiquette is practiced when eating with most Ghanaians. Food is often spicy, and may take some getting used to. Most larger restaurants serve western food as well as native Ghanaian food.

Tipping: *Dash* (from the Portuguese word *das*, meaning "give") is a common Ghanaian form of compensation in money, goods, or favors for services rendered. With the exception of services performed by waiters or bellhops, *dash* is normally paid before the service is given. *Dash* is paid for services ranging from watching a car to expediting the movement of goods in and out of the country. The system of *dash* is discouraged by the government, but is widely practiced.

Personal Appearance: Casual dress is the rule for most occasions, although a suit and tie or dress are required for more formal occasions. Shorts, however, are not acceptable public attire. Western dress is the norm in urban areas, with officials often wearing the traditional *kente* cloth robes on ceremonial occasions. Men in rural areas wear the robes every day. The design of the cloth often reflects the status, purpose, and attitude of the wearer. Women usually wear the traditional long wrap-around skirt, separate top, and head scarf. Guests in Ghana should respect the people's concern for modesty and neatness.

THE PEOPLE

General Attitudes: Ghanaians are proud of their diverse backgrounds. They are also proud of their position as the first sub-Saharan colony to gain independence from European powers. Although they have been greatly influenced by western civilization, the people are striving to develop a nation and culture that is uniquely "African." Ghanaians are generally sociable and take life at a relaxed pace.

Population: The population of Ghana is approximately 13.2 million, and is growing at a rate of 3% annually (0.9% in U.S.). The population-density rate is 110 people per square mile (58 in U.S.). About 99.8% of the population is black African; there are over 100 different ethnic groups, each with its own language and culture. Major groups include the *Fante* in the coastal areas, the *Asante* in the south central area, the *Ga* and *Ewe* in the south, and the *Hausa* and *Moshi-Dagomba* in the north. The .2% non-black population are Europeans and others. The capital is Accra, with a population of 750,000.

Language: Because of the diversity of language and dialects used by the various ethnic groups, no one native language can serve as the national language. Therefore, mainly because of Ghana's long exposure to British culture, English is the official language and is used in school, business, and government. There is currently a movement to make several of the local languages official languages. Some widely-spoken African languages include Akan (spoken by 44% of the people), Mole-Dagbani (16%), Ewe (13%), and Ga-Adange (8%). Most Ghanaians are at least bilingual.

Religion: Traditional African beliefs and practices still play a major role in the lives of the people of Ghana; approximately 45% of the people are animists. Approximately 43% of the people belong to various Christian religions, and 12% are Muslims. Many so-called "religious" practices are inseparable from the life and culture of Ghanaians and are retained regardless of religious affiliation.

Holidays: Holidays include Independence Day (March 6), Good Friday, Easter Monday, Republic Day (July 1), Christmas, and Boxing Day (December 26).

LIFESTYLE

The Family: The details of the family structure vary from one ethnic group to another. Some groups have a matrilineal family organization, in which inheritance is passed down through the wife's family instead of the husband's. In these groups, the chief responsibility for the family falls on the woman. Polygamy (having more than one wife) is also practiced by some Ghanaians. The elderly members of the family are deeply respected and exert a great deal of influence in family decisions. Ghanaians will normally sacrifice their own desires and ambitions for the sake of the family unit.

Dating and Marriage: Many marriages are still arranged by the families, although the children have the right to reject undesirable arrangements. More westernized practices of dating are also found among a growing minority of urban youth. Marriage in rural areas commonly follows tradition, which does not prohibit a man from taking more than one wife. The Christian marriage covenant with its monogamous (single-wife) restrictions is also becoming prevalent. Traditionally, the groom pays the bride's family a "bridal token" to indicate responsibility for the new bride.

Social and Economic Levels: Only about 50% of the people are engaged in economic activities. About one-fourth of the people live in absolute poverty. Luxuries such as cars are rare in Ghana.

Recreation: Soccer is the national sport. Ghanaians are also fond of field hockey, horse racing, track and field, tennis, and boxing. The Ghanaians also enjoy the theater, movies, cultural presentations, and music and dance festivals. Various ethnic-group festivals are celebrated throughout the country.

Diet: The diet consists mainly of yams, cassava (a starchy root), maize, plantain, and rice. Ghanaians enjoy hot and spicy food, and most of their meals are accompanied by a pepper sauce made with meat, fish, or chicken. Ghana also provides a variety of tropical fruits and vegetables to supplement the diet.

THE NATION

Land and Climate: Ghana lies on the Guinea Coast of west Africa, and is about the same size as the state of Oregon. The country is entirely in the tropics. The south is dominated by low lying plains alternating between grass cover and mangrove. The West and southern interior are tropical-forest areas. The Volta River country is covered with savannah woodland and swamps. The dam on the Volta River has created the longest man-made lake in the world (Lake Volta). The north is primarily dry grassland. Sixty percent of the land is covered by forests and brush, and 19% is used for agriculture. The north has 2 equal seasons: rainy from April to October, and hot and dry the rest of the year, with temperatures reaching 100° F. In the south, rain is expected between April and June, and again in September and October. Temperatures in the south range from about 74° F. in October to 86° F. in June.

History and Government: Ghana takes its name, though not its modern boundaries, from one of the great inland trading empires that flourished in West Africa from the fourth to the eleventh centuries A.D. The fabled university city of Timbuctu (now in Mali) was part of ancient Ghana. Because of the diversity of the ethnic groups, the history of the country is quite varied. Modern history begins with contacts with Portuguese traders in 1470. They developed gold mining and slave trading in the area. The control of the "Gold Coast" (which became Ghana in 1957) fell into British hands in the 19th century, and after 74 years of battles with the Asantes of the interior, the British gained control of the present area of Ghana in 1901. The Convention People's Party (CPP), under the leadership of Kwame Nkrumah, won the legislative elections in 1951, and for the first time the black majority controlled the government. On March 6, 1957, Ghana became the first black African colony to gain independence from Britain. Three years later, the country became a republic and Nkrumah, a communist, was elected president. While Nkrumah was visiting Peking in 1966, he was deposed by a military coup. General A. A. Afrifa ruled until general elections were again held in 1969. After 3 years of civilian rule, the military again took over the government in 1972, and Prime Minister Kofi Busia was dismissed. In 1979, former Flight Lt. Jerry J. Rawlings, with a group of junior officers and enlisted men, overthrew the government, arrested dozens of government officials, and executed 8 of them, including 3 former heads of state. Rawlings drafted a new constitution, held elections, and just 4 months after gaining power turned the government over to newly elected Dr. Hilla Limann and the new national assembly. However, after 2 years of civilian rule, Rawlings again seized the government in a coup and took control in December, 1981. Parties have now been outlawed, the constitution suspended, and a seven-member Provisional National Defense Council (PNDC) rules Ghana.

Economy: The Ghanaian economy centers largely on agriculture, which employs over 60% of the people. Cocoa accounts for about 70% of the country's exports. Other important agricultural products include root crops, corn, sorghum, millet, and peanuts. Mining is also an important part of the economy. Ghana is the world's fifth largest producer of diamonds and the seventh largest producer of gold. Manganese, bauxite, and aluminum are also important minerals. Industry employs only about 17% of the people. Since the completion of 2 hydroelectric projects, Ghana has been able to develop some heavier industry, including an aluminum smelter. Important industries are lumbering, light manufacturing, and fishing. Average annual gross national product (GNP) per capita is about $760 ($14,300 in U.S.), and the economy is declining at a rate of 7% annually. The inflation rate is over 32% annually, the highest rate in Africa and the fifth highest in the world (6% in U.S.). About 12% of the people are unemployed (about 8% in U.S.). The standard monetary unit is the *cedi*.

Education: Ghana is striving to increase the availability of primary education. Schools are organized on 3 levels: primary (6 years), junior secondary (3 years), and senior secondary (3 years). Today, every administrative district has at least 1 high school. Currently, about 30,000 students now study above the secondary school level, including students at the 3 full-fledged universities found in Ghana (Legon, Kumasi, Cape Coast). The literacy rate (in English) is about 30%.

Health: Although the government is working to increase the quality and availability of medical care, medical practice is not yet equal to the standards of western medicine. Malaria and other tropical diseases are still present in Ghana. Many of the people rely on traditional forms of herb medicine. It is necessary to clean all fruits and vegetables before eating them. Except in the modern-urban areas visitors should either drink bottled water or boil and filter water. For further medical information, contact International Health Consultants, PO Box 34582, Bethesa, MD 20817.

For Further Information

Because space is so limited in this *Culturgram* and needs are so varied, no suggested readings are included. We recommend a visit to your local library or bookstore. Check *Books in Print* and various cataloging systems for country-specific titles. Review *Encyclopedia Britannica* or similar comprehensive summaries. The U.S. government publishes *Country Profiles* which many libraries subscribe to. Computer searches (DIALOG, SDC, BRS, ISI) are now available at most major libraries. Contact the Embassy of Ghana, 2640 16th Street, N.W., Washington, D.C. 20009, or the National Tourist Board of Ghana, Sontheimer and Company, 445 Park Ave., New York, NY 10022.

How to Use This Culturgram

Quickly read the whole text as an overview. Then circle or give priority numbers to specific questions you have or ideas you want to pursue. Use the *Culturgram* as a guide to check on regional differences and current situations.

Maps

Culturgram maps are meant only as simple geographical orientations. Boundary representations are not necessarily authoritative. Different sources also vary spelling, transliterations, and accents.

Rev. 1/88

CULTURGRAM*

Hong Kong

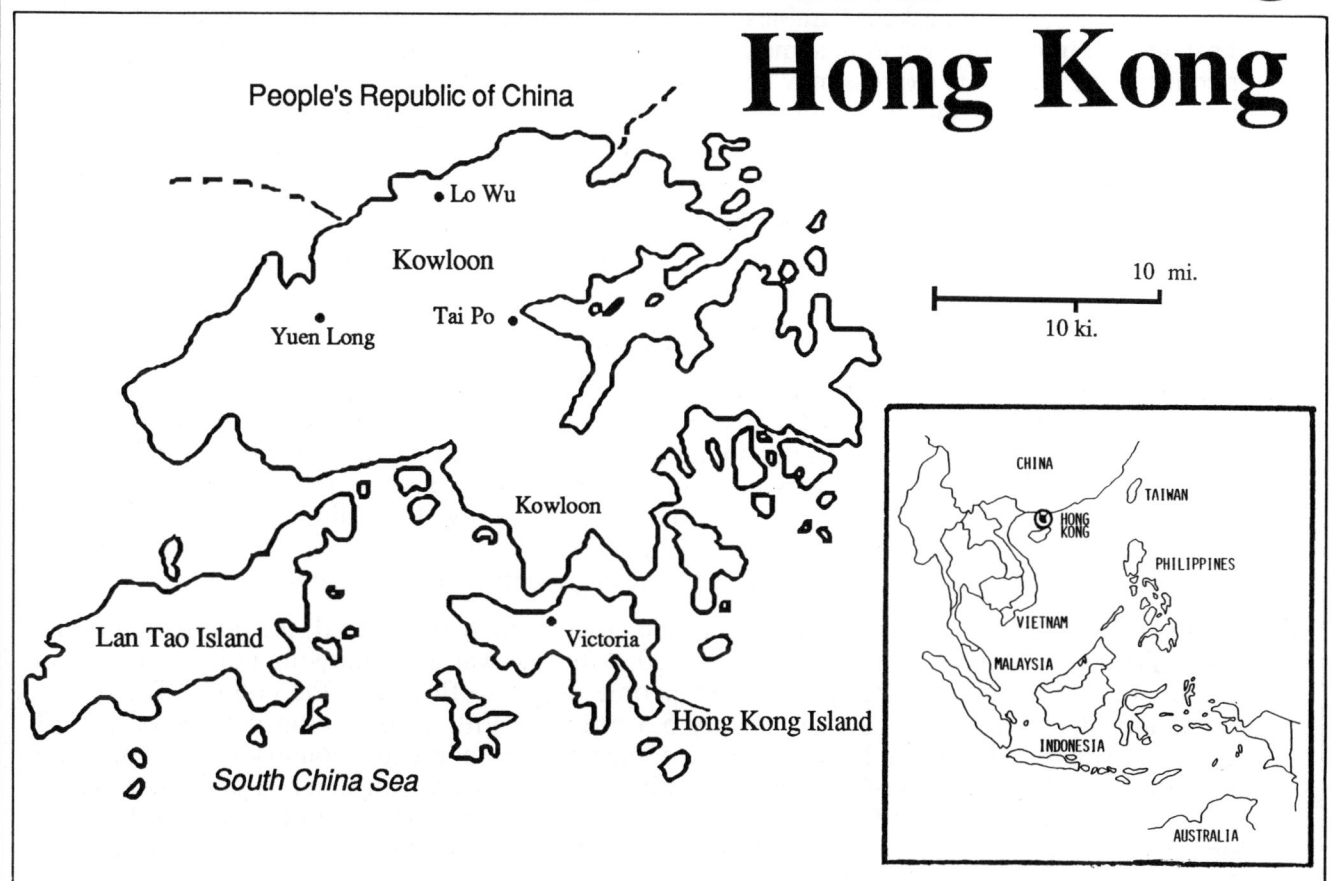

People's Republic of China

CUSTOMS AND COURTESIES

Greetings: The Chinese practice reserve and modesty in dealing with others; aggressive behavior is offensive. Humility or self-demeaning comments are normal in describing one's self or accomplishments. Sincere compliments are given and appreciated, but the Chinese try to deny praise. Polite conversation usually includes inquiries about one's health, business affairs, or school activities. English greetings are generally understood and accepted.

Visiting: A guest at someone's home should take a gift of fruit or candy for the host. Gifts are offered and received with both hands. Shoes are not usually removed when entering a home. Correct social manners include generosity; often the first person to reach the cashier at the ferry terminal will purchase tickets for the entire group. Visitors should sit when invited to do so, and maintain good posture. A special effort should be made to greet and show respect to older people.

Eating: Visitors at a home are usually offered tea, warm water, or a soft drink. Chopsticks are the eating utensils used at every meal. Dishes of food are typically placed in the center of the table. Everyone helps themselves by taking food from the central plates with chopsticks and placing smaller portions in their own personal bowls of rice. It is proper to hold the rice bowl close to one's mouth when eating. The host will try to refill the guest's bowl with more rice and other food until politely refused. It is traditionally inappropriate to eat food on the street.

*Culturgrams are briefings to aid understanding of, feeling for, and communication with other people. Culturgrams are condensations of the best information available. Your insights will be appreciated. If you have refining suggestions, please contact Brigham Young University David M. Kennedy Center for International Studies, Publication Services, 280 HRCB, Provo, Utah 84602 (801) 378-6528. Copyright © 1986. All rights reserved. Printed in the USA.

Public Meetings: When appointments are made, people are generally on time. An older person may feel awkward when being interviewed and should be helped to feel comfortable and relaxed before any questions are asked. Parables and idioms common to Western cultures do not usually translate well into Chinese and in some cases have no meaning at all. However, almost any story or concept one wishes to express may be conveyed by using a Chinese example. By doing a little research and by using examples from the Chinese culture, ideas may be communicated effectively. When using an interpreter, it is best to explain the ultimate goal of one's address and, if specific quotes are to be used, to let the interpreter see them in advance. Loud talking is not appropriate.

Gestures: When sitting down, visitors should place their hands in their lap and keep their feet on the floor. Women may cross their legs. Blinking the eyes at someone is impolite. The open hand, rather than the index finger, should be used for pointing. Beckoning is done with the palm down.

THE PEOPLE

General Attitudes: Hong Kong is referred to as the "Pearl of the Orient." It is a place of natural beauty, impressive modern structures, and, most importantly, resilient, adaptable and energetic people. The Confucian ethic of proper social and family relationships forms the foundation of Chinese society. The Chinese are very conscious of their social position in relation to the people they deal with. An individual's actions reflect on the entire family. The Chinese are concerned with "saving face" by avoiding direct conflicts and will try to allow a person to escape from an embarrassing situation with dignity. Therefore, causing a person to lose face must be avoided.

Population: During the Japanese occupation of Hong Kong in World War II, the population of the colony decreased to an estimated low of 600,000. After the war and following political upheaval on the Chinese mainland, large numbers of people began to flow into the colony. Today, the population of Hong Kong is approximately 5.5 million. With a population-density of 11,182 people per square mile, Hong Kong is the third most densely populated country in the world and the most densely populated in Asia. The population is currently growing at a rate of 1.3% annually (0.9% U.S.). More than 60% of the people live in the city. Hong Kong is an ethnically homogeneous country; approximately 98% of the population are of Chinese descent. Most of the Chinese are Cantonese, with roots in nearby Guangdong Province.

Language: Hong Kong maintains 2 official languages: Chinese and English. Street signs, telephone directories, and government documents are written in both. Although dialects from all provinces of China are heard in Hong Kong (Putonghua, formerly known as Mandarin, Shanghainese, etc.), the Cantonese dialect dominates. Most of the students in Hong Kong study English, and English-speaking visitors will have few communication problems in hotels, banks, business offices, or in most shops and restaurants. Policemen with red shoulder patches on their uniforms speak English. The Chinese are delighted with Westerners who speak Chinese. A visitor who succeeds in using a word or phrase in Cantonese will find himself highly complimented.

Religion: The Chinese have a heritage of diversity with respect to moral philosophy and formal religion. Strong elements of Taoism and Confucianism, both of which originated in China, and Buddhism, imported from India, remain in the religious life of many Hong Kong residents. Folk religious practices and ancestor worship are also widespread. Many homes contain brightly decorated boxes with pictures of deceased relatives, smoldering incense sticks, or symbolic offerings of fruit. Marriages and funerals are special ceremonial events. There is little congregational worship in the Western sense. The faithful observe special occasions with visits to shrines and temples or perform informal rites on the sidewalks near their homes. Nearly all Christian denominations are also represented. Approximately 10% of the people are Christian.

LIFESTYLE

The Family: Chinese family members are bound by a strong tradition of loyalty, obedience, and respect, as reflected by one of the lowest divorce rates in the world. Families are traditionally large and several generations may live together under one roof. Currently, the average family size is 4.5 people (3.1 in U.S.). Harsh economic conditions and differences between traditional values and those imported from the West are sources of stress for many Hong Kong families. The Chinese do not usually display affection in public.

Dating and Marriage: The former practice of marriages arranged by the parents of the bride and groom is no longer common, and dating in the Western style is becoming the norm. Many couples marry at an older age than their Western counterparts.

Social and Economic Levels: There is a wide range of economic levels in Hong Kong. The few private homes on Victoria Peak are luxurious. In the public housing estates, tens of thousands live in high-rise concrete communities in one- or two-room apartments. Some squatters reside in shacks on rooftops or hillsides, and very small fishing vessels are homes to Hong Kong's "boat people" (0.6% of the population). Approximately 7% of the people live in absolute poverty. However, televisions, telephones, and refrigerators are quite common in Hong Kong homes.

Diet: Rice is the staple food. Chinese dishes are often prepared with fish, pork, chicken, or vegetables. A great variety of fruits are also available. Business is often conducted over lunch or dinner. Lavish restaurant meals are traditional for weddings and other special events. Also, many familiar American fast-food restaurants and restaurants specializing in a variety of cuisines are located in Hong Kong.

Work Schedules: Hard work is the basic element of life for most Chinese. A six-day, forty-eight hour work week is normal. Business hours are from 9 a.m. to 5 p.m. 5 days a week, and from 9 a.m. to 1 p.m. on Saturdays. Smaller shops are usually open from early in the morning until late at night. Many people are found on the streets late into the evening.

Recreation: Movies and television are perhaps the most popular forms of entertainment. Beach outings and picnics are also popular. Favorite sports include ping pong, soccer, skating, squash, tennis, swimming, horse racing, basketball, and boating. The noise of *Mah-jong* tiles (a tile game that is a cross between domino and cards) being slapped on a board often fills the streets.

Holidays: The Chinese New Year, usually in late January or early February, is the most important holiday. Week-long festivities include parades, visiting relatives, paying one's debts, and the display of messages of prosperity and longevity on doorways. The Ching Ming Festival in April is similar to the American Memorial Day. Mid-Autumn Festival is a harvest holiday celebrated with lanterns and moon cakes. The Queen's Birthday, Easter, and Christmas are also observed.

THE NATION

Land and Climate: Hong Kong is a British territory occupying a mere 400 square miles on the south coast of China. It is comprised of the tip of the Chinese peninsula adjoining Guangdong Province, 2 large islands (Hong Kong and Lantau), and more than 200 smaller islands. Its total land mass is approximately one-third the size of Rhode Island. The climate is tropical with seasonal monsoons. Average precipitation during the rainy season (May to September) is 85 inches. Temperatures during those months are generally from 80 to 90° F., and the humidity is high. The territory is vulnerable to devastating typhoons which sweep up from the south during the rainy season. The most moderate temperatures occur from October to December. It is cold and damp from January to March. Sweaters and coats are commonly worn during the winter months.

History and Government: China ceded Hong Kong Island to Great Britain in 1842, following British occupation during the so-called Opium War. *Kowloon* (Nine Dragons), the tip of the peninsula directly north of Hong Kong Island, became part of the colony in 1860 under terms of the Convention of Peking. In 1898, China leased the New Territories, extending from Kowloon to the Chinese border, to Britain for 99 years. This lease is due to expire in 1997. In December 1984, Britain and China signed a joint declaration on the future of the territory. The declaration went into effect in May 1985. It says that Hong Kong will become a Special Administrative Region (SAR) of the China on July 1, 1997. The agreement provides for the continuation of Hong Kong's unique social, economic, legal, and other systems for fifty years after 1997, and for Hong Kong's smooth transition to its new status as an SAR. Hong Kong is administered by the Hong Kong government, which was developed from the basic pattern applied in all British-governed territories. A governor, who is the representative of the Queen, and two councils head the government. The Executive Council advises the governor, while the Legislative Council enacts laws and controls the finances. A new system for indirect elections was introduced in 1945 as part of the continuing development of representative government in Hong Kong. The government has achieved remarkable success in dealing with a host of extremely severe social problems by adopting a pragmatic managerial philosophy.

Economy: Only a fraction (9%) of Hong Kong's small land mass is arable, and natural resources are scarce. Because of this, shipping, commerce, and industry have become vital to its survival and economic success. *Hong Kong* means "Fragrant Harbor," and the harbor, with its constant parade of freighters and junks is the key to business. It is a free port; no tariffs are levied on imports or exports. Duties are levied only on tobacco, liquors, methyl alcohol, hydrocarbon oils, cosmetics, and non-alcoholic beverages. In per capita terms, it is one of the top 10 trading nations in the world, and no other country has a higher percentage of its people engaged in manufacturing (36%). Chief among the products of Hong Kong's light industries are textiles and clothing, plastics, electronics, and toys. Tourism is also a significant source of income. Only 2% of the people are employed in agriculture, one of the smallest percentages in the world. Land capable of supporting crops is worked intensively; the main crops are rice and vegetables, but Hong Kong is dependent on outside sources, primarily China, for over 80% of its food. The economy is growing at a healthy rate of over 8% annually and average annual gross national product (GNP) per capita is about $6,330 ($14,300 in U.S.). Unemployment is only 3% (7% in U.S.), and underemployment remains at a low level of 1.1%. The inflation rate was 3.2% in 1985 (6% in U.S.).

Education: Scholarship is a long-standing Chinese tradition, and formal education is valued highly by citizens of Hong Kong. A free, nine-year education program is required of all children. The quality of the schools, government-sponsored or privately-supported, varies considerably. Admission to the better secondary schools is based on competitive examinations. There are three government financed post-secondary institutions and five technical institutes in Hong Kong. The two universities in Hong Kong allow entrance to only 12,000 students, so large numbers of students seek higher education abroad. Some students do not return to Hong Kong after completing their studies elsewhere. Hong Kong's literacy rate is nearly 90%.

Transportation: The newly completed subway system offers rapid transit to major Hong Kong Island and Kowloon locations. An electrified train systems connects Kowloon and the New Territories. There is also an extensive bus and train system. Taxis and minibuses are widely available. A ferry service connects the islands and the mainland.

Health: Excellent medical care is available in all hospitals and clinics, although the government facilities are often crowded. Extremes in sanitary conditions can be seen. Life expectancy is the highest in the world (76 years), and the death rate is one of the lowest. For further medical information, contact International Health Consultants, PO Box 582, Bethesda, MD 20817.

For Further Information

Because space is so limited in this *Culturgram* and needs are so varied, no suggested readings are included. We recommend a visit to your local library or bookstore. Check *Books in Print* and various cataloging systems for country-specific titles. Review *Encyclopedia Britannica* or similar comprehensive summaries. The U.S. government publishes *Country Profiles* which many libraries subscribe to. Computer searches (DIALOG, SDC, BRS, ISI) are available at most major libraries. Contact: Embassy of Great Britain, 3100 Massachusetts Ave., N.W., Washington, D.C. 20008, or the Hong Kong Tourist Association, 548 Fifth Ave., New York, NY 10036; 421 Powell St. #200, San Francisco, CA 94102; 333 North Michigan Ave., Suite 2323, Chicago, IL 60601.

How to Use This Culturgram

Quickly read the whole text as an overview. Then circle or give priority numbers to specific questions you have or ideas you want to pursue. Use the *Culturgram* as a guide to check on regional differences and current situations.

Maps

Culturgram maps are meant only as simple geographical orientations. Boundary representations are not necessarily authoritative. Different sources also vary spelling, transliterations, and accents.

Rev. 1/88

CULTURGRAM*

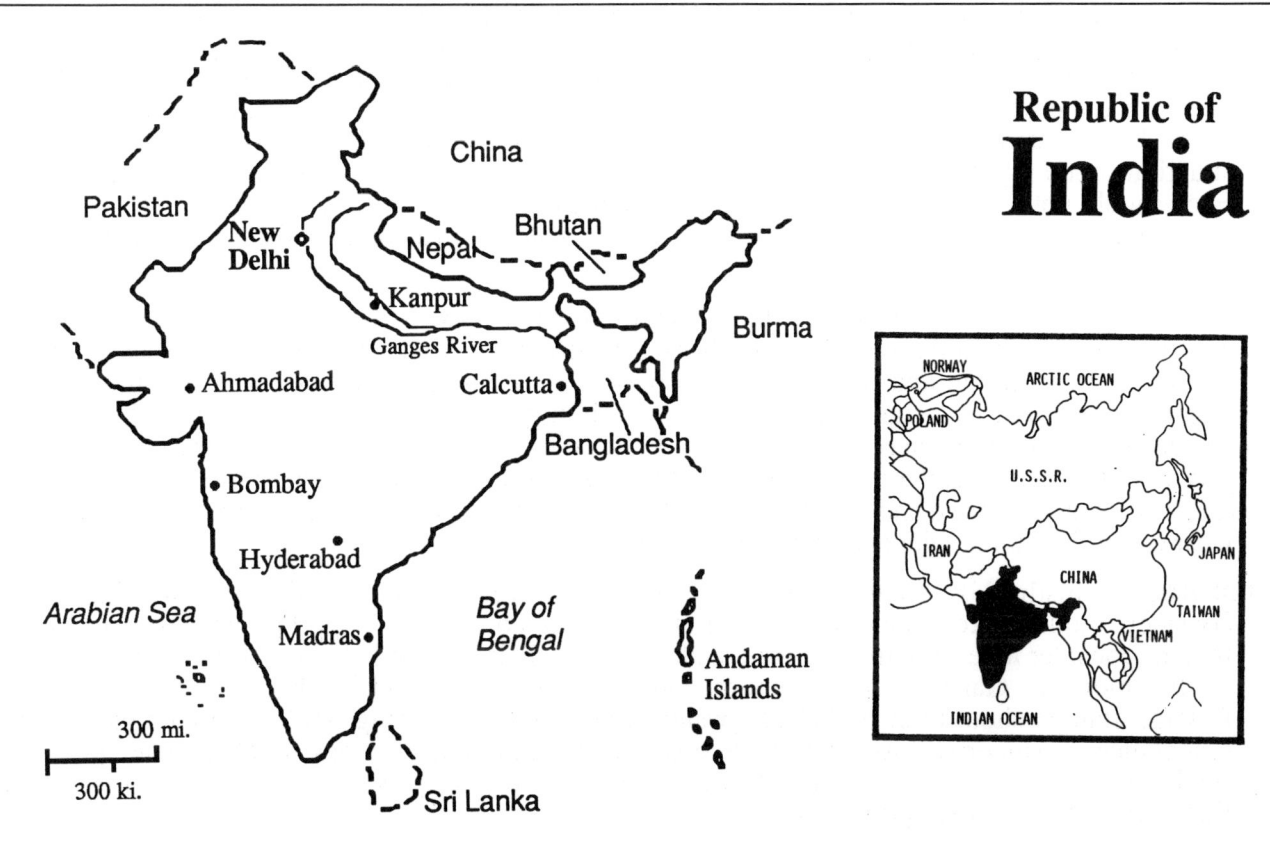

Republic of India

CUSTOMS AND COURTESIES

Greetings: The *namaste* (bending gently with palms together below the chin) is generally used. Indians do not usually shake hands or touch women in formal or informal gatherings. This is a sign of respect for a woman's privacy. Educated women, however, shake hands with westerners as a courtesy. It is polite to use titles such as professor and doctor, Mr., Shri, or the suffix *ji* with a last name to show respect. One should use the right hand for the *salaam* gesture of greeting and farewell with Muslims. Indians usually ask permission before taking leave of others.

Visiting: At social gatherings, guests are often adorned with a garland of flowers. The garland should be removed immediately, as an expression of humility, and carried in hand. India is a male-oriented society. Orthodox Muslim women are usually kept from the view of men outside their families. Women often stay out of the conversation and usually do not attend social functions. When the host and guests go out together, the host insists on paying for everything. Guests may repay the host by giving gifts such as specialty foods (fruits, sweets) from other areas of the country, or by giving gifts to the children in the family. Some Indians cannot invite you to their homes because of religious, financial, or spacial limitations. Indians do not wear footwear inside their homes, and visitors should remove their shoes when entering a home. Tea or coffee with sugar and milk stirred in is usually offered to guests. Fruits or sweets may also be offered. It is polite for guests to initially refuse refreshments. When guests leave the host arranges for their transportation, providing he has a car, and accompanies the guests to the gate or beyond. When invited to a social function, Indians are too polite to say no. If they cannot attend they will usually say "I'll try." People generally take coconuts, flowers, and fruit to the temple as offerings to show their religious zeal and dedication. In temples saffron powder, holy water from the Ganges river, and sometimes food are offered to visitors as *prasad*, or blessings from the Lord. It is discourteous to refuse such gifts. Women cover their heads when entering sacred places.

*Culturgrams are briefings to aid understanding of, feeling for, and communication with other people. Culturgrams are condensations of the best information available. Your insights will be appreciated. If you have refining suggestions, please contact Brigham Young University David M. Kennedy Center for International Studies, Publication Services, 280 HRCB, Provo, Utah 84602 (801) 378-6528. Copyright © 1986. All rights reserved. Printed in the USA.

Eating: When invited for a meal, it is customary to bring sweets, flowers, or fruit to the host family. Compliments on decor, clothes, etc., are appreciated. If the family uses no cutlery, it is advisable to assure them that you enjoy eating with your hands. The right hand should be used for eating and for giving or receiving objects. Conversation generally comes before the meal and guests should leave soon after eating. Men, elderly people, and children usually eat first with the guests, and the women eat after guests have finished. The guest is usually given large helpings of food. The *namaste* gesture is the most polite way to show one has had enough. In uncomfortable situations one might say, "I'm sorry, that's not our custom," and the host will likely understand. Food should not be taken from the eating area. Hindus are careful that their food is not touched by people outside their caste or religion. When drinking water from a communal container, the lips do not touch it.

Personal Appearance: Women in India usually wear *sarees* —traditional, long, and colorful dresses. Younger ladies wear slacks, shirts, and dresses. Men generally wear western-style clothing. Both single and married women may wear a *bindi*, or red dot, on their foreheads. Traditionally this was a sign of good posture, femininity, and gracefulness, but in modern times has become more often an optional beauty aid, the color of the *bindi* often matching the wearer's *saree*. After marriage, the dot, accompanied by a white powder on the upper forehead, signifies that a woman is married and that her husband is alive; widows do not wear a *bindi*. Women also wear colorful clothing with considerable jewelry.

Gestures: Whistling is very impolite. Women should never wink or whistle, as such behavior is considered unladylike. Public displays of affection are considered inappropriate in India. Most Indians consider love to be divine, and couples express their love and affection only in the privacy of their homes. Garlands of flowers displayed at bazaars should not be sniffed or handled. Postage stamps should not be licked—water is provided. Grasping one's own ears expresses repentance or sincerity. Apologies are essential if your feet or shoes touch another person. Beckoning is done with the palm turned down and pointing is often done with the chin. Backslapping is not appropriate.

Traveling: When taxis have no meters, it is advisable to settle on the price before getting in. On trains, except for "air conditioned" class, one must bring personal bedding, toiletries, tissues, towels, and drinking water. Travel to some parts of the country is limited because of a lack of roads and other services. India has 9 major ports and 3 national airline corporations.

THE PEOPLE

General Attitudes: The Indian people are religious, family-oriented, and philosophical, and believe strongly in simple material comforts and rich spiritual accomplishments. Abundant expressions of gratitude are typically saved for real favors rather than routine courtesies. Physical purity and spiritual refinement are highly valued. Acceptance of incidents as the will of fate is widespread. Many urbanized women are "westernized," but traditional values of modesty and humility continue to be important to most Indian women. National hero Mahatma Gandhi's ideals of humility and self-denial are highly respected. Social harmony is important.

Population: The population of India is approximately 762.5 million, the second largest population in the world (China is first). The population-growth rate is over 2% annually. The population density is about 470 people per square mile (58 in U.S.). India is one of the most ethnically diverse countries in the world. Religion and language, however, separate the people more than race does. About 72% of the people are Indo-Aryan; 25% are Dravidian; the remainder is composed of Mongoloid and other races.

Language: There are more than 1600 languages and dialects in India, 24 with more than 1 million speakers. There are 15 official languages. Hindi, spoken by 30% of the people, is the national language. English is spoken widely in government and business. Hindustani is spoken widely throughout northern India.

Religion: India is the birthplace of Hinduism, Jainism, Sikhism, and Buddhism, and is the adopted homeland of Zoroastrianism. About 83.5% of the people are Hindu. Hinduism is associated with the caste system, which has been abolished by the constitution, although it is still practiced by more traditional Hindus. About 10.7% of the people are Muslims and 2.6% are Christians. Christianity was traditionally associated with the "untouchable" class. About 1.8% are Sikhs and .7% are Buddhists. The remainder belong to various tribal and other religions.

LIFESTYLE

The Family: The basic social unit is the family; it takes precedence over the individual. In most families aunts, uncles, and other relatives live together. The elderly are respected and are cared for in their old age by their families. Traditional families are large, with at least 6 children. Modern, urban families are smaller, with 2-4 children. Due to the large population in India, the government is currently trying to promote family planning. In fact, the Indian government spends more on family planning than any other government in the world.

Dating and Marriage: Customs are different and becoming more westernized, but traditional marriages are still arranged by the parents, with the consent of the bride and groom. Marriage is very sacred and divine to most Indians. A marriage is considered to endure beyond death. Conventional dating and divorce are rare. India's divorce rate is one of the lowest in the world. For an Indian woman, chastity is the most treasured virtue of womanhood. Weddings are times of great celebration and feasting, and are often expensive for the bride's family.

Social and Economic Levels: The effects of the extensive caste system in India can still be easily seen. Class consciousness is very apparent. A wide gap separates the few who are rich and the many who are poor. About 30% of the people live in absolute poverty, and there are still people living on the verge of starvation. The caste system still limits social mobility, but not as much as in the past.

Diet: Indian meals are wholesome, and prepared mostly from scratch. Breakfast, lunch, snacks, and dinner are served daily. Coffee and tea are served with breakfast and at snacktime. Water is commonly served with all meals. Wheat bread *roti* is the staple food in the north, while rice is the staple in the south. Curry (eggs, fish, meat, or vegetables in a spicy sauce) is a popular dish. Different varieties of cereals and vegetables are also eaten. Hindus eat no beef, and Muslims, no pork. Vegetarianism is widely practiced. All castes have different food laws. After meals, betel leaves and nuts are commonly served to aid in digestion.

Recreation and the Arts: More movies are produced in India than in any other country in the world. Every major city has 100-150 modern theaters, some with elevators and restaurants. Music concerts and dance performances are very popular. Indian dancing is religious in origin. The hands and arms are used to tell stories. Indian temples and frescoes are magnificent. The Taj Mahal is a classic example of Muslim architecture. The ancient Sanskrit classics are among the world's greatest literature. Hockey, cricket, soccer and rugby are national sports.

Holidays: National holidays are Republic Day (January 26), Independence Day (August 15), Mahatma Gandhi's Birthday (October 2), and Christmas (December 25 and 26). Also, 22 days each year are dedicated to various religious and sacred holidays.

THE NATION

Land and Climate: India is the seventh largest country in the world, roughly one-third of the size of the United States. The majestic Himalaya mountains form India's northern border. The Ganges plain below is fertile and densely populated. Below that is the Deccan plateau. Approximately half of the country is currently under cultivation, and one-quarter is forested. The climate varies from tropical in the south to continental in the northern mountains. The 3 basic seasons are March-May (hot summer), June-September (rainy), and October-February (cool winter).

History and Government: The Indus Valley civilization dates back over 5,000 years. From about 500 B.C., Aryans speaking Sanskrit merged with Dravidians (natives) to create the classical Indian society. Buddhism flourished in King Asoka's reign, 3rd century B.C., but declined afterward. The Gupta Kingdom, 4-6th century A.D., was a golden age of science, literature and the arts. Arab, Turk, and Afghan Muslims ruled successively from the 8th to the 18th centuries. Following this Portuguese and Dutch traders came, but the English eventually assumed political control of

India. After World War I, the continuing nationalist movement was led by Mahatma Gandhi. He organized a series of passive-resistance campaigns and advocated civil disobedience to British rule. In 1947, Britain granted independence to India, but due to the politics of the Muslim league the country was separated into a secular India and Musim Pakistan. The partition brought about religious riots, killings, and mass migrations. Gandhi attempted to stop the religious violence, but was assassinated on January 30, 1948. On January 26, 1950, India became a parliamentary republic in the British Commonwealth and Jawaharlal Nehru became prime minister. When Nehru died in 1964, Lal Bahadur Shastri succeeded him as prime minister. Upon Shastri's sudden death, Indira Gandhi, Nehru's daughter, was chosen prime minister in 1966. She was defeated in 1977 by Morarji Ranchhodji Desai and his Janata Party, but Gandhi was re-elected in 1980. Religious violence erupted again in 1984 in Punjab province, where Sikh nationalists clashed with Indian soldiers. Hundreds were killed in disturbances originating on both sides. The storming of the Sikh Golden Temple by government troops caused even more social unrest and resulted in the assassination of Indira Gandhi by her own Sikh guards on Oct 31, 1984. Her son, Rajiv Gandhi, was chosen by the president of India to be prime minister and subsequently won a national election held in December, 1984. The parliament has 2 houses: the Lok Sabha (House of the People), and the Rajya Sabha (Council of State). There are 23 states and 9 union territories.

Economy: The Indian economy is predominantly agricultural. India is rich in natural resources and manpower. Since 1947, the government's goal has been to diversify the economy by accelerating the growth of industrial development. Today about 70% of the people are employed in agriculture. India ranks first in the world in the production of peanuts, second in rice and cheese, third in tobacco, fourth in wheat, cotton, milk, and butter, and fifth in sugarcane and rubber. Other important crops include other cereals, oilseed, jute, tea, and coffee. Despite being self-sufficient in food grains, some areas are occasionally affected by shortages. Important industries include textiles, food processing, steel, machinery, transportation equipment, cement, and jute processing. Tourism is also an increasingly important part of the economy. Despite a relatively large gross national product (GNP), because of the huge population, the average annual GNP per capita is only $210 ($14,300 in U.S.). It ranks as one of the smallest GNP-per-capita amounts in the world. The economy is currently growing at a rate of about 1.8% annually, and the country is still dependent on large amounts of foreign aid. Currently more than 10% of the people are unemployed or underemployed; there is a significant shortage of skilled labor and unemployment is rising. Inflation is typically higher than the U.S. The unit of currency is the *rupee*.

Education: Education is the primary concern of the various states. Under the Directive Principle of State Policy, schooling is free and compulsory from ages 6 to 14, but facilities are often inadequate. Plans call for extensive development of libraries to improve the literacy rate, which is now at 36%. India's book industry is growing to meet the increasing demand. India has 120 universities, 3,000 colleges and over 15 institutes dedicated to research in the arts and science.

Health: Malnutrition and poor living conditions contribute to the high death rate. While life expectancy has nearly doubled since independence, it is still only 56 years.. The government is working to expand health services. For further medical information contact International Health Consultants, PO Box 34582, Bethesda, MD 20817.

For Further Information

Because space is so limited in this *Culturgram* and needs are so varied, no suggested readings are included. We recommend a visit to your local library or bookstore. Check *Books in Print* and various cataloging systems for country-specific titles. Review *Encyclopedia Britannica* or similar comprehensive summaries. The U.S. government publishes *Country Profiles* which many libraries subscribe to. Computer searches (DIALOG, SDC, BRS, ISI) are now available at most major libraries. Contact Indian Embassy 2107 Massachusetts Ave., N.W., Washington, D.C. 20008, or the Government of India Tourist Office, 30 Rockefeller Plaza, N. Mezz., New York, NY 10020.

Rev. 1/88

CULTURGRAM*

Republic of Indonesia

CUSTOMS AND COURTESIES

Greetings: Indonesian culture is based on honor and respect for the individual. Letters begin with *Dengan hormat,* (with respect). Respect should always be remembered when greeting others. Men and women usually shake hands and bow the head slightly when introduced for the first time. Otherwise, it is unusual to shake hands in greeting. Indonesians shake hands when congratulating someone or when saying goodbye before a long trip. When one is introduced to older people, a slight bow is appropriate. Unless married or engaged, a man does not touch a woman in public, except to shake hands, even if he knows her well. It is not acceptable for foreigners to kiss in public. If a person has a prestigious title (such as doctor or professor), it should be used in conversation.

Visiting: Guests are welcomed warmly. A visitor should sit when invited but should rise when the host or hostess enters the room. Hosts will almost always serve a drink, but one should not drink until invited. It is polite, but not necessary, to remove one's shoes if the host or hostess is not wearing footwear. Shoes should be removed before entering carpeted rooms, feasting places, places of funeral viewings, or holy places, especially mosques. Sunglasses should be removed when speaking to someone or when entering a home. It is polite to bring flowers when invited to dinner with more westernized Indonesians. Gifts are generally not expected by traditional Indonesians, but compliments and notes of appreciation are always welcome. Gifts should be accepted graciously; it is impolite to refuse anything. Indonesians do not generally open gifts in the presence of the giver.

*****Culturgrams** are briefings to aid understanding of, feeling for, and communication with other people. Culturgrams are condensations of the best information available. Your insights will be appreciated. If you have refining suggestions, please contact Brigham Young University David M. Kennedy Center for International Studies, Publication Services, 280 HRCB, Provo, Utah 84602 (801) 378-6528. Copyright © 1986. All rights reserved. Printed in the USA.

Eating: Although there are many restaurants along the streets, eating while standing or walking on the street is inappropriate. Running water is found only in large cities. Usually, water should be boiled or otherwise prepared for drinking. Finishing a drink implies desire for the glass to be refilled. Food served in homes is usually safe, but care should be taken in buying food from street stands. Many westernized Indonesians eat with a spoon and fork, but more traditional families eat with their hands. Generally the fork is used in the left hand and the spoon in the right. It is impolite to eat or drink until invited to do so by one's host. Both hands are kept on the table while eating. Hostesses appreciate compliments on the food, but humorous remarks about the food are a serious breach of etiquette. At restaurants, tips are usually included in the bill. Toothpicks should not be used in public.

Public Meetings: Typical meetings are formal and proper. Respect is paid to those conducting meetings. Indonesians greatly value a quiet voice, an unassuming attitude, and agreement by consent. The worst possible insult is to embarrass another, so necessary disagreement and criticism should be handled privately. Laughing at another's mistakes is very offensive.

Personal Appearance: Public dress is left up to the individual, provided it is modest. Indonesians are conservative dressers and slow to accept new styles. Shorts, tank tops, thongs, and the like are not appropriate. A shirt and tie are appropriate for businessmen. A suit coat is not worn except for very formal occasions, such as weddings.

Gestures: Gestures are not used for calling someone, except to a child or a *becak* (a pedicab-like vehicle, pronounced "betchalk") driver. Waving one's hand with the palm facing down signals another person to come. Approval is sometimes shown by a pat on the shoulder, but touching the head of another is considered very disrespectful. The left hand should not be used to shake hands, touch others, point, eat food, or give or receive objects. Standing with hands in pockets or on hips is interpreted as defiance or arrogance and should be avoided. Crossing the legs while sitting is usually considered inappropriate, but if they are crossed, one knee should be directly over the other. Yawning should be avoided, but if one must yawn, a hand should be placed over the mouth.

Traveling: On public transportation systems, a person is expected to give his or her seat to the elderly, and men are expected to offer their seats to women. Taxis and *becaks* are always available; a houseboy or bellhop will help call one. The customer should not get in until the driver has been told the destination point and a fare has been agreed upon.

Shopping: In stores in which bargaining is appropriate, the reasonable price is usually about one-half to two-thirds the first given price. People usually do not give large bills unless they have asked first and know change is available. In some large department stores, prices are fixed.

THE PEOPLE

General Attitudes: Indonesians value loyalty to family and friends more than individual advancement. They rarely disagree in public, seldom say no (but rather say *belum*, "not yet"), and always have time for others. Punctuality, while important, is never emphasized at the expense of personal relations. Indonesians often view westerners as too quick to anger, too serious about themselves, and too committed to the idea that "time is money."

Population: Indonesia has a population of 173.1 million, which is the fifth largest in the world. The population-growth rate is about 2.1% annually (0.9% in U.S.). The population-density rate is approximately 223 people per square mile, although the island of Java is much more densely populated. Indonesia has more than 60 ethnic groups, each having its own customs, culture and language. Approximately 45% of the people are Japanese, 14% are Sudanese, 7.5% Madurese, 7.5% coastal Malays, and the remaining 26% belong to various other ethnic groups. The westernized farmers of Java and Bali form the largest cultural group. They are predominantly Muslim. Members of this group have strong social and spiritual values, and are highly developed in the arts of native dance, music, and drama. The commercially oriented traders of the coastal region, mostly Muslim, have a high regard for religious learning and the law. Some northern areas are strongly Christian. The tribes of Borneo and West Irian have strong kinship bonds, animistic religions, and a clan-oriented economic and social life.

Language: Although the official language is Bahasa Indonesian (a modified form of Malay), more than 200 languages and dialects are spoken. English is taught as a second language in the schools. Many of the older people also speak Dutch.

Religion: Ninety percent of Indonesia's population are Muslim. Another 5% are Christian (mainly protestant), and 3% are Hindu. Confucianism and Buddhism are also present (mainly among the Chinese). There is a strong feeling of national pride and veneration of ancestors among Indonesians.

LIFESTYLE

The Family: Traditionally, the Indonesian people have encouraged large families. Members of the extended family often live under the same roof or nearby. Loyalty and cooperation among family members are highly valued.

Dating and Marriage: Except in a few areas, the women wear no veils and have rights in property settlements, inheritances, and divorces. As in other Muslim countries, a man may have as many as four wives. Arranged marriages have generally given way to marriages of individual choice in urban areas, but are still common in rural areas.

Social and Economic Levels: There are both poor and rich in Indonesia, as is reflected by the income distribution: the richest 10% of the population receives about 34% of the national income with the poorest 20% only getting 6.6%. Approximately 51% of the people live in absolute poverty. Few homes have running water. A low crime rate prevails in Indonesia.

Diet: Rice is the main crop and staple food. Vegetables, fish, and hot sauces are often served with the rice. Tea is the most common drink. Fresh fruits are widely available and are the most common dessert.

Work: Most businesses close for 2 to 3 hours in the middle of the day. Business and government offices close at midday on Friday for worship. Many businesses also close on Saturday and Sunday.

Recreation: Indonesians enjoy sports of all types. Soccer is very popular among the youth. Indonesians are consistently the best in the world in badminton. Bicycling is a major means of transportation and exercise. Volleyball and tennis are also popular.

Holidays: Indonesians celebrate National Independence Day (August 17), Ascension of Mohammed, Idul Fitr (first day of the tenth lunar month), Idul-Adha (eleventh day of the twelfth lunar month), and the Muslim New Year. Lebaren, the day after Muslim Fast, is a holiday celebrated by all Muslims.

THE NATION

Land and Climate: The islands of Indonesia stretch in a 3,000 mile arc along the equator. There is a total of 13,500 islands, together about one-fifth the size of the United States. The dry season is from June to November, with temperatures ranging from 80° to 90° F., and the wet monsoon season is from November to March. The dry season does have some rainfall. Average annual precipitation is from 70-150 inches.

History and Government: When Christopher Columbus discovered America, he was looking for the East Indies and access to the rich spice trade. Most of those islands are a part of present-day Indonesia. Indonesia was a Dutch colony for several hundred years. Early in the 20th century, resistance groups began fighting for independence, which resulted in independence on August 17,

1945. Attempts by the communist party to gain control in 1965 were thwarted, and the party is presently illegal in Indonesia. Although there are free elections in theory, issues and candidates are carefully screened by the ruling party.

Economy: Indonesia is a country rich in natural resources, much of which remain undeveloped. Agriculture still employs 64% of the people and accounts for 53% of production. Indonesia is the world's second largest producer of rubber and third in rice. It also ranks fifth in soybean and timber production. Other agricultural products include copra and tea. Industry is playing an increasingly important role in the economy and currently employs about 7% of the people. Petroleum (owned and operated by the government), textiles, mining (copper and nickel), cement, and chemical fertilizers are all important industries. Trade employs about 12% of the people. The average annual gross national product (GNP) per capita is only $530 ($14,300 in U.S.), but the economic growth rate has been nearly 7% over the last 10 years. It is currently 4.5%. The inflation rate is typically higher than in the U.S. The monetary unit is the *rupiah*.

Education: Education is compulsory between ages 8 and 14, although facilities are still inadequate in outlying areas. Each of Indonesia's 27 provinces has at least 1 university or academy. The literacy rate is estimated to be about 64%.

Transportation: Because of its geographic layout, Indonesia has one of the best transport systems in the world. The main islands are served by major international airlines. Indonesia has some of the most accessible airfields in the world, although compared to western standards, most are of poor quality. Inter-island and mass transit systems are not yet adequate to meet all of the needs of the people. Recently, more people have been able to afford cars, but there are still few paved roads. Taxis are available in the cities. Big cities also have good rail transport systems, and buses are also available. The most common means of transportation are the bicycle and the *becak*.

Health: Medical facilities are reasonably good in the major cities, but are very sparse in the rural areas. The average life expectancy is from 45 to 50 years. For further medical information, contact International Health Consultants, PO Box 34582, Bethesda, MD 20817.

For Further Information

Because space is so limited in this *Culturgram* and needs are so varied, no suggested readings are included. We recommend a visit to your local library or bookstore. Check *Books in Print* and various cataloging systems for country-specific titles. Review *Encyclopedia Britannica* or similar comprehensive summaries. The U.S. government publishes *Country Profiles* which many libraries subscribe to. Computer searches (DIALOG, SDC, BRS, ISI) are now available at most major libraries. Contact the Embassy of Indonesia, 2020 Massachusetts Avenue, N.W., Washington, D.C. 20036, or the Indonesian Tourist Promotion Board, 323 Geary St., San Francisco, CA 94102. The U.S. Embassy in Indonesia is located at Medan Merdeka Selatan 5, Jakarta.

How to Use This Culturgram

Quickly read the whole text as an overview. Then circle or give priority numbers to specific questions you have or ideas you want to pursue. Use the *Culturgram* as a guide to check on regional differences and current situations.

Maps

Culturgram maps are meant only as simple geographical orientations. Boundary representations are not necessarily authoritative. Different sources also vary spelling, transliterations, and accents.

Rev. 1/88

CULTURGRAM*

Islamic Republic of Iran

CUSTOMS AND COURTESIES

Greetings: A handshake is the customary greeting. A slight bow or nod while shaking hands shows respect. Iranians generally stand when someone enters the room for the first time and again at leave-taking. Iranians, including men, kiss each other on the cheek as a greeting and a sign of affection. Close friends and children may be called by their first names. To shake hands with a child shows respect to his parents. A man should wait for the lady to extend her hand first.

Visiting: One should smile and greet every member of the family. Guests are the center of attention and are expected to be kind, intelligent, and able to converse on a variety of subjects. Even if excused from doing so, visitors should always take off their shoes before entering carpeted areas. A polite guest also compliments the host generously and accepts compliments in return. Guests should always mention the ownership of articles being complimented; otherwise the host may feel obligated to give the article to the guest. Hospitality is a cherished tradition in Iran. The Iranian philosophy is "a guest is a gift of God." When invited to dinner, it is customary to bring the hostess a flowering plant, cut flowers, or candy. Customarily, Iranians do not open gifts upon receiving them. If offered gifts or invitations from a friend, it is polite to decline a few times before accepting. It is also polite to thank the giver several times. The place of honor is always given to the oldest man present.

Eating: A host will often prepare the finest Persian food and may insist that the guests eat several servings. Iranians are very hospitable and may offer visitors tea with other foods and drinks. To

---

*Culturgrams are briefings to aid understanding of, feeling for, and communication with other people. Culturgrams are condensations of the best information available. Your insights will be appreciated. If you have refining suggestions, please contact Brigham Young University David M. Kennedy Center for International Studies, Publication Services, 280 HRCB, Provo, Utah 84602 (801) 378-6528. Copyright © 1986. All rights reserved. Printed in the USA.

decline the tea graciously and thank the host is not considered impolite. A cold juice or soft drink may be requested instead. Water is clean and safe in Tehran and other cities with filter systems. Generally, food is eaten with the right hand, and food or objects are passed with the right or both hands.

Personal Appearance: Iranians often dress formally; however, upon retiring to their homes at lunch time or in the evening, Iranians often dress in pajamas to feel more comfortable. They may also receive guests in this apparel. Women dress modestly, with covered arms and heads. No flashy styles or colors are worn. Currently, the Islamic regime does not allow men to wear short-sleeved shirts. Women are required to wear thick, opaque stockings in pubic.

Gestures: In conversation, a smile and the use of hand gestures may aid in communication. Crossing one's legs when sitting in front of a group is acceptable, but to slouch in the chair or to stretch one's legs is offensive. Out of respect, men and women do not always maintain eye contact in conversation. Men and women should not hold hands or show affection for each other in public. However, women may show affection for women, and men for men. To beckon, wave the fingers with the palm down. To tilt the head up quickly means "no." To twist the head means "what?" and tilt it down means "yes." To extend the thumb is vulgar. It is also considered rude to show the sole of one's foot.

THE PEOPLE

General Attitudes: The Iranian people as a whole like foreigners, even Americans. Their apparent dislike for Americans is, in fact, a contempt for the U.S. government's foreign policy toward Iran. Modernization began in the 1970s, but the recent fundamental Islamic revolution has curtailed most of the modern trends.

Population: Iran's population is approximately 45.2 million, and is growing at the high yearly rate of about 3.1% (0.9% growth rate in U.S.). Approximately one-third of the people live in cities and large towns. Tehran, the capital, is the largest city, but the national urban population is divided among various large centers: Tabriz in the north, Isfahan in the center, Abadan in the oil-producing gulf region, and Shiraz in the south. Since the Islamic Revolution in 1979, the government has encouraged more people to return to farms. Tribal life has been a traditional part of Iranian society; nomadic or semi-nomadic groups form 17% of the population. The population density is about 50 people per square mile (58 in U.S.).

Language: Iran's official language is Persian (Farsi), with many dialects. Turkish is also widely spoken in the north; there are 14 million Iranians of Turkish background. Also, Arabic is spoken in the southwest. French is the major cultural language and English is also used, especially for business.

Religion: Shiite Islam (believers are called Moslems or Muslims) has been the state religion of Iran since 1500 A.D. and is strongly identified with Iranian nationalism. Approximately one-tenth of the world's Moslems are Shiite and Iran is the most populous Shiite Moslem country. Shiite Islam reveres the prophet Muhammad's daughter, Fatima, her husband, Ali, their two sons, Hassan and Hussein, and their descendents (*Imams*). Imams are regarded as holy men. The twelfth Imam disappeared and it is believed that he will reappear to guide Moslems in the future. The Koran, the scripture of Moslems, is composed of revelations from the angel Gabriel to Muhammad. These revelations spoke of prophets also mentioned in the Bible, including Adam, Noah, Abraham, Isaac, Jacob, Joseph, Moses, and Jesus. The Moslems are adamant that Jesus is not the son of God, but a revered prophet. Since the revolution, a conservative and fundamentalist type of Islam has been imposed on the people by the clergy (*Mullahs*). Other religious groups, such as Jews, Bahais, and Protestants, have reported persecution. No proselyting of other religions is allowed.

LIFESTYLE

The Family: The family unit is very strong in Iran and provides its members with identity, security, and social organization. The father rules the house with undisputed authority. Large families with many children, especially boys, are desirable. It is lawful to have more than one wife, but the practice is not widespread. The average family size in Iran is 5 people (3.1 in U.S.).

Dating and Marriage Customs: Iranian girls generally marry between the ages of 18 and 25. Men may have to marry later because of military service or time spent earning enough money to start a family. Daughters in more traditional families stay at home and are not allowed to talk to strangers until married. New attitudes emphasizing school, work, more freedom in selecting marriage partners, and less cousin marriages have developed in recent years, especially in the urban centers.

Social and Economic Levels: The average family income is usually adequate to feed and clothe a family. Traditional economic gaps between the social classes are diminishing as the new government has had a leveling effect on society in general. The upper and middle classes often have cars, appliances, televisions, and telephones, although the recent revolution and war has limited the availability of such luxury items.

Diet: Diet varies throughout the country. Most Moslems do not eat pork and some do not eat shellfish. Rice and wheat bread are staples, usually eaten with a meat-and-vegetable stew. Yogurt, fresh vegetables, and white cheese are also eaten. Fresh fruit is a favorite dessert. The consumption of alcoholic beverages is prohibited.

Business: The business week runs from Saturday through Thursday. Hours are usually from 8 a.m. to noon, and from 2 to 6 p.m. Some businesses are only open until noon on Thursday, with most businesses closed on Friday, the Muslim day of worship. To keep a client waiting is not necessarily an insult. In fact, tea and fruit may be offered while waiting. Bargaining, especially in the bazaar, is expected.

Recreation: Iranians enjoy spectator sports such as soccer, wrestling, weight lifting, karate, and basketball. The cinema is also a popular leisure-time activity for the urban population. Mountain towns are popular for skiing in the winter. Attending poetry reading sessions, strolling through the streets, visiting tea houses, and shopping in the bazaar are still favorite forms of recreation.

Holidays: Friday is the Moslem day of rest, and most businesses are closed. The most important religious holiday is Ashura, when believers parade in the streets recalling the martyrdom of Hussein. The biggest national holiday is the Iranian New Year (March 21 to April 2). All businesses close, and the people visit one another, exchanging gifts.

THE NATION

Land and Climate: Iran is the 17th largest country in the world—about the size of California, Arizona, New Mexico and Texas combined. Most of Iran is a mountainous plateau, 4,000 feet above sea level, with a desert in the east and a narrow coastal plain in the south. Summers are hot and dry; winters in the higher altitudes are cold, with snow in the northern part of the country.

History and Government: As the world's oldest monarchy, Iran celebrated its 2500th anniversary in 1971. A feudal state ruled by an all-powerful Shah, Iran became a constitutional monarchy in 1906. But in 1921 a new dynasty led by Reza Shah Pahlair took and centralized power in the monarchy. Reform measures in recent decades gave women the right to vote and called for the distribution of more land among peasants, the distribution of a larger share of factory profits among workers, the nationalization of forests, the creation of a literacy corps to teach in rural areas, and the sale of some state factories to private enterprise. These reforms, however, were not entirely successful. In 1978, the reigning Shah, Reza Pahlavi, fled the country as control of the government was assumed by Ayatollah Khomeini and his followers. Khomeini had been in self-exile. The new government leaders have encouraged a return to traditional Islamic values. In March 1980, Bani-Sadr was elected as the first president of the Islamic Republic of Iran. He was, however, forced to flee into exile in 1981 as internal violence broke out, including the bombing death of the prime minister and the chief of the revolutionary council. Since September 22, 1980, Iran has been at war with its eastern neighbor, Iraq. Severe damage has been inflicted on the oil facilities of both sides. Since the seizing of U.S. hostages in 1979, U.S.-Iranian relations have been severed. As a result of recent conflicts, Iran is a major source of instability and civil disorder in the Middle East.

Economy: The average gross national product (GNP) per capita is approximately $1,700 ($14,300 in U.S.). Energy production is the most important economic activity in Iran. In 1979, Iran was ranked fifth in the world in total energy production. It was also ranked as the world's second largest petroleum exporter and the fourth largest crude petroleum producer. Also, Iran is a major producer of natural gas. Largely because of its strong energy activity, Iran had the second fastest export growth rate in the world in the 1970s. However, the continued war with Iraq has greatly damaged Iran's oil production and has caused a decline in exports. Despite the economic importance of energy, agriculture is the chief industry in Iran. It's principal crops are grains, rice, tobacco, cotton, fruit, oil seeds, and sugar. The Iranians are renowned for their production of fine Persian carpets, delicate miniature paintings, and intricate silver work. Inflation is typically high in Iran.

Education: Children begin school at age 7. Although facilities are still inadequate to provide primary education for all children, income from petroleum is being used to fund a program of school construction and teacher training. Special programs teach adult villagers how to read and write. Since the revolution, Islamic education is the only kind available. Secular education is considered inferior to religious instruction if conflicts arise. The literacy rate is about 40% in Iran. The University of Tehran has over 24,000 students, and there are more than 10 provincial universities, as well as many other smaller universities.

Health: For specific medical information, contact International Health Consultants, PO Box 34582, Bethesda, MD 20817.

For Further Information

Because space is so limited in this *Culturgram* and needs are so varied, no suggested readings are included. We recommend a visit to your local library or bookstore. Check *Books in Print* and various cataloging systems for country-specific titles. Review *Encyclopedia Britannica* or similar comprehensive summaries. The U.S. government publishes *Country Profiles* which many libraries subscribe to. Computer searches (DIALOG, SDC, BRS, ISI) are now available at most major libraries. Contact the Iran Permanent Mission to the U.N., 622 Third Ave., New York, NY 10017, or the House of Iran, 10 West, 49th St., New York, NY 10020.

How to Use This Culturgram

Quickly read the whole text as an overview. Then circle or give priority numbers to specific questions you have or ideas you want to pursue. Use the *Culturgram* as a guide to check on regional differences and current situations.

Maps

Culturgram maps are meant only as simple geographical orientations. Boundary representations are not necessarily authoritative. Different sources also vary spelling, transliterations, and accents.

Rev. 1/88

CULTURGRAM*

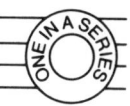

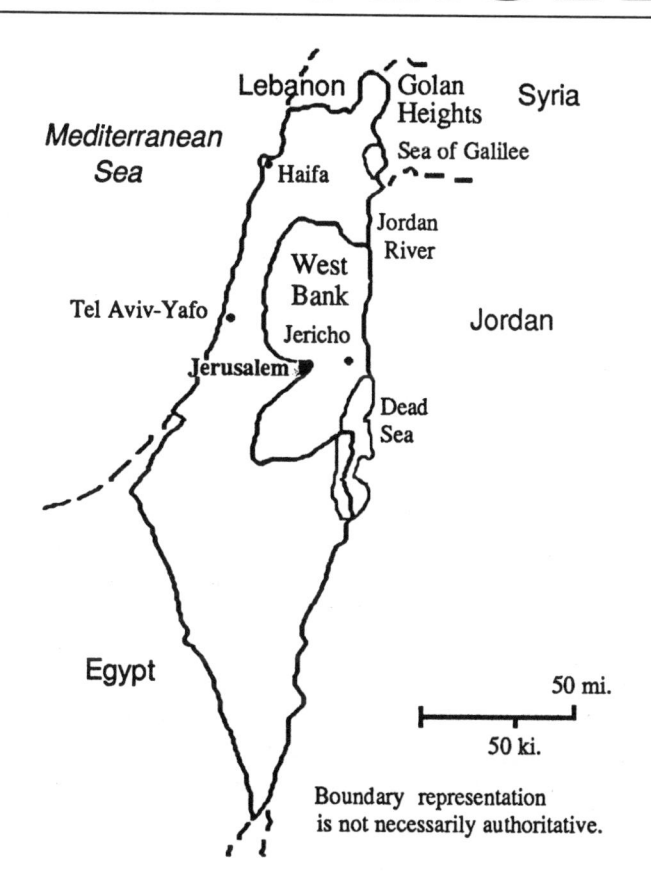

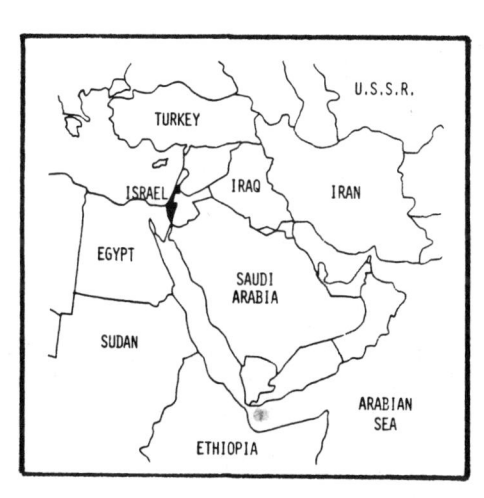

State of Israel

CUSTOMS AND COURTESIES

Greetings: "*Shalom*" is the usual greeting for either "hello" or "good-bye". Greetings are informal and handshakes are common. Among Israelis, good friends pat each other on the back or shoulders when greeting each other.

Visiting: Israelis are very hospitable and frequently invite newly made friends over to their homes. Invitations to visit are usually sincere and are not made casually, as is often the case in other cultures. Punctuality is expected as most Israelis are time conscious. Israelis are generally informal about visiting, and enjoy stopping by friends' homes often; an invitation is not always necessary with friends. Speech or actions that convey pride will not be appreciated by the Israelis. Israelis are open to questions and like to ask questions themselves. They appreciate those who take an interest in them, and in their various hobbies and studies. If you would like to give your host a gift, a book would be an excellent choice, since Israelis are eager readers with very inquisitive minds.

Public Meetings: When speaking to a group of people, it is appropriate to be informal and to use humor. It is important to be well informed about the subject matter and to be concise and to the point when speaking. Israelis expect speakers to strongly support their opinions with facts and evidence. Do not be surprised or offended by difficult questions from the audience. Quotations should be exact and paraphrases should be identified as such.

*****Culturgrams** are briefings to aid understanding of, feeling for, and communication with other people. Culturgrams are condensations of the best information available. Your insights will be appreciated. If you have refining suggestions, please contact Brigham Young University David M. Kennedy Center for International Studies, Publication Services, 280 HRCB, Provo, Utah 84602 (801) 378-6528. Copyright © 1986. All rights reserved. Printed in the USA.

Personal Appearance: Many Israelis are fashion-conscious, especially in the larger cities. The men are casual dressers, with shirts often unbuttoned at the neck and untucked. Ties and suits are generally considered too formal and are worn only on special occasions. The women also dress casually, and both men and women wear shorts and sandals during the long hot season. Because of the heat, cotton clothing is the most comfortable.

THE PEOPLE

General Attitudes: Israel is a land of informality. Titles are even less important in Israel than they are in the United States. Army officers and enlisted men call each other by their first names and often by nicknames. Visitors should not be offended or embarrassed by being called by their first names. Jewish immigration is officially encouraged, and much immigration has taken place. The return of the Jewish people to Israel has brought great joy to Israelis. Their society is a changing one that exhibits contrasts of old meeting new. On the streets, for example, one may see Talmudic students with long earlocks wearing long black coats side by side with stylish women and men in blue jeans. The Israelis are very devoted to their culture and country.

Population: The population of Israel is about 4 million people, excluding East Jerusalem. Currently the annual growth rate is 1.6% (0.9% in U.S.), but since 1970, the average annual growth rate has been much higher. The population density in this small country is 412 people per square mile (58 in U.S.). Nearly 90% of the people live in the cities, the fourth highest urbanization rate in the world. Excluding occupied areas, 85% of the people are Jews. The other 15% consists primarily of Arabs and members of the Druze and Circasean ethnic groups. Also, nearly 1 million Arabs live in Judea and Samaria (West Bank), administered by Israel since the war of 1967.

Language: Hebrew is the official language of Israel. Arabic is also used officially for the Arab minority. English is frequently used in commerce and is spoken by most Israelis. French or Arabic is compulsory in high school, and English is taught from the fifth grade on. Nearly all Israelis speak at least 1 foreign language.

Religion: The city of Jerusalem and the surrounding areas have played an important role in the development of several of the world's major religions, including Judaism, Christianity, and Islam. Corresponding to the ethnic divisions in the population, 85% of the people are Jewish. Most Israeli Jews are not orthodox, but do cling to some traditions. They are generally reluctant to change religions because of their heritage and values. The Sabbath is strictly observed by Orthodox Jews, from sundown on Friday to sundown on Saturday. Also, 11% are Muslims and 4% are Christians. The Christian minority is approximately half Greek Orthodox and half Greek Catholic Arabs, with a handful of Christians of other denominations. Israel is also the spiritual center of the Bahai religion, a small sect that worships beauty. State law requires that all workers be given one rest day a week (Friday for Moslems, Saturday for Jews, and Sunday for Christians).

LIFESTYLE

The Family: Families are very important in Jewish culture. They tend to be rather small; the average family size is 3.8 people (3.1 in U.S.). The father is the patriarch and exercises considerable influence in the home. Women are encouraged to work outside the home because of a limited labor force, and a need for increased income.

Marriage Customs: Israeli parents feel a deep responsibility to prepare and provide for a child's future. Thus, when a couple decide to get married, their parents handle all the business aspects of the marriage. It is not uncommon for the parents of both the husband and the wife to stay together in the same house for a few days to plan the wedding. Marriages are a great social event in Israel. Most Jewish marriages are performed by a rabbi. Oftentimes the marriage consists of a large dinner party with a band and hundreds of guests, although this tradition varies depending on the cultural background of the families involved. The singing and dancing often lasts well into the night.

Social and Economic Levels: Although Israel as a country is not as wealthy as many western countries, the people enjoy a relatively high standard of living. Israelis enjoy comfortable surroundings, and most homes have the modern appliances familiar in the West. The people live in either the city, a *moshav*, (a small, farming village), or a *kibutz* (a rural commune). Labor unions are very strong in Israel and play an important role in the lives of their workers.

Diet: Because of the diverse cultural backgrounds of Arabs and immigrant Jews, a wide variety of cuisine from many parts of the world is available in Israel. Some of the more popular dishes include *kabob* (meat and vegetables on a skewer) from the eastern Mediterranean region, Russian *borscht* (beet soup), and the now-popular chicken soup. *Gefilte* fish, a dish of baked or stewed stuffed fish brought to Israel by European Jews, is popular as a Sabbath dish because it can be cooked ahead of time and served cold. Vegetable salad, finely cut up and mixed with olive oil, lemon juice, and spices, is a staple and often eaten 2 or 3 times a day. Beef is usually eaten only once a week at the Friday evening Sabbath meal. *Falafel* (filled pocketbread) is comparable to the American hamburger in its popularity. Chicken and fish are eaten more frequently than beef. Fruit is plentiful, as are eggs. Fruit juices are generally a part of lunch or dinner. For health reasons, the drinking of water and soft drinks is strongly urged, particularly during the hot spring and summer seasons. Israelis tend to drink much less alcohol than most Americans or Europeans.

Recreation: Movies are very popular. Music also has great appeal to the people. Musical concerts are generally sold out far in advance. Football (soccer) and basketball are the most popular sports, along with swimming, hiking, and camping. Baseball and American football are virtually unknown. The most popular leisure activity in Israel, however, is visiting with friends, families, and neighbors in the evening after work. Many enjoy visiting in the living room over a snack and a cup of coffee.

Holidays: Jewish holidays include the Jewish New Year, or Rosh Hashanah (around September or October), the Day of Atonement, or Yom Kippur (the tenth day of the Jewish New Year), the Feast of Tabernacles (the fifteenth to twenty-second day after Rosh Hashanah), Hanukkah, or the Festival of Lights (last part of December), Pesach, or Passover (exactly 6 lunar months and 2 weeks after New Year's Day), Holocaust Day (13 days after Passover), Memorial Day (20 days after Passover), Independence Day (21 days after Passover), and Pentecost (50 days after the Passover). Dates are based on the lunar calendar.

THE NATION

Land and Climate: Excluding the occupied territories, Israel is nearly the same size as the state of Massachusetts. The weather is striking in its diversity. The southern part of the country (the Negev Desert) is dry most of the year and the northern part has a Mediterranean climate. Irrigation makes Israel's land arable year round. The intense sun makes a hat necessary for protection. Israel has 7 months of dry summer (April through October) and 5 months of cold, wet winter.

History and Government: The Holy Land, from which the present state of Israel has emerged, has had a long history of different rule. A Hebrew kingdom was established from the 12 tribes of Israel during the reign of King David nearly 3000 years ago. After the rule of Solomon, it was split into two states—Israel and Judah. These were later destroyed by Assyria and Babylonia in the eighth and sixth centuries B.C. After the Persian conquest of the Middle East, many Jews returned to the Holy Land and established a state there, including the reconstruction of a temple. The land later fell to the Greeks and then to the Romans. During the Byzantine era, the number of Jews dropped sharply because of persecution. In the seventh century A.D., Palestine was conquered by the Muslims. The Turks ruled Palestine for 400 years until the beginning of World War I. In the 1890s, Zionism, an international movement, was founded by Theodor Herzl to restore Palestine to the Jews. After World War I, the area came under British control. Finally, in 1947, the United Nations agreed to divide Palestine into 2 independent states, one Jewish and one Arab. On May 14, 1948, Israel was proclaimed independent and the British withdrew. That same day Egypt, Iraq, Jordan, Lebanon, Syria, and Saudi Arabia attacked the newly created Israeli state. Since that time 4 other wars have broken out between Israel and its surrounding Arab neighbors. In 1956, with the help of Britain and France, Israel invaded Egypt's Sinai region, but was soon forced to withdraw. In a six-day war in 1967, Israeli forces fought against Jordanian, Egyptian, and Syrian forces, capturing Jerusalem, the Sinai peninsula, the West Bank of the Jordan, the Gaza strip, and the Golan Heights. In October of 1973, Egyptian and Syrian armies launched an attack on Israel, necessitating the deployment of U.N. peace-keeping troops in the area. In 1979, a peace treaty between Israel's former Prime Minister Menachem Begin and Egypt's President Anwar Sadat was signed and Israel began withdrawing from the Sinai and the Gaza strip. A fourth war erupted when Israeli troops crossed into Lebanon in the summer of 1982 and entered Beirut, the Lebanese capital, as part of a crusade against the Palestinian Liberation Organization. U.N. troops were brought in and a cease-fire was negotiated. The figurehead head of state is the president. The head of the government is the prime minister. Israel is a parliamentary republic with a legislative assembly (*Knesset*) of 120 members, but has no written constitution.

Economy: The annual gross national product (GNP) per capita in Israel is about $6,093 ($14,300 in U.S.) and is growing at a rate of 2 to 3% annually. Chief agricultural products include citrus and other fruits, vegetables, beef, dairy, and poultry products. Major industries include food processing, diamond cutting and polishing, textiles and clothing, chemicals, metal products, and, more recently, electronic and computer-related products. Inflation has been very severe in Israel, averaging more than 50% annually over the past 6 years, but reaching 190% in 1983. However, pressure from the labor unions has kept salaries rising at the same rate as the cost of living, thus maintaining a high standard of living. More than 8% of Israel's national income goes to the poorest 20% of the people, the fourth highest percentage in the world. The *shekel* is the unit of currency.

Education: The government provides both religious and secular school systems and the people are free to choose either. School is free and compulsory until the 10th grade, but some high schools (8th through 12th grades) charge tuition and have strict admittance and performance requirements. Secondary education can lead to a vocation or to university studies. Israel's universities are among the world's finest. Most schools, including universities, hold class 6 days a week. Financial help for students who are in need is available from the government and other sources. There is an Arab education system (primary and secondary), whose classes are taught in Arabic. The literacy rate is 88% for the Jews and 70% for the Arabs.

Transportation: "Sherut" taxis may be used for faster and more convenient travel in between cities. These are large cars that carry up to 7 passengers at a time on fixed routes. There are also railway links between major population centers. In all cities, except Haifa, buses and trains stop their services on the Jewish Sabbath and holy days. However, taxis and private cars are still available.

Health: Facilities are mostly socialized through the Histradrut (Federation of Labor), the union to which most workers belong, but private doctors are readily available. For further medical information, contact International Health Consultants, PO Box 34582, Bethesda, MD.

For Further Information

Because space is so limited in this *Culturgram* and needs are so varied, no suggested readings are included. We recommend a visit to your local library or bookstore. Check *Books in Print* and various cataloging systems for country-specific titles. Review *Encyclopedia Britannica* or similar comprehensive summaries. The U.S. government publishes *Country Profiles* which many libraries subscribe to. Computer searches (DIALOG, SDC, BRS, ISI) are now available at most major libraries. Contact the Embassy of Israel, 3514 International Dr., N.W., Washington, D.C. 20008, or the Israel Government Tourist Office, 350 Fifth Ave., New York, NY 10118.

How to Use This Culturgram

Quickly read the whole text as an overview. Then circle or give priority numbers to specific questions you have or ideas you want to pursue. Use the *Culturgram* as a guide to check on regional differences and current situations.

Maps

Culturgram maps are meant only as simple geographical orientations. Boundary representations are not necessarily authoritative. Different sources also vary spelling, transliterations, and accents.

Rev. 1/88

CULTURGRAM*

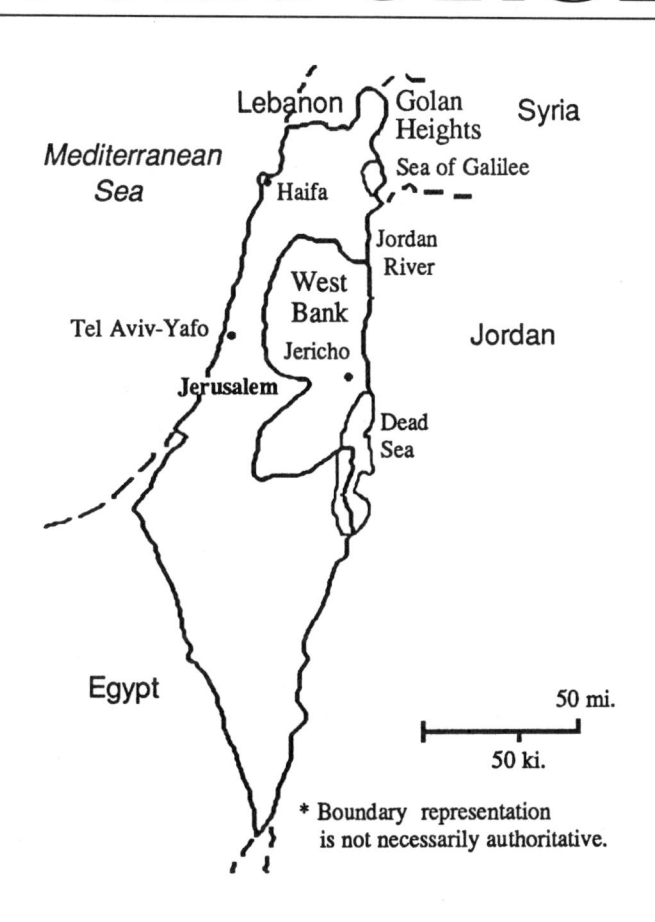

Israel and Occupied Territories
(Palestine)

*Boundary representation is not necessarily authoritative.

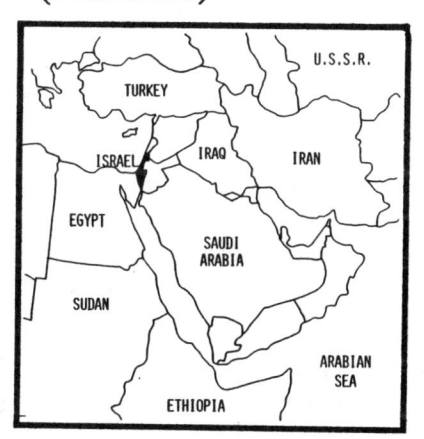

NOTE: Two *Culturgrams* have been prepared on the Israeli/Palestinian area: one centers on the Jewish culture and the other on the Arab culture. Political statements concerning the current turmoil in this area are purposefully avoided. Rather, the attitudes and feelings of the people of either culture are portrayed.

CUSTOMS AND COURTESIES

Greetings: *Al-Salaam Alayakum* (Peace to You) is the usual greeting among the Palestinian Arabs. A handshake is also common. A kiss on either cheek is frequent among close friends of the same sex. A pat on the back or shoulder is a sign of affection. There are also various other greetings that express welcome or goodwill. Friends call each other by first names while elderly and respected people are called "Abu...," meaning "Father of..." For example, "Abu Ahmed" refers to the father of Ahmed, whose personal name might be Ibrahim.

Visiting: Usually visitors must be invited before visiting someone, but close friends do not need an invitation; they can drop in at any time. When visiting a Palestinian Arab, it is polite to ask about his family, religion, and work. Personal questions, however, should be avoided. Visitors should try to be tactful in dismissing ideas or refusing food.

Personal Appearance: Villagers wear the traditional dress, which consists of long, loose robes that cover the entire body. The head is covered with a special head cover. To

---

*Culturgrams are briefings to aid understanding of, feeling for, and communication with other people. Culturgrams are condensations of the best information available. Your insights will be appreciated. If you have refining suggestions, please contact Brigham Young University David M. Kennedy Center for International Studies, Publication Services, 280 HRCB, Provo, Utah 84602 (801) 378-6528. Copyright © 1986. All rights reserved. Printed in the USA.

be respected by Palestinian Arabs, women should dress modestly; bare shoulders, short dresses, shorts, or tight pants or tops are inappropriate. Such dress could lead to misconceptions and harassment. In the cities, dress is casual, but businessmen usually dress more formally.

THE PEOPLE

General Attitudes: Palestinian Arabs are taught courage, bravery, hospitality, and generosity. They feel that the establishment of the State of Israel in 1948 was unfair and marked the beginning of their persecution. Palestinian Arabs do not feel that they are receiving basic human rights, and that if they express their political views concerning their homeland, they might be imprisoned or expelled. They respect Judaism, but condemn Zionism as having left them without a sovereign state. They are sensitive to references to the Holy Land as "Israel," since they still believe it is Palestine.

Population: There are approximately 4.5 million Palestinian Arabs, the majority of whom live in 3 main areas: the declared state of Israel, the West Bank, and the Gaza Strip (both occupied by Israel since 1967). About 2 million live in refugee camps in other countries in the Middle East. The rest of the Palestinian Arabs live in countries throughout the world. There are also 23 Bedouin tribes that live in tents in the area and have retained their traditional customs.

Language: The language of Palestinian Arabs is Arabic. A high percentage also speak English or French. Since the Israeli occupation, Hebrew is required as a second language in public schools by the Israeli government. However, because many have very little contact with the Israelis, not all Palestinian Arabs can speak Hebrew.

Religion: Approximately 80% of the Palestinian Arabs are Muslims. The rest are Christian, mainly Greek Orthodox or Roman Catholic. The Arabs feel that being Palestinian is the main factor that unites them as a group. Muslims and Christians normally respect each other. Arab Muslims and Christians combined represent about 15% of the total population of the area; the remainder is Jewish.

LIFESTYLE

The Family: Families are often large and play an important role in Palestinian Arab life. The father is the patriarch and the mother takes care of the housework and children. Few women work outside the home. Most of the families consider their traditional values threatened by the surrounding society. Palistinians encourage their children to cherish their heritage.

Dating and Marriage: Dating is strictly forbidden, even for some engaged couples. Girls marry at about age 18 and boys at age 22 or older. Cousin marriage is common among the Muslims. Mixed marriages between Christians and Muslims, however, are not common.

Social and Economic Levels: Palestinian Arabs who live in the occupied territories are affected by a high inflation rate. They are usually paid less than the Israelis. The establishment of Palestinian businesses and buildings is restricted by the Israeli governing authorities.

Diet: Lunch is the main meal of the day. Spicy food is typical of the Middle East. *Falafel* (filled pocketbread) is very popular among Palestinians. Other popular foods are stuffed grape leaves and spiced rice with nuts. Turkish coffee, tea, and fruit juice are common beverages.

Recreation: Soccer and basketball are the most popular sports. Playing cards, attending movies, and visiting with friends, especially neighbors, are also enjoyable activities.

Holidays: Palestinian Arabs observe both Muslim and Christian holidays. Schools are out on Friday and Sunday. Shops close according to the owner's religion. Ramadan is the month of fasting during which Muslims fast during the daylight hours. There are 2 big celebrations that visitors will see in areas predominately inhabited by Palestinian Arabs: Christmas in Bethlehem and Easter in East Jerusalem.

THE NATION

Land and Climate: The weather is striking in its diversity. The southern part of the country (the Negev Desert) is dry most of the year. Irrigation makes the Holy Land arable year round. The intense sun makes a hat necessary. The Holy Land has 7 months of dry summer (April through October) and 5 months of cold, wet winter.

History: Palestine is the traditional name given to the area known in Christendom as the Holy Land. It includes present-day Israel, the West Bank, and the Gaza Strip. The Holy Land has had a long history of different rule, largely because of its central location connecting the continents of Asia and Africa. A Hebrew kingdom was established from the 12 tribes of Israel during the reign of King David nearly 3000 years ago. After the rule of Solomon, it was split into 2 states—Israel and Judah. These were later destroyed by Assyria and Babylonia in the eighth and sixth centuries B.C. After the Persian conquest of the Middle East, the exiled Jews returned to the Holy Land and reestablished a state there, including the reconstruction of a temple. The land later fell to the Greeks and then to the Romans. During the Byzantine era, the number of Jews dropped sharply because of persecution. In the seventh century A.D., Palestine was conquered by Muslims. The Turkish Muslims ruled Palestine for 400 years until the beginning of World War I. The control of the Ottoman Empire over Palestine ended after World War I when the League of Nations granted Palestine as a mandate to Great Britain. The Balfour Declaration was issued in 1917. It pledged British support of the establishment of a national home for the Jews in Palestine; but it also insisted that nothing be done to prejudice the civil and religious rights of the existing non-Jewish communities in Palestine. The 2 goals conflicted and resulted in dissent throughout the British mandate, which was finally dissolved in 1948 with the partition of the country into 2 areas—one, Arab, and the other, Jewish. The latter was immediately declared the independent nation of Israel. Arabs, who had opposed the partition, immediately declared war. The conflict has continued until the present with hostilities erupting into open war in 1948, 1956, 1967, and 1973. After the 1967 war, Israeli forces occupied the West Bank, Golan Heights, the Gaza Strip and the Sinai. East Jerusalem was also controlled by the Israelis. The status of the Sinai and the Gaza Strip has changed in recent years; however, the West Bank and East Jerusalem are still under Israeli occupation. The status of the occupied territories has yet to be determined.

Government: In the occupied territories, the great majority of the inhabitants are Palestinian Arabs. The Palestinian Liberation Organization (PLO) is considered by a majority of Palestinians to be the legitimate representative of the Arab community. The 530-member Palestinian National Council (PNC), which is a part of the PLO, is recognized as the parliament in exile. Currently Yassir Arafat is the leader of the PLO, but other factions within the PLO have recently surfaced. These other factions do not recognize Arafat as their leader. Mayors with limited municipal powers are elected by the residents of the area. However, in the past, conflicts have arisen between some of the mayors and the Israeli government, resulting in the firing of some mayors. There are 4 Arab members in the *Knesset* representing the Arabs inside the state of Israel proper, although many Palestinians feel that the members do not represent Palestinian national interests properly. Also, the Israeli government has attempted to promote rural-based leagues in order to gain more cooperation from the Arabs. However, the leagues have little support from the Palestinian people, who view them as an attempt to divide their ranks.

Economy: The annual gross national product (GNP) per capita in Israel and the occupied territories is about $6,093 ($14,300 in U.S.). The economy is growing at a rate of 2 to 3%

annually. Agriculture and tourism are the 2 main sources of income for Palestinian families. However since 1967, the Israeli government has regulated various facets of these industries. Chief agricultural products include citrus and other fruits, vegetables, beef and dairy products, and poultry products. Major industries include food processing, diamond cutting and polishing, textiles and clothing, chemicals, metal products, and, more recently, electronic and computer-related products. Inflation has been very severe in Israel, averaging more than 50% annually over the past 6 years, but reaching 190% in 1983. The unemployment rate is about half that in the U.S. Palestinian Arabs also depend on help from Arab countries, the United Nations, and the PLO for development and building of streets, schools, and hospitals in the occupied territories. The *shekel* and Jordanian *dinar* are the accepted units of currency.

Education: In the occupied territories, educational opportunities are fewer than in other areas of the country because of the limited number of schools, books, and materials. Despite this, Palestinian Arabs have the highest rate of literacy in the Arab world (70%). Besides the public schools, there are private schools that are supported by worldwide Christian and Muslim organizations.

Transportation: Buses are the primary mode of mass transit. Taxis may be used for faster and more convenient travel between cities. There are also large cars that carry up to 7 passengers at a time on fixed routes. A system of railways links major population centers.

Health: The United Nations Relief and Work Agency (UNRWA) assists the refugee camps on the West Bank and the Gaza strip by providing medical care for the Palestinian Arabs. Hospital and medical care are difficult to obtain in the occupied region. For further medical information, contact International Health Consultants, PO Box 34582, Bethesda, MD 20817.

For Further Information

Because space is so limited in this *Culturgram* and needs are so varied, no suggested readings are included. We recommend a visit to your local library or bookstore. Check *Books in Print* and various cataloging systems for country-specific titles. Review *Encyclopedia Britannica* or similar comprehensive summaries. The U.S. government publishes *Country Profiles* which many libraries subscribe to. Computer searches (DIALOG, SDC, BRS, ISI) are now available at most major libraries. Contact the Committee on the Exercise of the Inalienable Rights of the Palestinian People, United Nations, United Nations Plaza, New York, NY 10017. You may also contact Embassy of Israel, 3514 International Dr. NW, Washington D.C. 20008 or the Israel Government Tourist Office, 350 Fifth Ave., New York, NY 10118.

How to Use This Culturgram

Quickly read the whole text as an overview. Then circle or give priority numbers to specific questions you have or ideas you want to pursue. Use the *Culturgram* as a guide to check on regional differences and current situations.

Maps

Culturgram maps are meant only as simple geographical orientations. Boundary representations are not necessarily authoritative. Different sources also vary spelling, transliterations, and accents.

Rev. 1/88

CULTURGRAM*

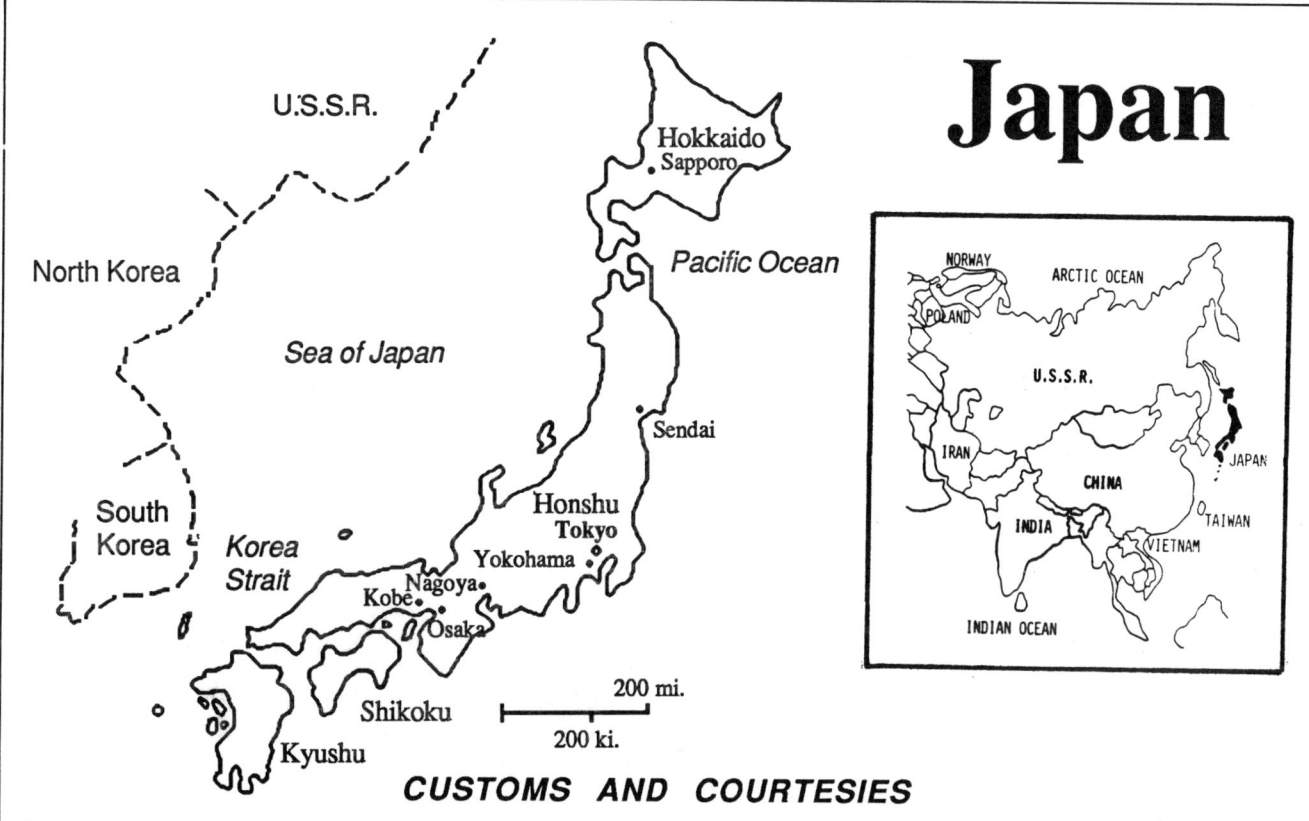

Japan

CUSTOMS AND COURTESIES

Greetings: A bow is the traditional greeting. Upon meeting, Japanese will often bow to each other. Guests should try to bow as low and as long as the other person is bowing, but not lower. This signifies humility. Western-style handshakes are also becoming increasingly popular. The Japanese are quite formal in introductions and at social events. They always use the name and title of their guests. It is polite to reciprocate this custom. The use of first names without a title is reserved for family and friends.

Visiting: Shoes should be removed before stepping from the enclosed porch into a Japanese-style home. Western-style buildings, however, may be entered with shoes on. After the shoes are removed, they are placed together pointing toward the outdoors. Slippers should also be removed before entering rooms with the immaculate straw mat floors *(tatami)*. Japanese traditionally emphasize modesty and reserve. When offered tea or fruit, one should express a slight hesitation to accept it. It is also advisable to deny compliments graciously. Guests should avoid excessive compliments to the host on items of decor; otherwise the host may feel obligated to give the items as gifts. When visiting, it is customary for guests to take a gift (usually fruit or cakes) to their host. Gifts should be given and accepted with both hands and a slight bow. The Japanese like to discuss their country and its accomplishments.

Eating: Eating while walking on the street exhibits poor taste. Snack foods are sold at street stands, but it is appropriate to stay at the stand until finished eating. The Japanese typically eat from their bowl while holding it at chest level instead of bending down to it on the table. Knives and forks are almost always available for the visitor who is not skilled with chopsticks.

Personal Appearance: Conformity, even in appearance, is one of the distinct characteristics of Japanese people. The general rule is to act in a manner similar to, or in harmony with, the crowd. Men wear suits and ties in public; women wear modest and clean dresses. It is advisable to avoid colors that are conspicuous. The accepted style of clothing is usually European rather than

---

*Culturgrams are briefings to aid understanding of, feeling for, and communication with other people. Culturgrams are condensations of the best information available. Your insights will be appreciated. If you have refining suggestions, please contact Brigham Young University David M. Kennedy Center for International Studies, Publication Services, 280 HRCB, Provo, Utah 84602 (801) 378-6528. Copyright © 1986. All rights reserved. Printed in the USA.

American. During the summer months (from June to August) men generally do not wear their coats. Handkerchiefs are usually carried.

Gestures: It is impolite to yawn in public. A person should sit erect placing both feet on the floor. Legs can be crossed with one knee directly over the other or they can be crossed at the ankles. Beckoning is done with the palm down instead of up, and pointing is done with the entire hand. Shaking one hand from side to side with the palm forward means no. Laughter does not necessarily signify joy or amusement; it can also be a sign of embarrassment or distress. The mouth should be covered when using a toothpick or yawning. Also, it is best to avoid chewing gum in public. It is not uncommon to see members of the same sex strolling hand in hand.

Traveling: Japan is rich in culture and history and has many places to visit. The forests and mountains, pagodas and temples, traditional festivals, and the famous Kabuki theater are some of the many tourist attractions. Generally speaking, cultural and historical centers are located south of Tokyo, while picturesque countryside is found to the north. There are two types of lodging: *hoteru* (hotels) are Western style, and *ryokan* (inns) are Japanese style. Both taxi and bus service are readily available and quite inexpensive.

THE PEOPLE

General Attitudes: Practicality, hard work, and devotion to economic progress characterize the modern Japanese. Society is group oriented and people identify strongly with their group (business, club, etc.). Loyalty to the group and to one's superiors is essential and takes precedence over personal feelings. Businesses provide the Japanese with prestige and benefits. Employees usually remain with a company for life. To be fired is often considered a disgrace to self and family. The family system is strongly evident in many areas of society. Group unity is strong and leaders seek consensus on most decisions. The Japanese feel a deep obligation to return favors and gifts. Age and tradition are honored but are usually not allowed to stand in the way of progress. The crime rate in Japan is one of the lowest in the world, and is only one-fifth the rate in the United States.

Population: The population of Japan is 120.7 million and is growing at 0.6% annually (0.9% in U.S.). This is the equivalent of almost half the population of the United States living on only four percent of the land area. With a density of 767 people per square mile (58 in U.S.), Japan is the third most densely populated country in the world. Approximately 45% of the total population is concentrated in three major metropolitan areas: Tokyo (the capital, and second largest city in the world), Osaka, and Nagoya. Nearly 80% of the population live in urban areas. Japan's population is 99% homogeneous, with only a small number of Koreans, Chinese, and native Ainu.

Language: Japanese is the official language. Although spoken Japanese is not closely related to spoken Chinese, the written language is directly related to Chinese ideographs adopted in ancient times. The Japanese also use two phonetic alphabets simplified from these ideographs *(hiragana and katakana)*. English is taught in all secondary schools and is often used in business.

Religion: The general attitude towards religion is humanistic. Traditionally, most Japanese practiced a combination of Buddhism and Shinto. Most households still observe some ceremonies of both religions, such as Shinto marriages and Buddhist funerals, and have small shrines in their homes. Religious celebrations and practices, however, are now a social tradition rather than the result of intense conviction, although some new minor religious movements have gained popularity in postwar years. Less than 1% of the population is Christian. Although there are many traditionally religious festivals, work is the "religion" of most. Meditation, ancestor worship, ritual cleansing, and a respect for nature's beauty and man's part in it are traditionally emphasized.

LIFESTYLE

Family: The family is still the foundation of Japanese society and is bound together by a strong sense of obligation and duty. The current trend is away from the traditional large, multigeneration families, but many aged parents still live with their married children. Contemporary families are usually smaller, consisting of husband, wife, and one or two children. Japanese average 3.4 people per family, compared to 3.1 in the U.S. In cities, high-rise apartments have become very common. Japan has the third highest abortion rate in the world—36% of all pregnancies are terminated.

Dating and Marriage Customs: In Japan, dating is a recent phenomenon. Young people begin dating at age 17 or 18. Movies and dining out are favorite dating activities. Marriage age averages about 25 to 27 for men and slightly younger for women. Traditionally, elderly friends of the family arranged the marriages, but now the individual couples decide.

Social and Economic Levels: The Japanese people live comfortably but not in luxury. Employees work hard and are paid good wages, including biannual bonuses from their companies. Workers usually retire at 55 years of age. Japanese have the highest life expectancy in the world—76 years (74 in U.S.). Sixty-eight percent of the population is economically productive, more than any other nation in the world.

Business Hours: Typical business hours are 8:00 a.m. to 6:00 p.m. with an hour break for lunch. Small shops and large urban shopping areas may stay open much later and do not close for lunch.

Diet: The Japanese diet consists largely of rice, fresh vegetables, seafood, and fruits. Although rice and Japanese tea are part of almost every meal, many people enjoy breakfast and lunch in Western style (toast and coffee, etc.). *Sushi* (uncooked fish) and *sukiyaki* (chopped meat and vegetables) are popular Japanese dishes.

Recreation: Baseball, soccer, volleyball, tennis, skiing, and jogging are popular in Japan. People also enjoy the traditional sports of sumo wrestling, judo, kendo (fencing with bamboo poles), and karate. Television and movies are very popular. Traditionally, highly stylized drama *(noh, kabuki)* and puppet theater *(bunraku)* are also enjoyed. People often go on outings to enjoy nature and seasonal changes.

Holidays: Holidays include New Year's, the biggest celebration of the year, when almost all businesses close and people visit shrines and relatives (January 1 to 3); Adults' Day (January 15); National Foundation Day (February 11); Vernal Equinox (March); Emperor's Birthday (April 29); Constitution Day (May 3); Children's Day (May 5); Senior Citizens' Day (September 15); Autumnal Equinox (September); Sports Day (October 10); Culture Day (November 3); and Labor Thanksgiving Day (November 23)

THE NATION

Land and Climate: Japan consists of four main islands and has 143,000 square miles of land area. It is somewhat smaller than the state of Montana. Seasonal changes correspond to those of the United States and are distinctly beautiful. The climate is temperate with warm, humid summers and relatively mild winters except on the islands of Hokkaido and northern Honshu, where the winters can be bitter cold. The months of June and July constitute the rainy season and September is the time of greatest typhoon activity. The islands are lush and green throughout much of the year.

History and Government: Japan is known historically as the Land of the Rising Sun, as symbolized in the flag. Founded some 2000 years ago, Japan's line of emperors has, according to tradition, continued to the present. From the 12th century until the late 19th century, however, feudal lords or Shoguns held political control. The current emperor, Hirohito, has been emperor since 1926. In 1895 the Japanese defeated China in a war fought over the right to rule Korea. Japan was also victorious in the Russo-Japanese War (ending in 1905), which led to world recognition as a military power. Involvement in World War I brought enhanced world influence and, at Versailles, Japan was one of the "big five." The post-war years brought great prosperity to a rapidly changing nation. Japan soon began to exercise considerable influence in Asia. Manchuria and much of China were subsequently invaded in an attempt to create an Asian co-prosperity sphere, with Japan at its head. On December 7, 1941, Japan launched a successful air attack on U.S. naval forces at Pearl Harbor. This tactic enabled the military machine of Japan to swiftly encircle most of southeast Asia. In 1943 the tide of the war began to turn in favor of the allies.

Two atomic bombs were dropped by the U.S. on Hiroshima and Nagasaki in the summer of 1945. Complete collapse of the empire and surrender ensued. A military occupation, chiefly American, lasted from 1945 to 1952. A new constitution was adopted in 1946 that renounced war and granted basic human rights. Since World War II, Japan has maintained only a small defense force, spending less than 1% of its annual gross national product (GNP) on defense. The country, however, continues to receive military support from the U.S. The government is a constitutional monarchy. The emperor is head of state but has no governing power. Legislative power is vested in the bi-

Diet, consisting of a House of Representatives (Lower House) and the House of Councillors (Upper House). In 1984 Yasuhiro Nakasone was reelected president of the ruling Liberal Democratic Party; he has been prime minister since 1982. Japan has 47 prefectures, each administered by an elected governor.

Economy: Japan is one of the most productive industrial nations in the world. The economy (the strongest in Asia) is currently growing at an annual rate of 4.2% annually. The inflation rate is typically higher than in the U.S., but unemployment is almost nonexistent (2%). Japan is not well endowed with natural resources, and more than 65% of the land is forested. Because of this, arable land is intensively cultivated, and approximately 30% of Japan's food must be imported. Major agricultural products include rice, sugar, vegetables, and fruits. Japan is the world's leading producer of fish (15% of the world total), and fourth in the production of eggs. Based on the promotion of manufacturing industries for the export market, Japan has achieved and maintained a very high rate of economic growth since 1945. Major industries are metallurgical and engineering industries, electrical and electronic industries, textiles and chemicals. Japan is the world's leading producer of television sets. It is second in the production of cars, radios, cement, and pig iron, and third in steel production. Trade imbalance has been a source of friction between Japan and the U.S. in recent years. The unit of currency is the *yen*.

Education: Japan has a very high literacy rate (99%) and reading is popular. The university entrance exams are difficult, and competition among students is strong. There are waiting lists of up to 6 years at major universities, demonstrating that success in Japan is based largely on education. Education is free and compulsory up to 15 years of age.

Transportation: A highly developed, very efficient mass-transit system of trains and buses is the principal mode of transportation. Convenient train and bus lines go almost everywhere. Over 16% of the people own cars, and traffic is heavy. There are three international airports, in Tokyo, Osaka, and Narita. Daily flights are available to the U.S. and most major cities in Asia. A visa is necessary to visit Japan.

Health: For specific medical information contact International Health Consultants, PO Box 34582, Bethesda, MD 20817.

For Further Information

Because space is so limited in this *Culturgram* and needs are so varied, no suggested readings are included. We recommend a visit to your local library or bookstore. Check *Books in Print* and various cataloging systems for country-specific titles. Review *Encyclopedia Britannica* or similar comprehensive summaries. The U.S. government publishes *Country Profiles* which many libraries subscribe to. Computer searches (DIALOG, SDC, BRS, ISI) are now available at most major libraries. Contact the Embassy of Japan, 2520 Massachusetts Ave NW, Washington D.C. 20008, or the Japan National Tourist Office Rockefeller Plaza, 630 Fifth Avenue, New York, NY 10111.

How to Use This Culturgram

Quickly read the whole text as an overview. Then circle or give priority numbers to specific questions you have or ideas you want to pursue. Use the *Culturgram* as a guide to check on regional differences and current situations.

Rev. 1/88

CULTURGRAM*

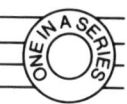

Hashemite Kingdom of Jordan

**Boundaries not Authoritative

CUSTOMS AND COURTESIES

Greetings: Jordanians greet each other and strangers warmly. Handshakes and a series of greetings and inquiries after each other's health are always given. Friends of the same sex often exchange a kiss on either cheek.

Visiting: In most Jordanian homes, both the husband and wife will receive visitors. It is considered a matter of honor to receive visitors and supply their needs. Guests may be expected to remain for a meal. Arabs always refuse offers of food twice, out of politeness, before accepting the third time. Therefore, if a guest wishes to decline an offer of food, he or she must refuse at least 3 times. It is considered polite (but not necessary) for a guest to leave a small amount of food on the plate, indicating that the host's generosity has been overwhelming and that the guest is absolutely finished. When invited for dinner or other occasions, guests may wish to take a gift; flowers or sweets (but no alcohol) are customary. When visiting a home, one should refrain from bringing up negative topics. The Palestinian-Israeli situation is a very delicate issue. If you wish to discuss this topic, approach it carefully.

Gestures: When sitting, avoid crossing the legs by resting one ankle on the other knee. Pointing the sole of one's foot at another person is considered insulting.

---

*Culturgrams are briefings to aid understanding of, feeling for, and communication with other people. Culturgrams are condensations of the best information available. Your insights will be appreciated. If you have refining suggestions, please contact Brigham Young University David M. Kennedy Center for International Studies, Publication Services, 280 HRCB, Provo, Utah 84602 (801) 378-6528. Copyright © 1986. All rights reserved. Printed in the USA.

THE PEOPLE

Population: Jordan has a population of 3.1 million. In size, Jordan is comparable to Maine. The population of the disputed West Bank, which until 1967 was part of Jordan but is presently occupied by Israel, is estimated to be over 800,000. The majority of the population is of Mediterranean descent. There is also a small minority of Circassian Russians. Many of the people live along the Jordan river. The capital city, Amman, occupies a central location and has an estimated population of 1 million. Approximately 70% of the population is urban; only 4% are considered Bedouin (nomads).

Language: Arabic is the official and most commonly used language. English is also widely spoken. Most professionals are bilingual.

Religion: About 90% of the population adheres to the Sunni branch of the Islamic faith. Christianity, represented by a half-dozen denominations, is the next largest body, followed by a number of non-Sunni Muslim groups. Each religious community has its own court system set up to judge in personal status matters, such as marriage, divorce, and inheritance.

LIFESTYLE

Role Relationships: In the Middle East, lines between age and social groups are still strong. Older people are honored and respected. Young men and women will generally not smoke, drink, or use slang in the presence of their elders and will try to assist them in any way possible. Within families, all generations converse easily and enjoy each other's company. In the workplace, employers look after employee interests and are considered responsible for a wider area of concerns than in the West. In many cases, the employer is regarded more like an uncle than a boss.

The Family: The family is unquestionably the most important unit in Jordanian society. The extended family — consisting of mother, father, children, grandchildren, and great grandchildren — shares a close relationship. Cousins are often as close as brothers and sisters are in the West. To be able to help any member of the family is considered a great honor. Older members of the family are revered. The U.S. custom of placing older family members in rest homes is considered reprehensible. Arabs love children and lavish a great deal of time and attention on them. Family size is beginning to decline because of educational and economic pressures, but it is still large by comparison to the United States.

Dating, Courtship and Marriage: Jordanian society is still conservative in dating and marriage practices. For the most part, families still have a significant role in arranging marriages. Young people often meet at universities or offices and persuade their parents to help them in their courtship and subsequent marriage, provided the parents approve. One-to-one dating is generally reserved for after the engagement party or until the marriage contract has been signed. Other important aspects of marriage include the large bridal token that is transferred to the bride's family as well as the substantial dowry given to the bride. Marriage is the norm, and all Jordanians expect to marry and have children. The divorce rate is much lower than in the United States.

Personal Appearance: Both sexes should adopt modest, conservative clothing when in the Middle East. In general, business suits for the men are appropriate for work. Women should have their shoulders covered and avoid low-cut, bare, or tight clothing, regardless of season. Summers in Jordan are hot and require cool cotton clothing. Increasing numbers of Jordanian women are adopting Islamic dress — a conservative floor length coat-dress, often with western styling, and a head scarf. Veiling is no longer common.

Economy: Amman has become a business center, particularly after the ongoing civil war and tensions in Lebanon forced companies to relocate. Amman has absorbed most of the country's growth. Jordan ranks well in quality of life indicators, even though it is not an oil producer and lacks an income that could support rapid development. Life expectancy, infant and child health care, and per capita income are all developing at a stable rate indicative of balanced growth.

Diet: Most meals include bread and meat, plus vegetables and fruits that are in season. Jordanian cuisine is generally not spicy. Islamic law forbids the consumption of pork and alcohol, and Muslims are careful to obey these restrictions publicly.

Work Schedule: On Fridays, commercial offices, government offices, and banks are closed. The University of Jordan, Yarmouk University, and Hauta University are closed Thursday and Friday. Shops may be open or closed on Friday, according to the discretion of the shopkeeper. Friday is the day of communal Muslim worship at the mosque and is not a workday. On other days, office hours are generally from 8 a.m. to 2 p.m. Shops are generally open all day.

Sports and Recreation: Soccer is the major sport; a soccer league provides national competition. Water sports, such as water skiing and scuba diving, are found in the Gulf of Aqaba.

Holidays: National holidays fall on fixed dates: Arbor Day (January 15), Labor Day (May 1), Independence Day (May 25), Great Arab Revolt and Army Day (June 10), Accession to the Throne Day (August 11), and King Hussein's Birthday (November 14). Religious holidays follow the Islamic lunar calendar, which is 10 to 11 days shorter than the Gregorian calendar. The ninth month of the year is Ramadan, when Muslims fast from sunup to sundown for the entire month. A major celebration, Eid al-Fitr, occurs at the end of Ramadan. Another holiday, Ed al-Adha, falls at the end of the Hajj (the pilgrimage to Mecca), which takes place 70 days after the end of Ramadan.

THE NATION

History: Compared with the majority of Middle Eastern Arab nations, the state of Jordan has a brief history. It did not come into existence until the 20th century. In 1921, Britain created Transjordan, pulling together a section of northwestern Arabia and the East Bank of the Jordan River. Prince Abdullah was proclaimed king. Over the years, the British slowly ceded power to local Arab officials and in 1946, Transjordan became independent. Jordan still has a strong British orientation, and it also has good relations with the U.S. In 1951, Abdullah was assassinated. His son Talal was proclaimed king, but due to ill health he was deposed by government officials. Shortly thereafter, Talal's 17-year-old son, Hussein, became the new Jordanian monarch. Hussein still rules today, making him one of the elder statesmen of both Middle East and world politics. Hussein's rule has been punctuated by regional wars and occasional internal unrest. These problems stem in large part from the refugee status of the Palestinian population who left their homes when Israel was declared an independent state (1948). The Arab-Israeli conflict has since changed from a local to a regional one as the surrounding Arab states took up the Palestinian cause. In 1979, the Israeli-Egyptian Peace Treaty was signed. Jordan rejected the treaty, saying that it endangered the status of the West Bank and Jerusalem. Since then, Jordan has been an active participant in international and inter-Arab discussions on possible solutions to the impasse between Israel, the Palestinians, and other Arab groups. The future status of the West Bank is a hotly disputed issue.

Government: King Hussein is the head of the Jordanian state. The government is a constitutional monarchy. Below the monarch is the National Assembly of Parliament, consisting of the House of Representatives and the Senate. The former are elected by universal suffrage, the latter appointed by the King. In early 1984, the Assembly was recalled after being recessed since the mid-1970s. The monarchy is hereditary, although in 1965 Hussein appointed his brother Hassan as Crown Prince. Hussein traces his lineage back to the Prophet Muhammad, thus providing legitimacy for his rule. Hussein is Commander-in-Chief of the Jordanian military, which is considered to be one of the best in the Middle East and was originally British-trained and U.S.-supplied.

Education: What Jordan lacks in natural resources it makes up for in human potential. Education, a primary concern of the government, is seen as a way to maximize that potential. Universal compulsory education has been established, consisting of 6 elementary years followed by 3 preparatory (or junior high) years. Beyond that, students may receive further schooling (either general or vocational), depending on available space. Jordan's literacy rate is approximately 70%, one of the highest in the Middle East.

Transportation: Jordan has good transportation systems and roads. Buses and taxis are available. Service taxis, which travel from one fixed spot to another, are widely used and easy to locate.

Health: Water, if cloudy, must be filtered and then boiled for 2 minutes. Major hotels provide boiled water. Boiled water must be used for brushing teeth, ice cubes, etc. Be sure that all food is well-cooked and served hot. All fruits and vegetables should be peeled before eating. Dust and air pollution are problems in Jordan and may cause increased sinus, bronchitis, and allergy symptoms; wearing contact lenses may also be uncomfortable. For further information, contact International Health Consultants, P.O. Box 34582, Bethesda, MD 20817.

For Further Information

Because space is so limited in this *Culturgram* and needs are so varied, no suggested readings are included. We recommend a visit to your local library or bookstore. Check *Books in Print* and various cataloging systems for country-specific titles. Review *Encyclopedia Britannica* or similar comprehensive summaries. The U.S. government publishes *Country Profiles* which many libraries subscribe to. Computer searches (DIALOG, SDC, BRS, ISI) are available at most major libraries. Contact the Embassy of Jordan, 3504 International Dr. NW, Washington, D.C. 20008, or the Jordan Information Bureau, 2319 Wyoming Ave., N.W., Washington, D.C. 20008. The U.S. Embassy in Jordan may be contacted at P.O. Box 354 Jebel Amman, Amman, Jordan.

How to Use This Culturgram

Quickly read the whole text as an overview. Then circle or give priority numbers to specific questions you have or ideas you want to pursue. Use the *Culturgram* as a guide to check on regional differences and current situations.

Maps

Culturgram maps are meant only as simple geographical orientations. Boundary representations are not necessarily authoritative. Different sources also vary spelling, transliterations, and accents.

Rev. 1/88

CULTURGRAM*

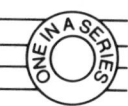

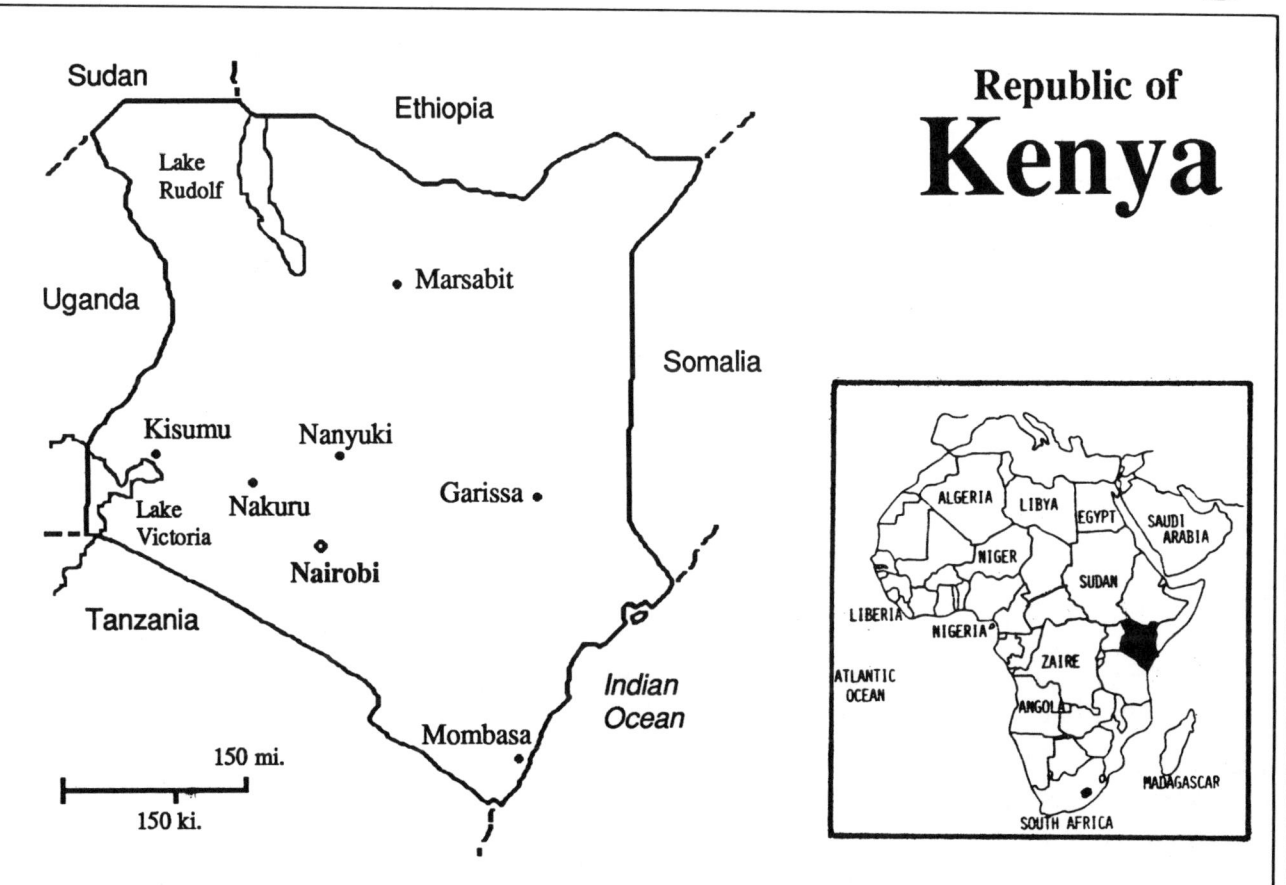

Republic of Kenya

CUSTOMS AND COURTESIES

Greetings: A handshake is generally used by men, women and children for greeting, although different ethnic groups have their own verbal greetings. Most of the people speak Swahili. The common greeting in Swahili is *Hujambo, hibari?* (Greetings, how are you?).

Visiting: When invited to a Kenyan home, it is appropriate to bring a small gift (cookies, chocolate bars, etc.) for the host. Flowers are usually used to express condolences. Wine is a common wedding gift.

Eating: When invited to dinner, visitors will find that adults eat together. Children are called in to greet the guests. As a rule, dinner is served first and socializing is done after dinner. Afternoon tea is a daily custom. European cuisine is prevalent in major cities and Nairobi has several excellent Indian restaurants as well as western style fast food establishments.

Personal Appearance: Visitors should be careful not to wear improper attire. Dress should be modest and conservative. Women should avoid wearing shorts in areas other than resort areas. In the cities, Kenyan men and women dress western style. In the rural villages, the people often wear a variety of traditional costumes.

*Culturgrams are briefings to aid understanding of, feeling for, and communication with other people. Culturgrams are condensations of the best information available. Your insights will be appreciated. If you have refining suggestions, please contact Brigham Young University David M. Kennedy Center for International Studies, Publication Services, 280 HRCB, Provo, Utah 84602 (801) 378-6528. Copyright © 1986. All rights reserved. Printed in the USA.

Shopping: Woodcarvings, animal skins, Masai beadwork and basketry, batik fabrics, Kisii soapstone pieces, and safari garb are popular items for visitors. Bargaining is expected in the markets and at roadside stands in the countryside.

Gestures: It is impolite to use only the left hand to give or receive a gift. It is advisable to follow the lead of the host in questions of etiquette. The verbal "tch-tch" sound should be avoided, as it is considered an insult

Photographs: It is best to obtain permission before photographing people close-up as many object on religious or other grounds. A tip is sometimes expected. Do not take photographs of military or other official buildings without permission.

THE PEOPLE

General Attitudes: The Kenyan people are generally warm, friendly and hospitable, and are cordial to Westerners. Social systems are group oriented. The individual is expected to be willing to sacrifice personal interests for the interests of the group. Kenyans are proud of their nation and its accomplishments.

Population: The population of Kenya is 20.2 million and is growing at the very high rate of 4.2% annually (0.9% growth rate in U.S.). About 97% of the population are native African, comprising 41 different tribes. The principal ethnic groups of the African population are Kikuyu (20%), Luo (14%), Luhya (14%), Kamba (11%), Kisii (7%), and Meru (5%). A small percentage of Arabs, Europeans, and Asians also live in Kenya. The capital is Nairobi, with a population of nearly 1 million. Only about 14% of the populace live in urban areas. The population density is 57 people per square mile (58 in U.S.).

Language: The national language is Swahili, but English is also an official language and is spoken widely. There are approximately 41 different languages spoken in Kenya.

Religion: The major religions found in Kenya are Christianity (66%), Islam (7%), and various traditional tribal religions (26%). Many people are devout in their religious beliefs.

LIFESTYLE

The Family: The family unit usually includes the extended family. There is much interaction between uncles, aunts, and cousins. In fact, children call their maternal aunts "mother," and their paternal uncles "father" in some rural areas. The average size of a Kenyan family is 5.6 people (3.1 in U.S.). Families live in much smaller houses than are found in the United States; an average house in Kenya consists of only 1.9 rooms. Urban families are usually smaller, and following tradition is considered less important.

Dating and Marriage: Dating starts at about age 18 in the urban areas, but is still uncommon in the rural areas. Men and women usually marry between the ages of 18 and 24. The brideprice system (where a payment is made by the husband's family to the wife's family) is still in effect, though money has been substituted for livestock as the medium of exchange. Usually the young people choose their partners, but then the wedding arrangements are completely handled by the families. In a few cases the marriages are still arranged.

Diet: The most common foods in Kenya are meat (goat, beef, lamb, chicken, fish), milk, *poshosti* (a stiff dough), *ugali* (corn meal porridge), pineapple, mango, papaya, red bean stew, and *kitumbura* (fried bread).

Recreation and Entertainment: Kenya is one of the most famous safari areas in the world. Leading attractions are the national park sanctuaries for lions, elephants, leopards, cheetahs, giraffes, zebras, gazelles, and other wild animals. The capital city of Nairobi also has a game park within the city limits. Soccer and track and field are national sports.

Kenya is famous for its world-renowned athletes such as Kip Keino, Ben Jipcho, Mike Boit and Wilson Waigwa. Kenya also offers superb fishing, mountaineering, golf, and year round water sports. Field hockey, cricket, and croquet are also popular among the urban population. The Kenya National Theater offers drama, concerts, and dance programs. There are many cinemas and night clubs. It is appropriate to stand during the Kenyan National anthem, which is played at all theaters and for all official functions.

Holidays: Kenyans celebrate New Year's Day (January 1), Good Friday (date varies), Easter Monday (date varies), Id-ul-Fitr (date varies), International Labor Day (May 1), Madaraka Day (birthday of the republic—June 1), Kenyatta Day (birthday of the first president of the republic—October 20), Jamhuri Day (Independence Day—December 12), and Christmas and Boxing Day (December 25 and 26).

Business Hours: Business hours are generally from 8:00 am to noon and from 2:00 to 5:00 p.m., Monday through Saturday. Government offices are open from 7:30 a.m. to 3:00 p.m. The average work week is 42 hours (40 in U.S.).

THE NATION

Land and Climate: Located on the equator, Kenya is slightly smaller than the state of Texas. It is noted for its striking topographical and climatic variety. The climate is generally cool (around 70° F.) in the highland areas of the south, but is hot and arid in the north and northeast. Along the coast it is also hot, but quite humid. There are 2 rainy seasons, the heaviest of which is from March to June; it is best to visit Kenya in the dry months, December through March.

History and Government: The first inhabitants of what is now Kenya were groups of hunting tribes (Dorobo or Bushmen) who lived in the vast plains of the area. They mixed and intermarried with groups of "Bantu" people from western Africa who had migrated to the same area. Other peoples from Arabia and North Africa also settled in this area and mixed with the indigenous people to produce a new race. These people developed the Swahili language. In 1498, Portuguese explorers arrived and established trading posts, but they were driven out by the Arabs in 1729. From 1740, Arabs ruled the Kenyan coast from a capital on the island of Zanzibar. In 1887, the British East Africa Company leased the Kenyan coast from the sultan of Zanzibar. Kenya became a British protectorate in 1895 and was organized as a crown colony in 1920. Kenya won independence on December 12, 1963, following a period of violent partisan uprisings. On December 12, 1964, Kenya became a republic within the Commonwealth of Nations. Jomo Kenyatta, a nationalist leader, served as its first president until his death in 1978. Daniel Arap Moi, the current president of Kenya, succeeded Kenyatta. There is only one legal political party in Kenya, the Kenya African National Union (KANU). The constitution of 1963 provides for a strong executive and a strong central government. The president is the head of state, president of KANU, and is the commander in chief of the armed forces. The vice president is appointed by the president from the members of the National Assembly. There is universal suffrage over age 18. Kenya is one of the most politically stable nations in Africa. It is ranked as the African country with the most freedom of the press. Kenya's major allies in the West are Great Britain and the United States, which are chief trading partners and suppliers of military and economic aid. The U.S. presence in Kenya includes over 5000 citizens and there are active U.S. AID and Peace Corps programs in Kenya. There are approximately 140 U.S. firms that have invested over 250 million dollars in Kenya.

Economy: Kenya, like some of its African neighbors, is considered a lower-middle income country. Kenya's gross national product (GNP) per capita is only $295 annually ($14,300 in U.S.) but is growing at a yearly rate of 2.1%. Kenya's economy centers on agriculture, though only 12% of the land has a high agricultural potential. Kenya's major crops include corn, coffee, tea, pineapple, sugar cane, sisal (used to make rope), and pyrethrum (a daisy-like flower used to produce a natural insecticide). Imports include machinery, transport equipment and crude petroleum. The tourism industry, centered in Nairobi, is also important to the Kenyan economy. As a result of the high population-growth rate and the large number of young people, 51% of the people are economically supporting the other 49%. The country suffers from a high inflation rate, which adds to the economic difficulties faced by Kenya. The monetary unit is the Kenyan *shilling*.

Education: Education through the eighth grade is compulsory. The government is also encouraging literacy education for adults. Complete education from primary through university levels is available to promising students or students who are able to pay tuition. Schools are operated by both the government and the private sector. Fees are charged from the fourth grade through technical and secondary levels. Teacher training is free, but teachers are bonded for 3 years after graduation. *Harambee* (self help) schools are common. Students are taught in their native language for the first three years of school, after which instruction is in English. The literacy rate is 47%.

Transportation: Both city bus systems and long-distance buses are available, but usually very crowded as only very few people own cars. Driving on the left-hand side of very narrow roads can pose a problem for American motorists. Air and rail transportation is also available. Guided tours into safari areas is also available, but a four-wheel drive vehicle is recommended.

Health: Malnutrition, malaria, typhus, and cholera are diseases still found in parts of Kenya, so immunizations should be kept current. In some rural areas Flying Doctor services are available. Most tour guides have prearranged services in case of an emergency. Water is safe to drink in most places, although some may prefer to drink only bottled water or soft drinks. For further medical information, contact International Health Consultants, PO Box 34582, Bethesda, MD 20817.

For Further Information

Because space is so limited in this *Culturgram* and needs are so varied, no suggested readings are included. We recommend a visit to your local library or bookstore. Check *Books in Print* and various cataloging systems for country-specific titles. Review *Encyclopedia Britannica* or similar comprehensive summaries. The U.S. government publishes *Country Profiles* which many libraries subscribe to. Computer searches (DIALOG, SDC, BRS, ISI) are now available at most major libraries. Contact the Embassy of Kenya, 2249 R. Street, N.W., Washington, D.C. 20008, or the Kenya Tourist Office, 424 Madison Ave, New York, NY 10017. The U.S. Embassy in Kenya is located at Moi/Haile Selassie Ave., Nairobi.

How to Use This Culturgram

Quickly read the whole text as an overview. Then circle or give priority numbers to specific questions you have or ideas you want to pursue. Use the *Culturgram* as a guide to check on regional differences and current situations.

Maps

Culturgram maps are meant only as simple geographical orientations. Boundary representations are not necessarily authoritative. Different sources also vary spelling, transliterations, and accents.

Rev. 1/88

CULTURGRAM*

Republic of Korea (South Korea)

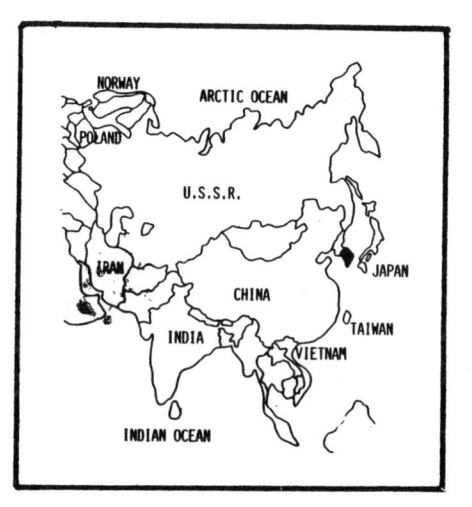

CUSTOMS AND COURTESIES

Greetings: Korean men greet their male friends by bowing slightly and shaking hands, either with both hands or with the right hand. Women, however, rarely shake hands. Young children bow and nod their heads unless invited to shake hands. One should pay complete attention to the person being greeted.

Visiting: If you have been invited to a home for dinner or a party, it is considered polite to bring a small gift, such as a basket of fruit, as a token of appreciation. Shoes are always removed upon entering. Talking or laughing loudly is often considered offensive. After a visit or interview, the host sees the guest to the door, or even outside, before saying goodbye. One should not open a gift at the time it is received. If money is given as a gift, it should be enclosed in an envelope.

Eating: Eating while walking in the street should be avoided. People usually eat first and wait to converse until after the meal. Making noises while eating is not considered impolite. In fact, this is a sign that the food is good. Guests should never joke about the food. Food or other items should be passed with the right hand, the left hand supporting the right forearm. Tipping in restaurants is not encouraged since the bill usually includes a 10% tip.

*****Culturgrams** are briefings to aid understanding of, feeling for, and communication with other people. Culturgrams are condensations of the best information available. Your insights will be appreciated. If you have refining suggestions, please contact Brigham Young University David M. Kennedy Center for International Studies, Publication Services, 280 HRCB, Provo, Utah 84602 (801) 378-6528. Copyright © 1986. All rights reserved. Printed in the USA.

Gestures: Although Korean men often hold hands in public, putting one's arm around another's shoulders or slapping a person on the back is considered inappropriate unless such a display is between very close friends. One must be particularly careful about touching older people and those of the opposite sex. Good posture while standing or sitting is important. In meetings and on formal occasions, visitors should cross their legs only with one knee over the other and with soles and toes pointed downward. In very formal situations, visitors should not cross their legs at all. Feet should never be put on a desk or chair. Hands should always remain in sight of the person one is talking with. Both hands should be used for handing something to another person and for receiving objects. It is polite to cover the mouth when yawning or using a toothpick.

THE PEOPLE

General Attitudes: Social stratification has been the rule for many centuries in Korea, making proper social relationships extremely important. Rituals of courtesy, formality in behavior, and dress, and extreme modesty when speaking of one's own accomplishments, status, wife, and, family are a part of the social tradition. Special deference and courtesy should be shown to the elderly. Reluctance to accept high honors is the mark of a true Korean gentleman. Compliments are graciously denied. Success depends greatly on social contacts. Traditionally, gifts were given before a favor was requested from a person, but this practice is now strongly discouraged. If one wishes to avoid an obligation, the best way to return a gift is with a short note of thanks with the last sentence saying, "I regret I am unable to accept it." Friendships are highly valued, and harmony in social interaction is important. Open criticism, abruptness, and public disagreement are avoided because Koreans feel that no one has the right to upset the feelings or tarnish the self-esteem of another. It is usually considered much better to quietly accept an injustice to preserve harmony than to assert one's individual rights. Koreans are justly proud of their country's cultural and economic achievements, which include the world's first movable metal-type printing, the first ironclad warship, and the rain gauge.

Population: The population of the Republic of Korea is about 42.6 million, and is growing at the annual rate of 1.5% (0.9% in U.S.). As a result of Korea's small land area, the population density rate is 985 people per square mile (58 in U.S.), and 3,463 people per square mile on arable land — the fourth highest rate in the world. Approximately 57% of the people live in urban areas. Although there is a small Chinese minority, South Korea is the most ethnically homogeneous country in the world.

Language: The official language is Korean, which is written with phonetic characters (*hangul*). Also, English is widely taught in high schools and many older Koreans remember Japanese from the colonial period of 1910–45.

Religion: Many Koreans are Shamanists (about 25%) who believe in folk religions. Also, approximately 18% are Buddhists and 13% adhere to basic Confucian traditions. Nearly 35% of the people are Christian, of which about 70% are Protestant. Next to the Philippines, Korea has more Christians than any other Asian nation. Christianity is growing 4 times faster than the population-growth rate, and many government officials are Christians. Many younger people are also Christian, while the older people tend to remain tied to traditional folk religions and Buddhism.

LIFESTYLE

The Family: The family is the foundation of society and is bound together by a strong sense of duty and obligation among its members. Although the modern trend is toward smaller family units, several generations often live in the same household. Currently, the average family size in Korea is 4.5 people (3.1 in U.S.). Koreans are group-oriented, and individuality is subordinate to one's group, such as family, school class, or business associations.

Dating and Marriage: Dating between young people is often in groups of 2 or 3 couples or 2 of one sex and 1 of the other. Movies are the most popular form of entertainment, but the youth also like hiking, taking small trips, and socializing at bakeries and tea houses. In some cases, marriages are still arranged by the families involved, but usually families only set up meetings and the couple has the final decision. Men marry at about 27 years of age and women at 24.

Social and Economic Levels: The average income is just enough to provide the necessities for a family. Many people have televisions, but few have telephones. Installing a private phone costs between $200 and $600 and is too expensive for most people. There are relatively few foreign cars in Korea because of high import taxes. Korea now manufactures its own cars and has an increasingly valuable export market.

Diet: Korean food is generally spicy. A Korean delicacy is *pulgogi* (barbecued beef slices), while common foods like *kimchi* (a highly spiced, pickled cabbage), *dok* (pounded rice cake), and boiled rice are also eaten. Also, Koreans eat large amounts of fish and soups. Dessert is not usually served, but when served, it consists of fresh fruit.

Work: Approximately 34% of the people are farmers, living mainly in rural villages and cultivating small plots. Nearly 25% are employed in mining and manufacturing–related industries and about 40% in services. Small family stores are usually open 7 days a week, from sunrise to 10 p.m. or midnight, but the larger department stores close earlier, usually about 7 or 8 p.m. The average workweek in Korea is 52.5 hours, the second longest in the world.

Recreation: Popular sports include soccer, boxing, baseball, basketball, tennis, *taekwondo* (the Korean art of self-defense), volleyball, hiking, track and field, and swimming. Simple visiting is also a favorite way to pass time.

Holidays: Korean holidays include New Year's Day (January 1–3), the Lunar New Year (January 15), Independence Movement Day (March 1), Arbor Day (April 5), Children's Day (May 5),Buddha's Birthday (observed in May according to the lunar calendar), Memorial Day (June 6), Constitution Day (July 17), Independence Day (August 15), Choo–Suk — Korean Thanksgiving Day (in September), Armed Forces Day (October 1), National Foundation Day (October 3), Korean Language Day (October 9), and Christmas (December 25).

THE NATION

Land and Climate: South Korea is slightly larger than the state of Indiana. It is bordered by North Korea on the north and is only 123 miles from Japan to the east at the closest points. Nearly 70% of the land is covered by forests; only 23% of the land is arable. The high humidity makes summer seem hotter and winter colder. The monsoon season occurs in the summer, from mid–July to mid–August. Spring and fall are the most pleasant times of the year, with seasonal changes corresponding to those in the Northern Hemisphere. Korea is traditionally known as the Land of the Morning Calm.

History and Government: Silla kings united 3 warring tribes in 668 A.D. A new kingdom, Koryo, ruled the Korean peninsula from 935 to 1392 and from 1392, the Yi dynasty ruled Korea. From 1637, Korea was a dynastic kingdom paying tribute to the Mongol rulers of China. In 1876, Korea was forced to open its ports to outside trade by Japan, ending its long period of isolation. In 1895, a war between China and Japan was fought on the peninsula. Ten years later, Russia's attempt to acquire Korea as a colony was halted by the Japanese. And in 1910, Korea was formally annexed by Japan as a colony, bringing an end to the 518–year reign of the Yi dynasty—one of the longest reigns in history. At the end of World War II, Korea was liberated from Japan, but the Soviet Union entered the northern part of Korea and the United States entered the south. The 2 major powers agreed on an administrative division along the 38th parallel, and a separate pro–Western government was established in the south soon after. Syngman Rhee became president. In June 1950, the North Korean army invaded the South, triggering a 3–year war. The United States and the United Nations came to the support of the South and China came to the support of the North. In July 1953, a cease–fire was achieved along the 38th parallel. Rhee resigned in 1960 under charges of election–rigging and political corruption. Although new elections were held the following year, General Park Chung Hee seized control of the government and was elected president 2 years later. In 1978, Park was reelected for a fourth term and continued to serve until he was assassinated in 1979 by the head of the Korean Central Intelligence Agency. A military coup followed and Chun Doo Hwan emerged as the new president. His party easily won a substantial majority in the parliamentary elections of March 25, 1981. In November of 1987, a new constitution was approved guaranteeing direct elections, for the first time in 16 years, as well as human rights. The country remains divided into North and South, though reunification talks have been held in recent years. All males must serve in the armed forces, usually for 3 years, and 34% of the country's central budget is used for the military.

Economy: Over the last 20 years, South Korea's economy has averaged nearly 10% growth annually. Currently, the average gross national product (GNP) per capita is $2,000 annually ($14,300 in U.S.). Traditionally, agriculture has been the most important sector of the economy, but today only 16% of the GNP comes from agriculture. Rice, barley, and fish are the main products. Major industries include textiles and clothing, food processing, chemicals, steel, electronics, and shipbuilding. The annual inflation rate in Korea is typically higher than in the U.S., while the unemployment rate is lower. South Korea has the second best distribution of income in the world — 10% of the country's GNP goes to the poorest 20% of the people.

Education: Education is the most highly valued aspect of Korean culture. Education brings wealth and success. Technical education is gaining popularity, although highly educated men have traditionally discouraged technical education. Education is compulsory between the ages of 6 and 12. The lack of teachers sometimes limits enrollment in secondary schools, and the selection of students traditionally has been based on highly competitive entrance examinations. However, examination tests for entrance to middle schools were abolished in 1969 and high school entrance exams were abolished in 1973. It is necessary, however, to pass rigorous entrance examinations in order to enter college. According to government officials, 78% of all school expenses are paid by the national government, and 22% by local authorities. The literacy rate is 90%.

Transportation: Public transportation is mainly by bus, subway, or taxi. The bus system is efficient and inexpensive. There is also a good subway system in Seoul. Taxis can be hailed on the street or summoned by telephone. Travel between cities is either by train, which is slow but inexpensive, or bus, which is faster but more expensive. Traffic accidents are common.

Health: For specific medical information, contact International Health Consultants, PO Box 34582, Bethesda, MD 20817.

For Further Information

Because space is so limited in this *Culturgram* and needs are so varied, no suggested readings are included. We recommend a visit to your local library or bookstore. Check *Books in Print* and various cataloging systems for country-specific titles. Review *Encyclopedia Britannica* or similar comprehensive summaries. The U.S. government publishes *Country Profiles* which many libraries subscribe to. Computer searches (DIALOG, SDC, BRS, ISI) are now available at most major libraries. Contact the Embassy of South Korea, 2600 Virginia Ave., N.W., Washington, D.C. 20037, or Korea National Tourism Corp., 460 Park Ave., Suite #400, New York, NY 10022. The U.S. Embassy is located at 82 Sejong-Ro, Chango-Ku, Seoul.

How to Use This Culturgram

Quickly read the whole text as an overview. Then circle or give priority numbers to specific questions you have or ideas you want to pursue. Use the *Culturgram* as a guide to check on regional differences and current situations.

Rev. 1/88

CULTURGRAM*

Republic of Lebanon

CUSTOMS AND COURTESIES

Greetings: Lebanese people take social amenities seriously. When meeting strangers, acquaintances, or friends, it is important to exchange greetings, to inquire about the person, the family, and in general to make polite small talk before getting down to business. Americans are sometimes taken to be unfriendly because they rush right into business matters. Handshakes are common to both men and women. Close friends and relatives often kiss each other on both cheeks upon meeting or departing. Titles such as "Dr." or "Professor" should be used consistently where appropriate. In Arabic, these titles are commonly used with the person's first name, but Lebanese are accustomed to hearing titles with last names in English and French.

Visiting: Hospitality is a prized tradition in Lebanon. People feel honored to have guests in their homes and love to chat. They appreciate genuine compliments on their homes, food, children, and accomplishments. Gifts of flowers or candy are appropriate when visiting. Hosts always serve guests something to drink, usually coffee or tea. This will often be prepared and served without asking the guest. Hospitality requires that it be accepted, so a word of polite explanation is in order if it is refused. Any topic may be discussed, but in view of the strong feelings of most Lebanese people toward the internal strife of recent years, guests would be wise not to express any precise political opinions until the views of the host have been determined. Arguments about local politics are inappropriate.

Eating: Unspoken rules of hospitality require the host to make the guest feel as welcome as possible and to try to get him to eat as much as possible. It is impolite not to try foods that are offered, but

---

*****Culturgrams** are briefings to aid understanding of, feeling for, and communication with other people. Culturgrams are condensations of the best information available. Your insights will be appreciated. If you have refining suggestions, please contact Brigham Young University David M. Kennedy Center for International Studies, Publication Services, 280 HRCB, Provo, Utah 84602 (801) 378-6528. Copyright © 1986. All rights reserved. Printed in the USA.

when a guest has had enough, it is not necessary to give in to urgings from the host. Western eating utensils are usually used, except for several foods that are eaten with pieces of broken Arabic bread used as a scoop. Pieces of lettuce are also used as scoops in eating *tabboule*, one of the national dishes. Meals often consist of many courses and can last several hours. It is not appropriate to discuss business during a meal.

Personal Appearance: Lebanese care about style. Western dress is the norm, and people of all classes make an effort to be clean, neat, and stylish. Outlandish fashions are rarely followed. Conservative suits for men and modest but fashionable attire for women are normal.

Gestures: "Yes" is signified by a nod; "no" is signified by an upward movement of the head or raised eyebrows, sometimes accompanied by a clicking sound made by the tongue. Gesturing to someone to come with your hands (the palm facing down and the fingers waved) is acceptable. Objects should not be handed to another to hold, as this may imply a servant status. Showing the palm with the fingers up is usually a sign of negation. A closed fist should never be waved in the air. The soles of the shoes should always be directed toward the earth and never toward another person, as this can be very offensive.

THE PEOPLE

General Attitudes: Lebanon is a good example of a traditional Third World society that has had a long association with the West and has been deeply influenced by it. Attitudes vary greatly; many traditional Arab attitudes and values remain, but people are "western" in various degrees. Compared to life in America, life in Lebanon is still fairly relaxed and slow-paced. People tend to care more about personal relationships than about "getting ahead." Most people are deeply involved in local political issues, but personal relationships and family ties are often much more important in determining loyalties than political ideologies. "Leftist" and "rightist" labels must be taken with a grain of salt. On a personal level, many people tend to have fatalistic attitudes about life, a probable reflection of the fact that it is more difficult to rise above the educational level or social class of one's parents than it is in the West. Friends will use titles with each other in meetings and will speak more formally than they would in other situations. In face-to-face contact with 1 or 2 other people, Lebanese tend to stand closer to each other and talk louder than Americans.

Population: The population of Lebanon is approximately 2.6 million and is growing at a small rate of 0.7% annually (0.9% in U.S.). The average population density is nearly 700 people per square mile (58 in U.S.), but is much higher in agriculturally rich areas. Beirut, the capital, is the only large city, although several other smaller cities are found along the coast. The mountains and the Bekaa Valley are filled with small, rural villages. Approximately 93% of the people are Arabs and 6% are Armenians.

Language: Arabic is the official language and is spoken by all. Many educated people also speak English or French. The Armenian minority also speaks Armenian and some of them also speak Turkish. Multi-lingualism is common, with some people speaking 3 or 4 languages well.

Religion: Lebanese society is based on religion. Every citizen carries an identity card on which a religion is listed. The official estimate is that 55% of the people are Christian and 44% Muslim or Druze (a sect that broke away from Islam in the Middle Ages). However, it is generally believed that the Muslims now constitute a majority. The largest Christian church is the Maronite Church, an Eastern-rite church. The 2 Islamic groups are the Sunni (the religion of most Arabs) and the Shiite (the religion of most Iranians). There is also a small Jewish minority.

LIFESTYLE

The Family: Lebanese families tend to be strong and close knit. Cousins and other relatives are expected to have close personal relationships. Upper class people tend to have small families while lower class people often have large families. Discipline in the family is strict, and children show respect for their parents and other elders. Family loyalty is a pervasive social value.

Dating and Marriage Customs: Traditionally, neither Christians nor Muslims dated and all marriages were arranged by the family. Now, Christians and upper class people have embraced modern dating customs, while Muslims or those of the lower classes continue to follow tradition. Since financial independence is considered a prerequisite for marriage, men often wait to marry until their late 20s or early 30s. Women usually marry in their early 20s. Christians are generally opposed to divorce, though it is allowed by Islamic law for Muslims. Public displays of affection, even between married couples, are not acceptable.

Social and Economic Levels: Lebanon is a class-based society. The wealthy have access to fine education, good jobs, and many luxuries. The urban poor and the rural peasants, on the other hand, have little access to education, and eek out a subsistence-level existence. Although each religious group has both rich and poor, Lebanese tend to see the Christians, especially the Maronite Christians, as a privileged class. The other Christian groups, the Sunni Moslems and the Druze are somewhat prosperous, while the Shiites are considered underprivileged. Although the economy is based on the free market and entrepreneurial opportunities are many, most people do not succeed in rising above the social class of their parents.

Diet: Three meals are eaten daily, the main one between noon and 3 p.m. This meal may last 2 or more hours. Except in upper class homes, the diet has less meat and more fruit, vegetables, bread, and rice than in the United States. Various stews are Lebanese specialties. The cuisine is often spicy and hot.

Work Schedule: A typical week involves 8 hours of work per day, Monday through Friday, and a partial day of work on Saturday. Sunday is usually not a work day.

Recreation: Soccer is the most popular Lebanese sport. Swimming at the beaches is also enjoyed in the summertime. Movies are well attended. One of the most common leisure activities is simply visiting friends and relatives.

Holidays: National, Muslim, and Christian holidays are celebrated. National holidays include Labor Day (May 1), and Independence Day (November 22). Ramadan is the biggest Muslim holiday; a month of fasting by day and feasting at night. Christians celebrate Easter, Christmas, and other holy days.

THE NATION

Land and Climate: Lebanon is slightly smaller than the state of Connecticut. Sixty percent of the land is desert, 10% forest, and only 27% is arable. Lebanon has a typical Mediterranean climate: warm and dry in the summer, rainy and cool in the winter. The coastal plain is much more hot and humid in the summer than are the mountains, so many people have summer homes in mountain villages. There is some snow (and skiing) at high elevations.

History and Government: A small part of modern Lebanon, known as Mount Lebanon, was a Maronite enclave in the vast Ottoman Empire. This area, and all of Syria, became a French protectorate when the French and British drove the Ottomans out of the area during World War I. Lebanon became a republic in 1926, but French troops did not withdraw from the country until 1946. The country was set up so as to insure the Christians a slight majority of power. The president was to always be a Maronite, while the prime minister was to be a Sunni Muslim. The Christians have refused to allow a census since 1932. However, since the Muslim birthrate is higher, it is generally accepted that the Muslims now form the majority. This fact, along with social disparities between the two, has led to a great deal of internal tension and strife, culminating in the civil wars of 1958 and 1975-present. A large number of displaced Palestinian refugees from Israel settled in Lebanon in 1948 and 1967, further complicating the internal problems. Well-armed Palestinians have generally sided with the Muslims in domestic Lebanese conflicts. In the summer of 1982, Israel invaded Lebanon and occupied the entire area south of Beirut. Many foreign powers have aided one Lebanese faction or another, including the U.S.S.R., Syria, Iraq, and Israel. Both

Syrian and U.N. troops (including the U.S., France, and Italy) have been deployed at various times as peace-keeping forces in Lebanon. With the election of Amin Gemayel in late 1982, many hoped that the internal conflicts would soon be resolved, but turmoil and instability continue to plague the country. The conflict is now in its 12th year.

Economy: Because of the destructive internal conflicts of recent years, accurate statistics are not available for the Lebanese economy. Average gross national product (GNP) per capita is estimated to be between $800 and $900 annually ($14,300 in U.S.) and growth is thought to have been negligible from 1974 to 1981. The economy depends largely on banking and tourism. Before the latest civil unrest, Lebanon was considered to be the banking center of the Middle East. However, the war totally destroyed the banking industry and most other sectors of the economy are now in ruin. Approximately 17% of the people are employed in agriculture. Important crops include citrus fruits, various grains, potatoes, tobacco, and olives. Food processing, textiles, cement, oil refining, and chemicals are the most important industries in Lebanon. Inflation and unemployment fluctuate significantly, but both are severe economic problems. The basic unit of currency is the *pound*.

Education: Low-cost government schools are available to all but are of low quality. Those who can afford to do so send their children to higher quality private schools. Law requires 5 years compulsory education, and approximately 93% of all children attend. Entrance into a university is by competitive examination. Approximately 75% of the people are literate and bilingual.

Transportation: Because of the destruction caused by the civil war, its subsequent conflicts, and the recent Israeli invasion, much of Lebanon's transportation system has been damaged or destroyed. Normally, one can get around Beirut in city buses, regular taxis, or "service" taxis. The latter charge a set price for a specific run and may pick up more than one passenger along the way. Similar transportation systems run throughout most of the country, depending on the area. Buses are boarded from the back door and exited from either the middle or front doors. Seats are usually given to women and older men. Taxis have red license plates and can be hailed by raising the hand. Most taxis are unmetered, so the fare should be agreed upon with the driver before the ride begins.

Health: Good medical care is generally available. Houses usually have 2 water systems, one to the kitchen and one for the rest of the house. The kitchen system is chlorinated and is safe for drinking; the other is not. Tourists staying only a short time are advised to avoid tap water altogether, since good bottled water is available. For further medical information, contact International Health Consultants, PO Box 34582, Bethesda, MD 20817.

For Further Information

Because space is so limited in this *Culturgram* and needs are so varied, no suggested readings are included. We recommend a visit to your local library or bookstore. Check *Books in Print* and various cataloging systems for country-specific titles. Review *Encyclopedia Britannica* or similar comprehensive summaries. The U.S. government publishes *Country Profiles* which many libraries subscribe to. Computer searches (DIALOG, SDC, BRS, ISI) are now available at most major libraries. Contact the Embassy of Lebanon, 2560 28th Street, NW, Washington, D.C 20008, or the Lebanon Tourist Office, 405 Park Ave., New York, NY 10022.

How to Use This Culturgram

Quickly read the whole text as an overview. Then circle or give priority numbers to specific questions you have or ideas you want to pursue. Use the *Culturgram* as a guide to check on regional differences and current situations.

Maps

Culturgram maps are meant only as simple geographical orientations. Boundary representations are not necessarily authoritative. Different sources also vary spelling, transliterations, and accents.

Rev. 1/88

CULTURGRAM*

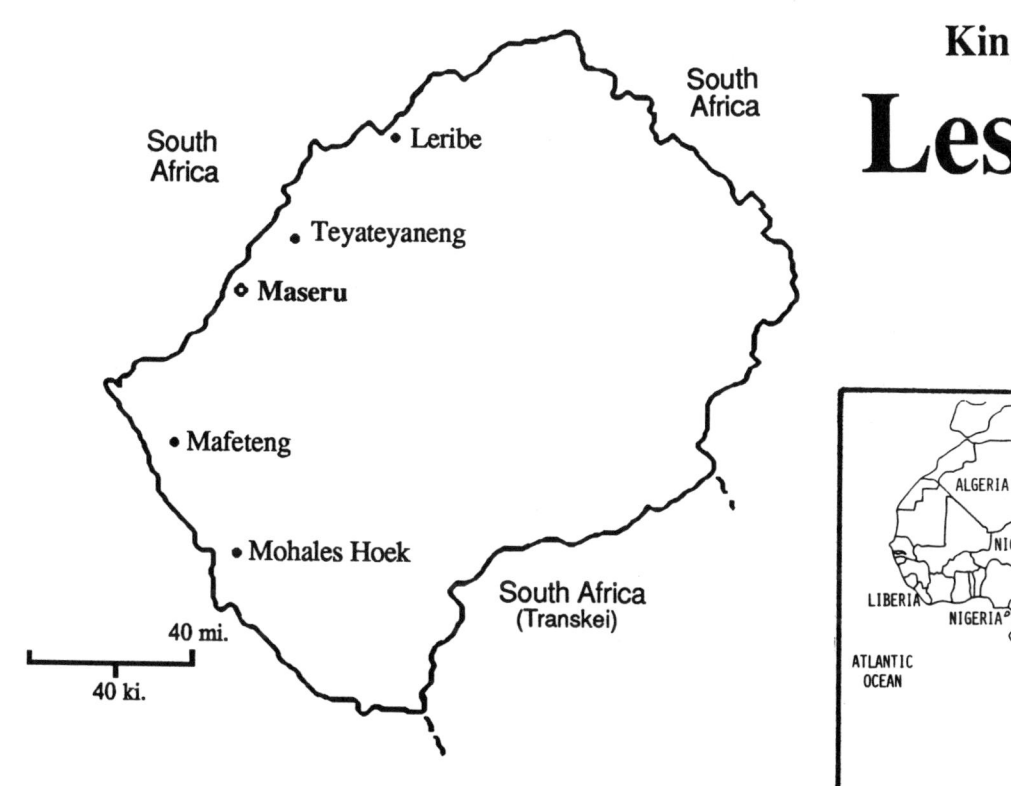

Kingdom of Lesotho

CUSTOMS AND COURTESIES

Greetings: In Lesotho (pronounced le-SOO-too), people generally greet each other with formality. There are distinctive greetings for men, women, children, young boys, and young girls. English greetings are also widely understood.

Visiting: When knocking on a person's door, one should also say *Koko* (are you there?) The person answers *Kena* (come in) and then it is appropriate to enter. It is considered extremely discourteous to enter without speaking. If one is invited to have tea with rural people, the visitor should expect a full course meal. The guests are not expected to help supply the meal.

Eating: The continental style of eating is observed in the capital city, Maseru, and in most hotels throughout the country. In the villages, it is proper to eat with the fingers. In Maseru, there are restaurants in the hotels and elsewhere that serve European and Chinese cuisine. There are also several western-style grocery and department stores.

Personal Appearance: The blanket (robe) is the traditional all-purpose covering and is still used by some people in Lesotho. The majority dress in conservative, western-style

---

*Culturgrams are briefings to aid understanding of, feeling for, and communication with other people. Culturgrams are condensations of the best information available. Your insights will be appreciated. If you have refining suggestions, please contact Brigham Young University David M. Kennedy Center for International Studies, Publication Services, 280 HRCB, Provo, Utah 84602 (801) 378-6528. Copyright © 1986. All rights reserved. Printed in the USA.

clothing. Women do not generally wear slacks or shorts. The *Basotho,* or people of Lesotho, are clean, neat, and very concerned about appearance.

THE PEOPLE

General Attitudes: The Basotho are generally a courteous, friendly people, who are hospitable to foreign visitors. Elderly people are treated with great respect. The citizens of Lesotho are proud of their independent nation.

Population: The population of Lesotho is 1.5 million and is growing at a rate of 2.5% annually, one of the lowest growth rates in Africa (0.9% in U.S.). Only about 5% of the people live in the cities (73% in U.S.), although urbanization is increasing at an exceptionally high rate. The population density of Lesotho is 84 people per square mile (58 in U.S.). Between the 16th and 19th centuries an influx of immigrants (refugees from tribal wars in surrounding areas) populated the region which led to the development of a distinct Basotho ethnic group. The result is a fairly homogeneous cultural entity. (Lesotho is 78% homogeneous compared to 50% in the U.S.) The Sotho make up the majority of the population with minority groups of Xhosa and Taung. Maseru is the largest city and has a population of about 75,000.

Language: The official languages are English and Sesotho. Sesotho is a Bantu language and is spoken by nearly all the inhabitants of Lesotho. A mistake in emphasis of a word may be considered a worse social blunder than an incorrect translation. The people respect foreigners who take the time to learn as much of their language as possible.

Religion: The Basotho are a relatively religious people. The Catholic religion has the largest following with 40% of the population; about 35% belong to various Protestant sects, and approximately 25% belong to traditional African religions.

LIFESTYLE

The Family: Lesotho is a strong patriarchal society that is centered on the nuclear family. Since many of the men are out of the country working, the women, especially in the villages, make many decisions and do most of the farm work. Women also work on the roads and in the service occupations. As a result of domestic violence and other factors, about 25% of the women are widowed, the highest widow rate in the world.

Social and Economic Levels: Most of the men work from 3 to 9 months in South Africa in mining, farming or industry. At any given time an estimated 200,000 workers are absent from Lesotho. The remaining workers are employed mainly in subsistence agriculture, raising livestock, and producing handicrafts. Over 65% of the population live in absolute poverty. Few people enjoy the convenience items common to most Americans.

Diet: The normal diet of the Basotho people consists of *mealie meal* (cornmeal), rice, potatoes, cabbage, and pumpkin. Beef and chicken are the most popular meats.

Holidays: Offices and shops may be closed on the following holidays: New Year's Day (January 1), Moshoeshoe's Day (March 12), National Tree Planting Day (March 23), Good Friday (date varies), Easter Monday (date varies), the King's Birthday (May 2), Ascension Day (date varies), Commonwealth Day (May 24), Family Day (first Monday in July), Independence Day (October 5), National Sports Day (first Monday in October), Christmas (December 25), and Boxing Day (December 26).

THE NATION

Land and Climate: Lesotho is a small mountainous country slightly larger than the state of Maryland and is located in the south-central part of the Republic of South Africa. Until 1976, when Transkei was given independence by South Africa, Lesotho was the only country in the world entirely surrounded by another. However, Transkei is not recognized as an independent state by any other nation than South Africa. It is divided into the lowlands, the foothills, and the highlands. A land of spectacular and beautiful mountains and a pleasant climate, it is becoming increasingly more attractive to tourists, most of whom are South African. Lesotho is a land of clear skies; the sun shines more than 300 days per year. The climate is temperate all year with a dry season from May to September. The dry season is also the best time to visit. January is usually the hottest month with maximum daytime temperatures of about 95% F. In June and July (winter) the average temperature is about 50% F.

History and Government: The history of Lesotho began when the Basotho nation came into being in 1818 under the leadership of Moshoeshoe I. He brought together remnants of Sotho-speaking groups that had been scattered throughout South Africa. In 1867, after the loss of extensive territory, the Basotho requested British protection against Boer advances from South Africa, and in 1868, Britain annexed Basutoland. Internal self-government was introduced in 1959. On October 4, 1966, Basutoland attained full independence as the Kingdom of Lesotho. When independence was granted in 1966, a constitutional monarchy was established, and Chief Leabua Jonathan became Prime Minister. In 1970 the constitution was suspended, and Jonathan has ruled by decree since then. Elections have not been held since 1970. The government consists of King Moshoeshoe II, the prime minister and his cabinet ministers, who are appointed by the king in accordance with the prime minister's advice. There is also an Interim National Assembly with only limited legislative powers.

Economy: Lesotho is a relatively poor country. The gross national product (GNP) per capita is only $455 annually ($14,300 in the U.S.). The economy, however, is growing at a rate of 2% annually, and is based on subsistence agriculture, livestock raising, and the earnings of its people employed outside the country in the mines. Nearly 90% of the population is employed in agriculture, although only 13% of the land is arable. Soil erosion is a major problem everywhere. Grazing rights are communal but arable land is allocated to individuals and families by the chiefs. Corn, wheat, sorghum, peas, beans, and potatoes are the main crops. Nearly all food produced is consumed by the Basotho. Manufacturing is only a small part of the economy. Also, there are a number of native crafts being revived: sheepskin products, pottery, candles, weaving, etc. Lesotho's geographic location and heavy economic dependence on the Republic of South Africa make it extremely sensitive to political and economic developments in South Africa. Although it sharply criticizes South Africa's racial policy, the government of Lesotho maintains vital economic and commercial ties with the Republic. Both the South African *rand* and the *maloti* (Lesotho currency) are used in Lesotho. The *maloti* is equal to and freely convertible into the *rand*. In addition, the *maloti* notes and coins are backed by the *rand*.

Education: The literacy rate in Lesotho is about 55%, which, though low by western standards, is one of the highest rates in Africa. The educational system is based on and has been greatly influenced by the British Colonial system. Primary education is made up of 7 levels called standards. At their completion, an examination is administered. If the student passes and the family can afford board and tuition, secondary education can begin. After another 3 years and an exam, a Junior Certificate is given. Two more years in high school and completion of another exam enables a person to attend the University of Lesotho at Roma.

Transportation and Communication: Maseru is a small city and it is easy to walk to the farthest points in the city. There are a few minibuses that travel around the city and go between other cities in the lowlands. Traffic moves on the left. To go further into the mountains you must take a national bus. The minibuses are crowded and are often driven carelessly. Both taxis and buses are a relatively cheap mode of travel. Air travel is also available between Maseru and some mountain cities. Telephone and telegraph service is available in and between the larger population centers.

Health: Tap water is safe in the Maseru area. Medical facilities in Maseru are also adequate. Lesotho has a flying-doctor service for emergencies. Life expectancy in Lesotho is 51 years (74 in U.S.), and the infant mortality rate is one of the highest in the world. For further medical information, contact International Health Consultants, PO Box 34582, Bethesda, MD 20817.

For Further Information

Because space is so limited in this *Culturgram* and needs are so varied, no suggested readings are included. We recommend a visit to your local library or bookstore. Check *Books in Print* and various cataloging systems for country-specific titles. Review *Encyclopedia Britannica* or similar comprehensive summaries. The U.S. government publishes *Country Profiles* which many libraries subscribe to. Computer searches (DIALOG, SDC, BRS, ISI) are now available at most major libraries. Contact the Embassy of Lesotho, Caravel Bldg., 1601 Connecticut Avenue, Suite 300, N.W., Washington, D.C. 20009, or the Department of Information, PO Box 353, Maseru, Lesotho. The U.S. Embassy in Lethoso may be contacted at P.O. Box 333, Maseru 100, Lethoso.

How to Use This Culturgram

Quickly read the whole text as an overview. Then circle or give priority numbers to specific questions you have or ideas you want to pursue. Use the *Culturgram* as a guide to check on regional differences and current situations.

Maps

Culturgram maps are meant only as simple geographical orientations. Boundary representations are not necessarily authoritative. Different sources also vary spelling, transliterations, and accents.

Rev. 1/88

CULTURGRAM*

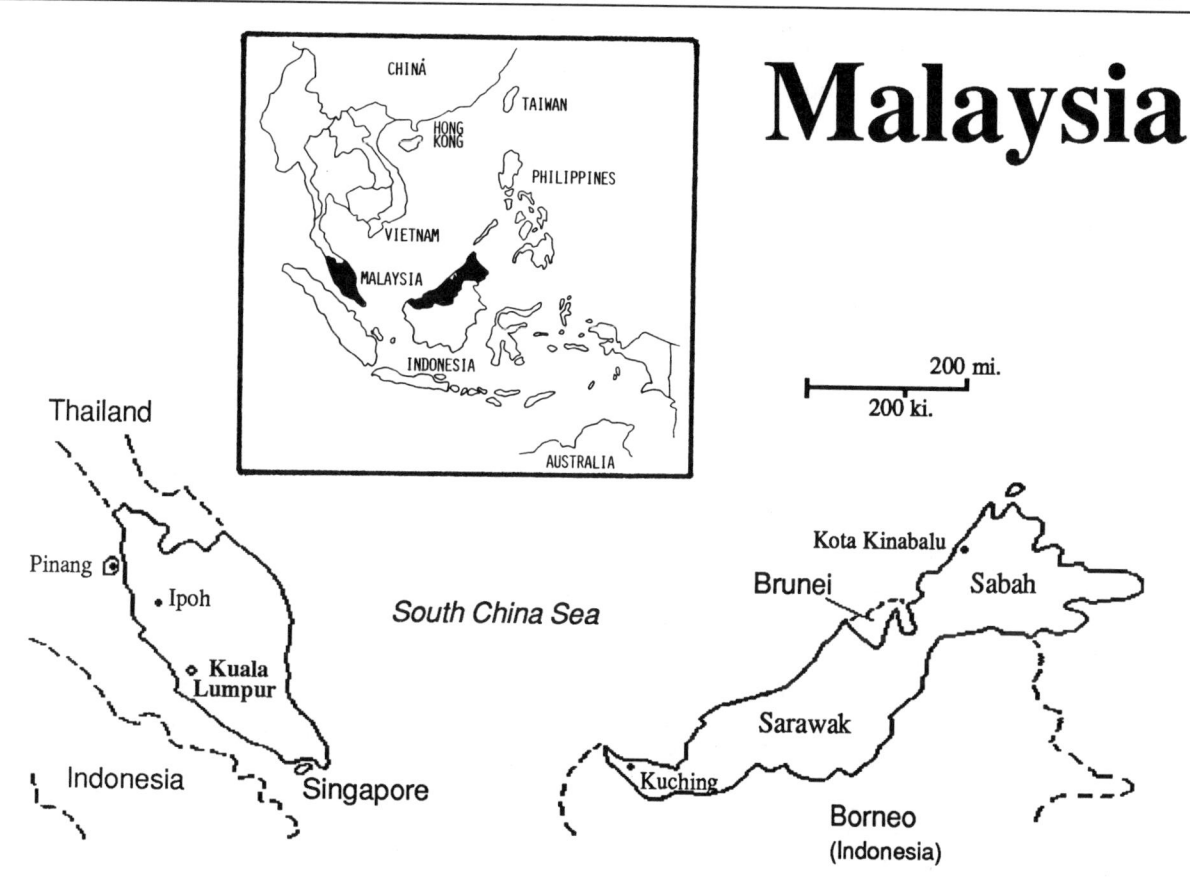

Malaysia

CUSTOMS AND COURTESIES

Greetings: A handshake is used only between men. A slight bow or nod of the head is common when greeting an older person. Women and elderly persons seldom shake hands, but may offer verbal greetings. When greeting close male friends, men use both hands to grasp the hand of the other. Business cards are sometimes exchanged after an introduction.

Visiting: Malaysians do not emphasize punctuality to the extent it is emphasized in the West. They may be late for appointments, since individuals are considered more important than schedules. Shoes should be removed when entering a home. The host will normally serve tea or coffee to the guests. If ice water is preferred, a polite request will not offend the host. Drinks are offered and received with both hands.

Eating: Eating customs differ among ethnic groups. Malays and Indians eat with their hands and with spoons. Chinese eat with chopsticks and spoons. Some cultural groups refrain from eating certain foods. For example, Muslims do not eat pork, and Hindus, and some Buddhists, do not eat beef. When using a toothpick or when yawning, the mouth should be covered. Tipping is not the rule in most restaurants, although some waiters may expect westerners to tip because they have been conditioned to expect it. Drinking water should be boiled, but tap water from the municipal water system is safe.

*****Culturgrams** are briefings to aid understanding of, feeling for, and communication with other people. Culturgrams are condensations of the best information available. Your insights will be appreciated. If you have refining suggestions, please contact Brigham Young University David M. Kennedy Center for International Studies, Publication Services, 280 HRCB, Provo, Utah 84602 (801) 378-6528. Copyright © 1986. All rights reserved. Printed in the USA.

Gestures: In Malaysia it is not polite to beckon to adults, with the exception of close friends. Beckoning is done with the palm turned down instead of up. Individual fingers should never be used for gesturing. Giving and receiving gifts with both hands shows respect. Objects should not be moved with the feet. A slight bow when leaving, entering, or passing by a group of people is a nonverbal "excuse me," but should only be done if the group is composed of people of position.

THE PEOPLE

General Attitudes: A person's ancestral background is often important to social status and future opportunities. Many people believe that successes and opportunities are the result of fate.

Population: The 15.7 million people that live in Malaysia are racially diverse and have many different cultural backgrounds. Ties between these groups have developed through educational, social, sports, and cultural organizations. The Malays and other indigenous people (Bumiputras) are the largest ethnic group and comprise about 50% of the population. They are mainly rice farmers, civil servants, or fishermen. The Chinese make up 35% of the population and live mostly in the Malaysian tin and rubber belt (peninsular Malaysia). Many Chinese engage in commerce in urban areas and as a result nearly all of the larger towns have traditionally had Chinese majorities. Recent Malay urbanization has begun to change this trend. The third largest ethnic group are the Indians who comprise about 10% of the population. They live mainly in Peninsular Malaysia. Malaysia's population is a young one, with 45 per cent of the people under the age of 15. The population-growth rate is 2.2% annually (0.9% in U.S.), while the population density is 100 people per square mile (58 in U.S.).

Language: Bahasa Malaysia (Malay) is the official language. All Chinese and Indians are required to learn Malay. English is also widely spoken and is a compulsory subject in all schools. The Chinese dialects are Hokkien, Cantonese, or Hakka. Most of the Indian community speak Tamil.

Religion: Islam is the official religion of Malaysia. The Malays are mostly Muslims, while some of the indigenous people in East Malaysia are Christians. Many also continue to adhere to ancient religious beliefs. The Chinese are chiefly Buddhist, with some Confucianist, and Taoist. Some believe in all of these religions simultaneously. There are also some Christians among the Chinese. The Indians are mostly Hindus, with a few Muslims and Christians. They hold strongly to their folk beliefs and customs, mixing these with various religious teachings. Despite the religious diversity, Malaysians enjoy complete freedom of worship and it is not uncommon to see mosques, temples, and churches all in the same neighborhood.

LIFESTYLE

The Family: Traditionally, the family system has been the most important social unit in Malaysia. It is common for two, three, or more generations to live together in the same house. Cooperation, loyalty, and unity are important in the family. Young people respect their elders. However, recent social changes have begun to affect the family structure. Now the trend is toward smaller families. Members of the extended family are now more likely to live in the same neighborhood, close to each other, but not in the same house. The older members of society complain that the youth are becoming less respectful.

Dating and Marriage Customs: In rural areas, dating is conservative. Dating often begins at age 17 or 18 and is not usually approved of by the family because it is felt that young people should concentrate on school studies. Some marriages are still arranged by the family, but the majority are not. People usually make their own choices about whom they marry, but often consult family members. Dating and marriage customs are much more liberal in the large modern cities.

Social and Economic Levels: As Malaysia continues to grow economically, the middle class continues to develop. However, there is still a wide disparity between the upper and lower classes. Ten percent of the people live in absolute poverty. Radios and televisions are owned by many of the people. Other luxuries, such as telephones and automobiles, are usually possessed only by the middle and upper classes.

Diet: Because of the wide cultural variety in Malaysia, a wide variety of foods are available. Rice is the dietary staple and fish is the main source of protein. Spiced foods such as hot peppers are also widely used. The variety of fruits is quite remarkable. Durians, large oval-shaped fruits, are the "king" of the fruits, along with pineapples, bananas, and papayas. Malaysians especially enjoy dining at restaurants.

Work: The business community is composed mostly of Chinese. The five and one-half day workweek is common, although some businesses operate 6 or 7 days a week.

Recreation: Popular sports include soccer, badminton, table tennis, basketball, field hockey, and tennis. Other recreation usually consists of watching television or going to movies. Rural people enjoy visiting friends and relatives.

Holidays: Malaysians celebrate New Year's Day, Hari Raya Haji or Idil-Adzha (date varies), Birth of the Prophet Mohammed (December 17), Chinese New Year (January or February), Labor Day (May 1), Wesak Day (May), Kadazan Harvest Festivals (May), Gawai Day (June 1), Merdeka or Independence Day (August 31), Deepavali (October or November), Hari Raya Puasa or Idil-Fithri (date varies), and Christmas (December 25).

THE NATION

Land and Climate: Malaysia has 2 different and distinct land regions: Peninsular Malaysia (about the size of Alabama) and the 2 states of Sabah and Sarawak (about the size of Louisiana) located in the northwest region of the island of Borneo. These 2 land areas are separated by 400 miles of the South China Sea. Together the total land area is about 129,000 square miles, or slightly larger than the state of New Mexico. Approximately 90% of the total land area is still covered with dense forests. Lying just north of the equator, Malaysia has a hot, humid climate with heavy rainfall. The temperature is generally between 70 and 90° F. There are 2 monsoon seasons on the peninsula—June to September in the southwest, and October to March in the northeast. Both bring heavy rainfall to the respective coastal areas.

History and Government: Portuguese traders first arrived on the Malay peninsula in 1511. Britain became interested in the area in 1786 when the British East India Company leased the island of Penang. By the early 1900s, Britain controlled all the Malay states as colonies or protectorates. In 1946, Penang and Malacca were united with 9 Malay states and became the Federation of Malaya in 1948. In that same year, communist insurrections erupted and guerrilla terrorism spread throughout the countryside until it was finally quelled in 1959. On August 31, 1957, Malaysia was granted independence from Britain. Six years later, the Federation of Malaya and the former British colonies of Singapore, Sarawak, and North Borneo (Sabah) united to become Malaysia in order to avoid a communist takeover in Singapore. However, tension mounted between the Malay-dominated government in Malaya and the Chinese-dominated government in Singapore, culminating in the creation of an independent Singapore in 1965. In 1969, racial tension resulted in widespread rioting in Kuala Lumpur, the capital of Malaysia. Since that time, great efforts have been made by the government to avoid the recurrence of racial rioting and to promote national unity. Many Chinese and Indians, however, claim that the Malay-dominated government favors the Malay people and overlooks the needs of non-Malays. This tension can be felt in conversing with non-Malays about the situation. The constitutional monarchy is headed by a paramount ruler, or chief of state, who is elected by 9 hereditary Malay rulers. As in England, the monarch is not politically active. Political power rests in the hands of the prime minister. Malaysia has a parliament with a 58-member Senate and a 177-member House of Representatives. All adults in Malaysia have the right to vote.

Economy: Malaysia has one of the highest per capita incomes in Southeast Asia. Gross national product (GNP) per capita is $1,750 annually ($14,300 in U.S.) and is growing at the high rate of 5.6% yearly. Approximately 42% of the people are employed in agriculture and about 32% in industry. Malaysia is the world's largest producer of rubber and exports large amounts around the world. Other major agricultural products include oil palm, rice, coconuts, timber, and pepper. Industrially, Malaysia ranks as the world's largest producer of tin. Also, rubber and oil palm processing and manufacturing, electronics, logging and timber processing, and petroleum are important industries in the Malaysian economy. Malaysia has the third highest energy production growth rate in the world. It continues to develop its large petroleum reserves. The unit of currency is the Malaysian *ringgit*, which is divided into 100 *sen*.

Education: Education is considered the key to social status and success. Six years of primary education and 3 years of secondary education are compulsory. After this, students take a public examination to determine whether they may continue school for 2 more years in a secondary school or a trade school, both of which require a modest tuition. There are 5 universities in Malaysia, all on the peninsula. There are also some teacher-training and other colleges in East Malaysia. Many Malaysians study abroad and higher degrees from well-known British, Australian, and American universities are valued. The literacy rate is approximately 65%.

Transportation: Bicycles, motorcycles, and automobiles are the principal means of transportation; buses, trains, or airplanes are used for longer trips. Taxis are metered and most drivers speak a little English. The steering wheel is on the right side of the car and traffic moves on the left side of the road. Driving in the cities can be frightening and dangerous. In some towns the trishaw is still available. Less than 13% of the people own automobiles.

Health: The average life expectancy is 68 years (74 in U.S.). Medical care is socialized, with private practitioners also available. Generally, adequate medical assistance is available to anyone who needs it. In rural areas, medical care is very inexpensive — often free or less than 1 *ringgit* (about 50 cents) per visit. A day in a hospital may cost 1% of a person's daily salary. Most private practitioners are Chinese and Indians. Mosquitos are a problem in the damp tropical climate of Malaysia. For further medical information, contact International Health Consultants, PO Box 34582, Bethesda, MD 20817.

For Further Information

Because space is so limited in this *Culturgram* and needs are so varied, no suggested readings are included. We recommend a visit to your local library or bookstore. Check *Books in Print* and various cataloging systems for country-specific titles. Review *Encyclopedia Britannica* or similar comprehensive summaries. The U.S. government publishes *Country Profiles* which many libraries subscribe to. Computer searches (DIALOG, SDC, BRS, ISI) are now available at most major libraries. Contact the Embassy of Malaysia, 2401 Massachusetts Ave., N.W., Washington, D.C. 20008, or the Malaysian Tourist Information Office, Transamerica Bldg., 5th Floor, 600 Montgomery St., San Francisco, CA 94111.

How to Use This Culturgram

Quickly read the whole text as an overview. Then circle or give priority numbers to specific questions you have or ideas you want to pursue. Use the *Culturgram* as a guide to check on regional differences and current situations.

Maps

Culturgram maps are meant only as simple geographical orientations. Boundary representations are not necessarily authoritative. Different sources also vary spelling, transliterations, and accents.

Rev. 1/88

CULTURGRAM*

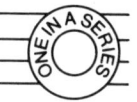

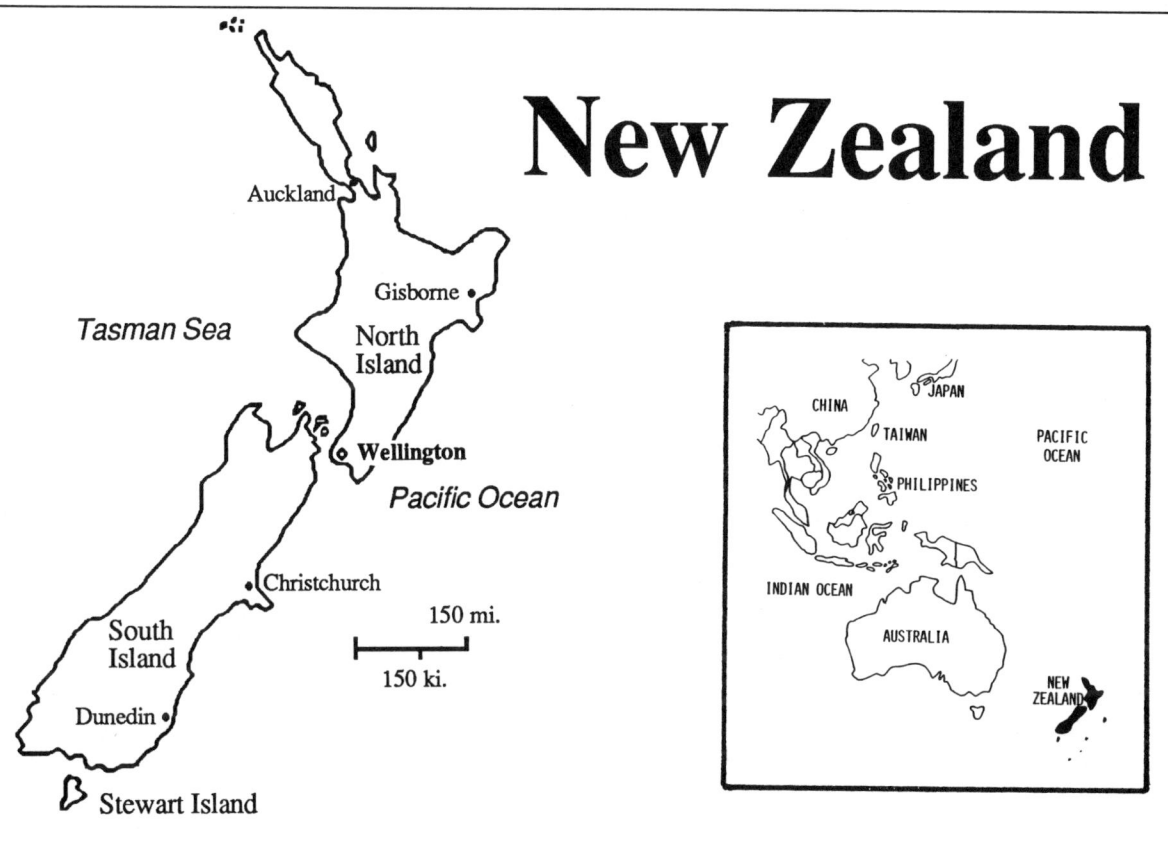

New Zealand

CUSTOMS AND COURTESIES

Greetings: Greetings in New Zealand range from American-style openness and Maori graciousness to formal British reserve, depending upon the person and the circumstances. Visitors should be prepared to be polite and formal until a more informal feeling can be sensed. Formal greetings are "How do you do?" or, "I'm very pleased to meet you!" (after an introduction). An informal greeting is "hello" or "good day." It is always appropriate to use titles in a formal situation—Mr., Miss, Mrs., Dr., etc. One should use first names only with intimate friends. New Zealanders greet one another by shaking hands (the two-handed variety isn't often used). Gentlemen usually wait for a woman to offer her hand first (if at all) in formal situations.

Visiting: Visitors are not expected to bring a gift or flowers for the host but may do so. In order to avoid embarrassment, one should not admire the host's property too openly or excessively.

Eating: New Zealanders eat continental style, with the fork in the left hand and the knife in the right. A drink is usually served at the end of a meal rather than during the meal, but guests may also request it during the meal. Tipping is not common at restaurants, hotels, etc. unless good service has been given several times by the same person. Even then a tip may be refused.

Gestures: Many of the same improper gestures used in the United States are also offensive in New Zealand. Waving at a friend is a sign of recognition. If a yawn cannot be suppressed, the mouth should be covered. One should not chew gum or use a toothpick in public, as many New Zealanders consider such behavior offensive and inappropriate.

*****Culturgrams** are briefings to aid understanding of, feeling for, and communication with other people. Culturgrams are condensations of the best information available. Your insights will be appreciated. If you have refining suggestions, please contact Brigham Young University David M. Kennedy Center for International Studies, Publication Services, 280 HRCB, Provo, Utah 84602 (801) 378-6528. Copyright © 1986. All rights reserved. Printed in the USA.

Traveling: On buses, men usually give their seats to women. Children are required by bus company regulations to stand and allow adults to be seated if there are insufficient seats. Otherwise, children must pay the full fare.

THE PEOPLE

General Attitudes: New Zealanders are open, friendly, and hospitable. They have a somewhat more relaxed lifestyle than Americans. Today's New Zealanders are, on the whole, a self-reliant, practical people, and aggressively modern in their approach to technology. They are noted do-it-yourselfers and love to work around their homes and gardens. New Zealanders have retained much of the characteristic reserve of the British in dealing with strangers. However, if accepted as a member of a local group, one will find the people very open, relaxed and informal. New Zealanders are very proud of their country, and especially appreciate visitors who have an understanding of their values and culture.

Population: The population of New Zealand is about 3.3 million and is growing at an annual rate of about 1.4% (0.9% in U.S.). The people are principally of two cultural backgrounds: 87% are of European origin, primarily British; another 9% are Maori, or native New Zealanders. The Maori population is younger and is increasing more rapidly than the European population. Polynesians from Tonga, Samoa and the Cook Islands have migrated to New Zealand since 1946 in search of work and have settled primarily in Auckland. Auckland now has the largest concentration of Polynesians in the world.

Language: English and Maoriare are the official languages. The Maoris speak their own language, although nearly all Maoris speak English in addition to their traditional language. Many Maori words have become a part of the English spoken in New Zealand. A *Kiwi* is a New Zealander, and a white person is a *Pakeha* (a Maori word meaning fairskinned).

Religion: Most residents of New Zealand are nominal Christians. There is no state religion, but the Anglican church has considerable influence. Of the 81% of the population that are Christian, Anglicans (known as Episcopalians in the U.S.) comprise 31%, Presbyterians 20%, Roman Catholics 16%, and Methodists 6%. In addition, 1% of the people are Hindu or Buddhist. Church attendance is typically low, except on religious holidays.

LIFESTYLE

The Family: Among those of European origin, the average family is still a husband, wife, and 2 children. There is an increasing number of "solo mums" (unmarried or divorced women with children), and the state recognizes common law marriages. Women now constitute over one-third of the work force. Among Polynesians, extended families are common, often with 3 or 4 generations living in the same house. The average family size in New Zealand is 3.7 people (3.1 in U.S.).

Dating and Marriage: Dating and marriage customs are similar to those found in the United States. However, a wedding breakfast for invited guests is more common than an American-style reception held in the evening.

Social and Economic Levels: Social and economic levels are generally high in New Zealand. Most families own their own homes, and nearly all have television sets, refrigerators, and other appliances. Housing is of high quality, generally single family dwellings on one-eighth acre lots. Approximately 10% of the national income goes to the poorest 20% of the population, the fifth largest amount in the world.

Diet: The New Zealand diet is quite British, with mutton and lamb, beef, fish and pork being very common. New Zealanders consume more meat and protein per capita than any other people in the world, but a large amount of vegetables are also eaten. Vegetables and fruits depend upon the season more than in North America. Breakfasts are hearty; lunches vary from light sandwiches to a complete meal; tea (dinner) is the main meal of the day with meat, vegetables, potatoes and a pudding (dessert). A light supper is sometimes served in the late evening. New Zealanders are famous beer drinkers and, increasingly, wine drinkers. Tea replaces coffee for most people and morning and afternoon tea breaks serve the same function as American coffee breaks. New Zealand ranks third in the world in consumption of tea per capita.

Business Hours: Normal shopping and business hours are from 9 a.m. to 5:30 p.m. Monday through Thursday, and 9 a.m. to 9 p.m. on Friday. A few centers are open on Saturday and corner "dairies" (convenience stores) are open seven days a week until late. Offices are open from 9 a.m. to 5 p.m. and banks are open from 9:30 a.m. to 4 p.m. Monday through Friday.

Recreation: New Zealanders love sports, and horse racing is at the top of the list. Rugby and association football (soccer) are also very popular in the winter. Cricket, tennis, lawn bowls, and track and field are popular summer games. New Zealand boasts many world famous teams and athletes. Since no area is far from the mountains, sea, or rivers, there are many opportunities for mountaineering, skiing, tramping (hiking), fishing, hunting, swimming, and sailing. New Zealanders work hard, but they also enjoy their leisure time. They spend considerable time in the outdoors, playing sports, gardening, or fixing up their homes.

Holidays: Public holidays include: New Year's Day (January 1), Waitangi Day (February 6), Good Friday and Easter Sunday, Anzac (April 25), Queen's Birthday (1st Monday in June), Labour Day (fourth Monday in October), Christmas and Boxing Days (December 25 and 26). In addition, each provincial district has an Anniversary Day, commemorating the founding of the province.

THE NATION

Land and Climate: About the size of the state of Colorado, New Zealand is a mountainous island nation some 1,200 miles southeast of Australia. The 2 principal islands are North Island and South Island. The more populous North Island has fertile agricultural land, the largest man made forest in the southern hemisphere, and a few isolated snowcapped volcanoes. The North Island also boasts of hot springs, mud pools and geysers in its thermal region. On the South Island, the Southern Alps provide magnificent scenery and opportunities for sports. There are many glaciers, lakes, rivers, and fertile plains. On the southwest coast there are fjords rivaling those of Norway. Both islands have many sandy beaches. Other islands are Stewart Island, off the southern tip of South Island, and the Chatham Islands, about 500 miles east of South Island. The climate is temperate, with plenty of sunshine, adequate rainfall, and few extremes in weather. Wintertime, however, may seem quite cold because of the high humidity. Seasons are the reverse of those in the northern hemisphere.

History and Government: Maori migrations probably began about 900 A.D. The Dutch explorer Abel Tasman discovered New Zealand in 1642 but never went ashore. In 1769, Captain James Cook of England landed in New Zealand. The Maoris ceded sovereignty to the British in 1840 in return for legal protection and rights to perpetual ownership of Maori lands. New Zealand went from provincial parliaments in 1852 to a central administration in 1877, and became a dominion in 1907. New Zealand made valiant contributions in both world wars. The country is an independent, self-governing member of the British Commonwealth. The government consists of a single-chamber legislature and a prime minister as the head of the government. A governor-general formally represents Queen Elizabeth II as head of state.

Economy: New Zealand has a modern industrialized economy comparable to some western European countries. Average gross national product (GNP) per capita is about $7,730 yearly ($14,300 in U.S.) and the economy is currently growing at an annual rate of 1.4%. Although only 13% of the population are employed in agriculture, New Zealand's international trade still depends heavily on exports of meat, wool, dairy products, and forest products. These products are processed in highly efficient factories at relatively low cost. Currently, New Zealand is one of the largest exporter of lamb, mutton and butter. It also ranks second in sheep production and first in wool. New Zealand is also a major producer of meat and meat products. Important industries include food processing, textiles, machinery, and wood and paper products. Today, the annual inflation rate is high (14%), but the unemployment rate is lower than in the U.S. The government maintains substantial control of prices and wages. New Zealand's monetary currency is the New Zealand dollar.

Education: Education is free and compulsory from age 6 to 15. Preschool education starts at three years and most children enter primary school at the age of 5. The curriculum is prescribed by the state and is rigorous; a series of competitive public examinations are given in the fourth, and sometimes fifth years of high school (grades 12,and 13). There are 6 universities, all run by the state. There is also an excellent system of technical education for those students who want to learn trades and professions for which a university degree is not required. An increasing number of the high school graduates go on to do university work and only about half of those who start actually complete a degree. The literacy rate is 98%.

Transportation: Since about 40% of the people have cars (the fourth highest percentage in the world); private car is the preferred mode of transportation. All major cities have good bus systems. Most people ride the bus to and from work. Taxis operate from stands or on call 24 hours a day, and in some cities they can be hailed from the street. Trains and modern airlines operate between cities and industrial centers. Ferries sail regularly between the two main islands.

Health: A comprehensive social security program covers the aged, disabled, sick, and unemployed. Public hospital services are free to citizens. Private hospitals and dental offices are subsidized. Medical facilities are generally good and readily available. For further medical information contact International Health Consultants, PO Box 34582, Bethesda, MD 20817.

For Further Information

Because space is so limited in this *Culturgram* and needs are so varied, no suggested readings are included. We recommend a visit to your local library or bookstore. Check *Books in Print* and various cataloging systems for country-specific titles. Review *Encyclopedia Britannica* or similar comprehensive summaries. The U.S. government publishes *Country Profiles* which many libraries subscribe to. Computer searches (DIALOG, SDC, BRS, ISI) are now available at most major libraries. Contact the New Zealand Embassy 37 Observatory Circle, N.W., Washington, D.C. 20008, or the New Zealand Tourist Information Office 630 Fifth Ave., Suite 530, New York, NY 10111

How to Use This Culturgram

Quickly read the whole text as an overview. Then circle or give priority numbers to specific questions you have or ideas you want to pursue. Use the *Culturgram* as a guide to check on regional differences and current situations.

Rev. 1/88

CULTURGRAM*

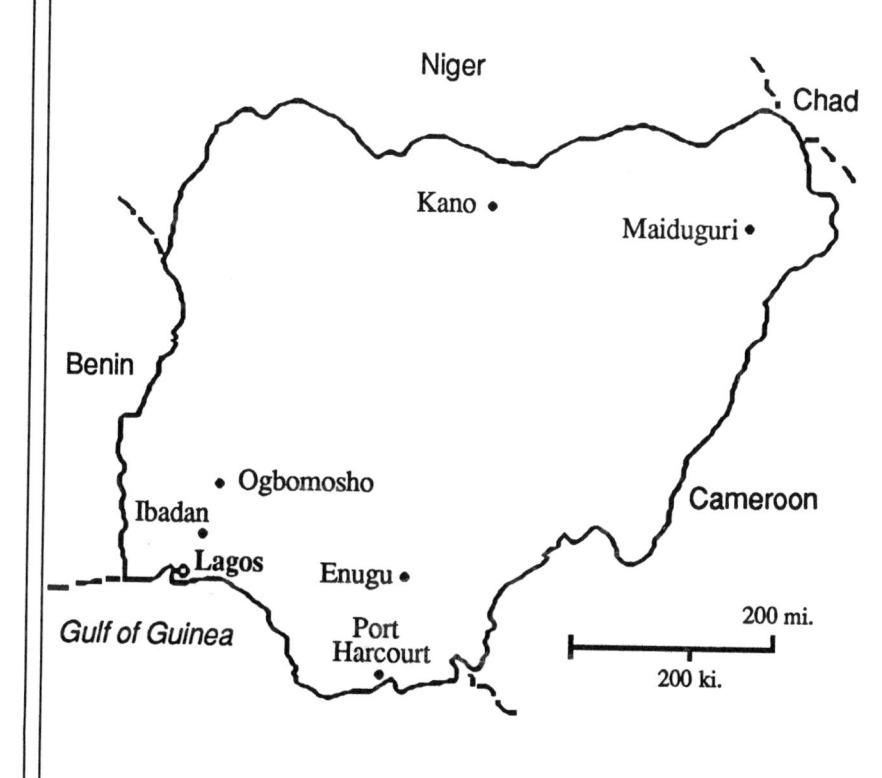

Federal Republic of Nigeria

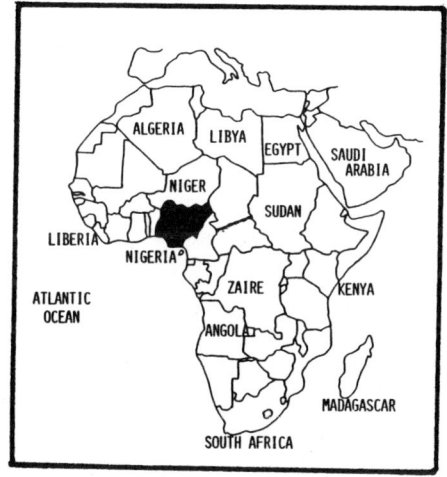

CUSTOMS AND COURTESIES

Greetings: In Nigeria, greetings are highly valued among the different ethnic groups. Refusing to greet another is a sign of disrespect. Because of the diversity of customs, cultures, and dialects in Nigeria, English is widely used in exchanging greetings throughout the country. "Hello" is the most popular greeting. More formal greetings, such as good morning, good afternoon, and good evening, are also appropriate, but visitors should avoid the use of colloquial expressions. Visitors are also encouraged to be courteous and cheerful when exchanging greetings, but not arrogant. Nigerians treat visitors with respect and, in return, expect to be treated with respect. Personal space between members of the same sex is much closer than it is in America. This may cause discomfort to those not accustomed to conversing at close quarters.

Visiting: Nigerians enjoying entertaining, and try hard to please their guests. Although they are generally not time conscious, they know about the western habit of punctuality and expect their western friends to arrive on time. Most Nigerians prefer "African time" (a slower, more flexible schedule) to western punctuality. Nigerians possess a rich heritage and hope for a bright future as a modern African nation, and thus can be offended by an attitude of superiority by visitors.

Tipping: *Dash* (from the Portuguese word *das*, meaning give) is a common Nigerian form of compensation in money, goods, or favors for services rendered. With the exception of services performed by waiters or bellhops, *dash* is normally paid before the service is given. If the service offered is not desired, a firm refusal is usually necessary. The government officially discourages

---

*****Culturgrams** are briefings to aid understanding of, feeling for, and communication with other people. Culturgrams are condensations of the best information available. Your insights will be appreciated. If you have refining suggestions, please contact Brigham Young University David M. Kennedy Center for International Studies, Publication Services, 280 HRCB, Provo, Utah 84602 (801) 378-6528. Copyright © 1986. All rights reserved. Printed in the USA.

certain kinds of *dash* that resemble bribery, such as payments for help in clearing customs, getting visas, or obtaining preferential treatment from government officials. However, the custom is still widespread. Visitors, as well as Nigerians, may be charged extra-high rates for taxis. Sometimes the going rate is not adhered to.

Personal Appearance: Dress varies according to the area and culture. In the Muslim north, dress is very conservative for both men and women. Dress is more casual in the non-Muslim east and west. Shorts are not appropriate attire for adults. For men, a shirt and tie are appropriate for formal and most other semi-formal occasions. Visitors will be most comfortable in cotton clothing—polyester is too warm. Traditional Nigerian men's dress is loose and comfortable. Although some women and young girls in the cities wear western dress, most women wear traditional long wraparound skirts, short-sleeved tops, and head scarves. The fabric is renowned for its color and patterns.

Gestures: Nigeria is a multicultural nation and gestures differ from one ethnic group to another. Generally, pushing the palm of the hand forward with the fingers spread is a vulgar gesture and should be avoided. One should not point the sole of the foot at another person. Using the left hand in eating (unless one is left-handed) or in receiving something from someone has a bad connotation. Nigerians often wink if they want their children to leave the room.

THE PEOPLE

General Attitudes: Individual Nigerians are proud of the unique cultural heritage of their particular ethnic group. There is some ethnic tension, but continuing efforts are gradually unifying the nation. The Nigerians are sensitive about their past status as a colony, and are striving to create a modern industrial society that is uniquely African, and not a "carbon copy" of western society. Because of negative connotations attached to the word tribe, Nigerians avoid its use. "Ethnic group" is a suitable substitute. Life in Nigeria moves at a relaxed pace which is in keeping with the Nigerian concept of time.

Population: The population of Nigeria is estimated to be about 91,178,000, making it the most populous nation in Africa. The population continues to grow at the high rate of 3.4% annually (0.9% in U.S.). The population density is about 171 people per square mile (58 in U.S.), the third highest rate in Africa. There are over 250 ethnic groups in Nigeria. The Hausa and Fulani in the north, the Yorubas in the west, and the Igbos in the east together account for about 60% of the population. Each of the ethnic groups has its own distinct culture. Because of traditions against numbering the population in many ethnic groups, census results are generally only estimates.

Language: English is the official language in Nigeria. However, because of the Nigerian accent, spoken English may be difficult to understand. Pidgin English (broken English) is widely spoken by uneducated Nigerians, and sometimes even educated people use Pidgin English to converse among themselves. Each of the ethnic groups also has its own distinct language. Hausa, Yoruba, and Igbo are widely spoken. Educated Nigerians are often fluent in several languages.

Religion: Nigeria is divided between the predominantly Muslim north (47%) and the Christian east and west (34%), with a strong minority of traditional African religions throughout the country (18%). Both the Christians and the Muslims have strong missionary activity inside the country. Nigerians may claim membership in a particular religion, and may also incorporate traditional African worship practices and beliefs into their daily life.

LIFESTYLE

The Family: Although the technical details of family structure vary from culture to culture, Nigerian families are generally male dominated. The practice of polygamy (having more than one wife) is not uncommon in Nigeria, but a man cannot take a second wife without the consent of the first wife. Although the protected status of Muslim women in Nigeria is similar to other Muslim countries, most other Nigerian women enjoy a great degree of freedom both in influencing family decisions and in engaging in open trade at the market place. Large families traditionally share the workload at home. Nigerians have deep respect for their elders. Children are trained to be quiet, respectful, and unassertive in their relations with adults. Marriage customs vary, but the payment of bridal token (money, property, or service traditionally given to the family of the bride by the husband) is common throughout the country.

Social and Economic Levels: Nigerians have the third highest average income in sub-Sahara Africa, but are still very poor by western standards. Homes are much smaller than in the U.S. Approximately 30% of the people live in absolute poverty.

Diet: The mainstays of the Nigerian diet are yams, cassava (a starchy root), and rice. Nigerians are fond of hot, spicy food. Their meals are normally accompanied by a pepper sauce made with fish, meat, or chicken. Climatic conditions also provide for a wide selection of fruits and vegetables to supplement the diet. Because of the tse-tse fly, dairy cattle are scarce in the coastal regions, but canned margarine, cheese, and powdered milk are used as dairy-product substitutes.

Business Schedules: Most businesses are open from 8:00 a.m. to 12:30 p.m., and then reopen from 2:00 to 4:30 p.m., Monday through Saturday. Government offices are open from 8:00 to 3:00 Monday through Friday, and a half-day on Saturday. Business appointments should be made in advance. Business is rarely discussed over the phone. Westerners are expected to be prompt, even though they may have to wait for some time after arriving.

Recreation: Nigerians enjoy many different sports, both as participants and spectators. Soccer, wrestling, polo, football, cricket, and swimming are all popular. Nigerians also enjoy attending movies. English-speaking movies are shown in many cities, and there are also several T.V. stations. Live theater and art exhibits are well attended.

Holidays: National holidays include New Year's Day (January 1) and National Day (October 1). Muslim holidays vary according to the shorter Muslim calendar, and include Maulid an-Nabi (birthday of Mohammed), the beginning of the month of Ramadan, Idul Fitr (end of Ramadan), and Idul-Adha (feast of sacrifice). Christian holidays include Good Friday, Easter Monday, Christmas Day and Boxing Day (December 26).

THE NATION

Land and Climate: Nigeria is about the same size as the states of California, Nevada, and Utah combined. Its geography is as diverse as its people and culture; about 24% of the land is arable, 35% forests, and 41% desert. The country ranges from the grassy plains of the Jos plateau in the north to the sandy beaches and mangrove swamps on the coast. Park lands and tropical rain forests dominate the central region. Nigeria is divided into three segments by the Niger and Benue Rivers, which meet in the center of the country and flow together to the Gulf of Guinea. These three segments correspond roughly to the boundaries of the three major ethnic groups. The climate is hot and humid year-round.

History and Government: Nigeria, with its many different ethnic groups, has a diverse history. The Hausa, located in the north, converted to Islam in the 14th century and established a feudal system that was solidified by the Fulani conquest in the 19th century. In the west, the Yoruba established the Kingdom of Oyo and extended its influence as far as modern Togo. The Igbo, located in the east, remained isolated. At the end of the 15th century, European explorers and traders made contact with the Yorubas and began a lucrative slave trade. In 1861, the British declared the area around the city of Lagos to be a crown colony, outlawed the slave trade, and annexed the remainder of the territory as a colony in 1914. When Nigeria became an independent republic in 1960, tension rose among the various ethnic groups. After 2 coups and much unrest, the Igbo-dominated eastern region attempted to secede from the country and establish the Republic of Biafra. Two-and-a-half years of civil war followed, and the Igbos were forced back into the republic. In 1979, national elections were held and a representative civilian government was established. This government, however, lasted only until late 1983, when a military coup left General Mohammed Buhari as military leader of the nation. Another coup occurred in the summer of 1985 and Major General Ibrahim Babangigia became the nation's new military leader. A new national capital has been under construction at Abuja, in the center of the country.

Economy: Although classified as a middle-income country by western standards, Nigeria's economy is one of the strongest on the African continent. Its gross national product (GNP) is the largest in Africa, and GNP per capita is about $760 annually ($14,300 in U.S.). The economy is currently declining at a rate of 5.5% yearly. Agriculture employs about 70% of the people and is an important part of the economy. Nigeria is a major producer of peanuts. Other important products include cotton, cocoa, yams, cassava, sorghum, corn, and rice. The discovery of large petroleum deposits has reshaped Nigeria's economy. Nigeria is currently the second largest exporter of petroleum to the United States, and is an active member of the Organization of Petroleum Exporting Countries (OPEC). It is the world's fifth largest exporter of petroleum and also produces a significant amount of rubber. Energy production continues to grow at a rapid rate. With the oil revenues, the leaders are working to create an industrial base, strengthen the agricultural sector, and generally improve economic conditions. Other important industries include mining (natural gas, coal) and processing (oil palm, peanuts, cotton, petroleum). The unit of currency is the *naira*.

Transportation and Communication: Nigeria is well linked by roads, railroads, and air routes, but traffic is heavy on the roads and often very hazardous. Few people own cars, but buses and taxis are plentiful in the cities. Although telephone systems are not yet comparable with those in the West, a new system provides adequate service. Nigeria has a relatively free and vocal press. Most newspapers are printed in English.

Education: The individual states provide primary and secondary education, and some states also provide higher education. The federal government supports almost all higher educational institutions. Although education for rural people is limited, government programs have recently doubled enrollment. Emphasis is on applied science and technology, with a goal to introduce more Nigerians into the skilled work force to replace foreign labor. Considerable numbers of Nigerians attend universities around the world, often on generous scholarships from the Nigerian government. In fact, more Nigerian students study abroad than from any other African country. The literacy rate is about 28%.

Health: As opportunity for education improves, so does the quality of health care. Hospitals currently offer adequate health care in the cities. Medical care in rural areas is still inadequate. The best medical treatment can often be found at the medical colleges. Nigeria has one of the highest infant-mortality rates in the world. Westerners not accustomed to Nigeria should boil the water for 20 minutes before using it, and fruits and vegetables should be cleaned before eating. For specific medical information, contact International Health Consultants, PO Box 34582, Bethesda, MD 20817.

For Further Information

Because space is so limited in this *Culturgram* and needs are so varied, no suggested readings are included. We recommend a visit to your local library or bookstore. Check *Books in Print* and various cataloging systems for country-specific titles. Review *Encyclopedia Britannica* or similar comprehensive summaries. The U.S. government publishes *Country Profiles* which many libraries subscribe to. Computer searches (DIALOG, SDC, BRS, ISI) are now available at most major libraries. Contact the Nigerian Embassy, 2201 M Street, N.W., Washington, D.C. 20037, or the Nigerian Tourist Association, 47 Marina, PO Box 2944, Lagos, Nigeria. The U.S. Embassy in Nigeria is located at 2 Kleke Crescent, Lagos, (P.O. Box 554), Nigeria.

How to Use This Culturgram

Quickly read the whole text as an overview. Then circle or give priority numbers to specific questions you have or ideas you want to pursue. Use the *Culturgram* as a guide to check on regional differences and current situations.

Maps

Culturgram maps are meant only as simple geographical orientations. Boundary representations are not necessarily authoritative. Different sources also vary spelling, transliterations, and accents.

Rev. 11/87

CULTURGRAM*

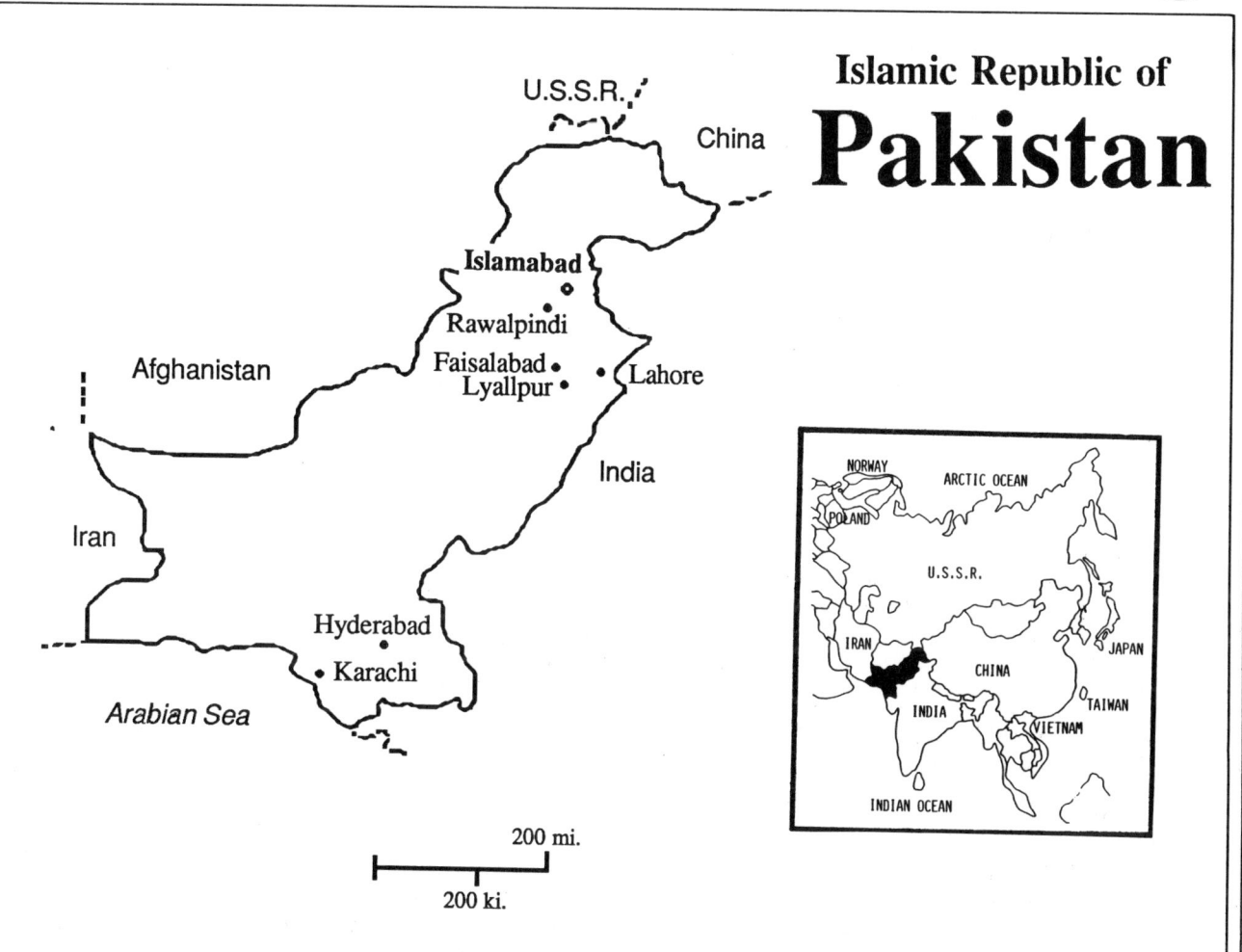

Islamic Republic of Pakistan

CUSTOMS AND COURTESIES

Greetings: A handshake is the most common greeting, although close friends may embrace. It is not appropriate for a man to shake hands with a woman, or to touch her in public. Hospitality is very important to the Pakistanis, and they will always try to make guests feel welcome. A title and last name should be used when addressing a Pakistani.

Visiting: Although the Pakistanis are not generally time conscious, they are aware of western attitudes towards promptness and will expect their western visitors to arrive on time. The people like to establish warm ties and a personal rapport with guests. They may be offended by the business-like attitudes of westerners. Visitors are often treated to coffee or tea and some other refreshment, and may be invited to eat a meal. It is important that visitors accept this hospitality. It is customary to socialize before a meal, and then to leave soon after the meal is finished.

Eating: Men will often eat before the women and children, especially at formal occasions, such as weddings. It is not unusual for a man to be invited to dinner without his wife. Even if his wife is invited, a man will sometimes come alone. Many traditional foods are eaten by hand, and it is important to use only the right hand when eating. Pakistani food is hot and spicy, and may require some getting used to.

---

*__Culturgrams__ are briefings to aid understanding of, feeling for, and communication with other people. Culturgrams are condensations of the best information available. Your insights will be appreciated. If you have refining suggestions, please contact Brigham Young University David M. Kennedy Center for International Studies, Publication Services, 280 HRCB, Provo, Utah 84602 (801) 378-6528. Copyright © 1986. All rights reserved. Printed in the USA.

Personal Appearance: While western wear has been the norm for Pakistani businessmen in the past, a recent government edict requires the wearing of national dress by all government employees. Adoption of the national attire is rapidly replacing western wear in Pakistan. The traditional or national apparel is called the *shalwar-kameez*, and includes trousers, a tunic, and a stole. The style, color, and complementary jewelry, vary throughout the country. Pakistani dress always covers the legs of the wearer. Shorts, skimpy dresses, and all types of revealing clothing are considered to be in poor taste and should not be worn in public.

THE PEOPLE

General Attitudes: Most Pakistanis are devout Muslims, and live according to the philosophy that the will of God is evident in all things. The people feel a deep pride in their own ethnic group.

Population: The population of Pakistan is approximately 99.2 million; it is the ninth most populous country in the world. The population is growing at an annual rate of 2.6 percent (0.9% in U.S.). The population-density rate is approximately 220 people per square mile (58 in U.S.). Pakistan's population can be divided into 4 major ethnic groups: the Punjabi is the largest group, comprising 65% of the population, followed by the Sindhi (11%), the Baluchi (9%), and the Pathan (8%). Pakistan also supports a large number of Afghani refugees who have fled from the current turmoil in Afghanistan.

Language: Because of the diversity of ethnic groups and the great difference between dialects in a single language, many languages are spoken throughout Pakistan. Urdu is the official language of the government, but is spoken by only 7% of the people. The different provinces in Pakistan are free to use their own regional languages and dialects. Major language groups include Punjabi (spoken by 64% of the people), Sindhi (12%), and Pushtu (8%). The remaining 9% speak a variety of other languages and dialects. Because of Pakistan's former status as a British colony, English is spoken by a majority of the educated population. English is used widely as a common tongue among peoples of diverse speech.

Religion: The uniting force of the people of Pakistan is the Islamic religion. About 97% of the people in Pakistan are Muslims. Islam pervades every facet of a Pakistani's life from birth to death, and people believe that their destiny is subject to the will of God (Allah). Muslims believe in all of the major Biblical prophets and patriarchs from Adam to Jesus. They also believe that Mohammed is the last and greatest of God's prophets. Muslims do not accept Jesus as the Son of God, although they believe in the resurrection and a final judgment. The Koran, composed of the revelations and teachings received by the Prophet Mohammed, is the chief scripture of Islam. In Pakistan, all law must now be based on Islamic principles, and the legal code is currently being rewritten to conform to these principles.

LIFESTYLE

The Family: Since Pakistan is overwhelmingly Muslim, the family remains the center of social life and support. Although increased modernization has brought many women into the work force, the male continues to reign as the head of the household. It is still common for the extended family, including a father and his married sons (and grandsons), to live together. The presiding male of the family has significant influence over the lives of all family members. The entire family celebrates the birth of a son. Although polygamy is permitted under Islamic law, Pakistan has made it illegal except in special circumstances. The government is presently stressing the need for family planning to help control explosive population growth. The average family size is 5.7 people (3.1 in U.S.).

Dating and Marriage: Individual choice of marriage partners has traditionally played little role in the marriage process, and arranged marriages are still the norm. Formal engagements may last from a few months to many years, as arranged between the heads of families. The Pakistanis view marriage as a union of 2 families as much as a union of 2 people. Both families are heavily involved in the preparations. A Muslim holy man, usually called *Qazi*, completes the marriage contract between the two families. The marriage celebration and ritual is very elaborate. Pakistan has been able to consistently maintain a low divorce rate.

Social and Economic Levels: Pakistan is a very poor country, facing many of the same problems as other developing nations of the world. Homes are among the smallest and most crowded in the world, averaging only 1.7 rooms in a home with 3.1 people per room. Most Pakistanis do not have many of the luxuries that are common in the West. About one-third of the population live in absolute poverty. Pakistan does, however, boast a fairly equitable income distribution, as 8% of the national income goes to the poorest 20% of the people.

Diet: The mainstay of the Pakistani diet is the *chapati* or *roti*, an unleavened bread similar to the Mexican tortilla. Food is generally hot and spicy, with curry being one of the common spices. The Pakistanis enjoy beef, lamb, and poultry, but are forbidden by the Koran from eating pork. With very few exceptions, it is now illegal to consume, sell, or distribute alcoholic beverages.

Recreation: Field hockey, cricket, and squash are 3 of the most popular national sports, and Pakistan has been a leader in world field hockey and squash competition for many years. Sports developed in Pakistan include wrestling, kabaddi, a form of team wrestling, and polo, which was picked up by the British and exported to England. Pakistanis also enjoy soccer, and tennis, both as participative and spectator sports.

Holidays: Secular holidays include Pakistan Day (March 23), May Day (May 1), Independence Day (August 14), Defense of Pakistan Day (September 6), Death of Quaid-e-Azam, the nation's founder, (September 11), and the birthday of Quaid-e-Azam (December 25). Muslim holidays vary from year to year according to the shorter Muslim calendar, and include Eid-al-Asha, the Feast of the Sacrifice, commemorating Abraham's obedience to the Lord in being willing to sacrifice his son Ishmail; the Fast of the month of Ramadan; Eid-i-Milad-un-Nabi, the birthday of the Prophet Mohammed; and Eid-al-Fitr, the Feast of the Breaking of the Fast, which ends the month of Ramadan and the pilgrimage, or *haji*, to Mecca. During the month of Ramadan, Muslims do not eat or drink between sunrise and sunset. Although non-Muslims are not required to obey the rules of the Fast, they are expected to refrain from eating in front of Muslims, to show respect for their customs.

THE NATION

Land and Climate: Pakistan is about the same size as the states of Texas and Oklahoma combined. The country is generally flat and arid, with the exception of the slopes of the Himalayas in the north. Total rainfall averages only about 8 inches a year. The regions of Sind in the south and Baluchistan in the west are desert, while the forested regions lie in the north. Pakistan's agriculture is supported by the irrigation of the Indus River valley, which runs through the center of the country. About 40% of the land is arable, and 24% is under cultivation.

History and Government: The history of modern Pakistan began with the arrival of Arab traders in the 8th century, who introduced the Islamic faith to the area. Muslim warriors conquered most of Pakistan in the 900s. By the 16th century, Muslim power had reached its peak under the Moghul dynasty. Although many of the Indians were converted to Islam, the majority of the population remained Hindu. By the 1800s, the British East India Company had become the dominant power in the area and the last Mogul emperor was deposed in 1859. After the period of British control over the subcontinent, the people began to push for independence from the Crown. Muslim leaders, particularly Mohammed Ali Jinnah and Liaquat Ali Khan, fearing that they would be swallowed up by the Hindu majority, organized the All-India Muslim league. In June 1947, the British conceded the necessity of a Muslim and a Hindu state, and Pakistan was formed from the Punjab area in the west and the Bengal area in the east. West and East Pakistan were separated by 1,000 miles of Indian territory. Conflict with India flared several times over the disputed Kashmir area, where the Muslim majority was being ruled by a Hindu minority. This dispute erupted into war in 1948, and a peace agreement was not reached until early in 1966. Tension between East and West Pakistan reached a peak in 1971, when East Pakistan proclaimed its independence from Pakistan and called their nation Bangladesh. Aided by India, Bangladesh succeeded in its revolution against Pakistani troops. In the vacuum of power created by the defeat, Zulfikar Ali Bhutto stepped in as leader, declared martial law, and strove to reestablish the confidence of the people. During a period of civil unrest in 1977, General Mohammed Zia ul-Haq, chief of staff of the army, seized control of the government and jailed Bhutto. Bhutto was convicted of murder and hanged in 1979. Elections have been postponed indefinitely. Relations with the United States suffered a major setback in 1979 when mobs of Pakistani Muslims attacked and burned the U.S. embassy, killing 2 Americans. After the Soviet invasion of neighboring Afghanistan, the U.S. increased economic and military aid to President Zia's government. Pakistan has endured prolonged and varied domestic turmoil since 1960.

Economy: Pakistan is primarily an agricultural country; over one-half of the people are employed in agriculture. The emphasis today is placed on using new high-yield grains to keep pace with the demands of the growing population. Extensive irrigation in the Indus valley has greatly increased agricultural output. Chief products include wheat, rice, sugarcane, and cotton. At the time of its independence, Pakistan had very little industry. Recent efforts by the government have increased the industrial capacity immensely. Industry now employs 22% of the people. Pakistan is a major producer of cotton fiber, which goes into the production of carpets, rugs, and mats—Pakistan's chief exports. Other industries are food processing, tobacco, engineering, chemicals, and natural gas. Pakistan is a major exporter of labor to the oil-producing regions of the Gulf. Consequently, these funds now represent the single largest source of foreign-exchange earnings, exceeding all other exports. Average annual gross national product (GNP) per capita is only $300, one of the lowest in the world ($14,300 in U.S.). Because of its poor economic situation, Pakistan is the fourth largest receiver of foreign aid, most coming from the United States and China. Currently, the economy is growing at the high rate of 4.6% annually. The standard unit of currency is the *rupee*.

Education: Pakistan suffers from a high rate of illiteracy, a characteristic of developing nations; only 24% of the people are literate. Government efforts in education have greatly increased the number of primary schools in the country. Efforts are being directed toward developing skilled technicians to aid in expanding the nation's industrial base. A lack of financial support, combined with the large number of school-age children, compounds the problem of education in Pakistan.

Health: Medical services in Pakistan are limited. Fully equipped hospitals are located in urban areas, and are generally understaffed and overworked. Outside of the cities, medical care is scarce. The ratio of doctors to patients is about 1 to 6,000. The government is striving to increase the number of doctors in the country, but many of the highly skilled medical personnel seek more lucrative employment abroad. For further medical information, contact International Health Consultants, PO Box 34582, Bethesda, MD 20817.

For Further Information

Because space is so limited in this *Culturgram* and needs are so varied, no suggested readings are included. We recommend a visit to your local library or bookstore. Check *Books in Print* and various cataloging systems for country-specific titles. Review *Encyclopedia Britannica* or similar comprehensive summaries. The U.S. government publishes *Country Profiles* which many libraries subscribe to. Computer searches (DIALOG, SDC, BRS, ISI) are now available at most major libraries. Contact the Pakistan Embassy, 2315 Massachusetts Ave., N.W., Washington, D.C. 20008, or Pakistan Tourism Development, 12 E. 65th St., New York, NY 10021. The U.S. Embassy in Pakistan is located at Diplomatic Enclave, Ramma 5, Islamabad, Pakistan.

How to Use This Culturgram

Quickly read the whole text as an overview. Then circle or give priority numbers to specific questions you have or ideas you want to pursue. Use the *Culturgram* as a guide to check on regional differences and current situations.

Rev. 1/88

CULTURGRAM*

Republic of the Philippines

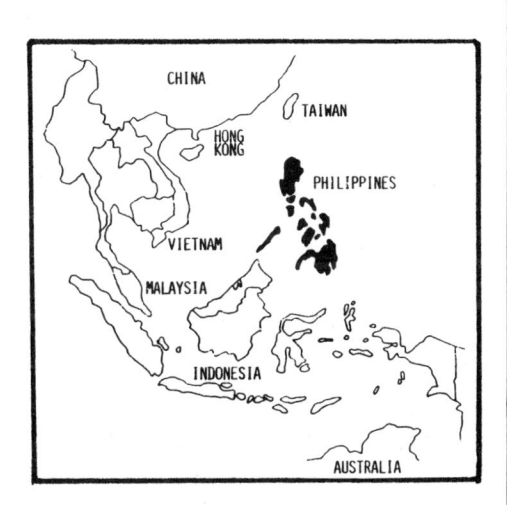

CUSTOMS AND COURTESIES

Greetings: Initial greetings are usually friendly and informal. Because English is commonly used in urban areas, normal English greetings are acceptable. The everyday greeting for acquaintances and friends is a handshake for both men and women. When greeting a young person, guests should allow the child to show respect. Older people should be shown respect and allowed to take the lead. When greeting a family, it is proper to greet the eldest first.

Visiting: Because of the long exposure to American custom and habit, most American social customs are understood and accepted in urban areas. Hospitality is important to Filipinos. They always try to make guests feel at ease. When visiting in a family's home, a guest should also be tactful and solicitous. Filipinos appreciate genuine love and concern expressed in an open and compassionate manner. Insincerity will not be appreciated and may be offensive. The word hostess should not be used when referring to the lady of the house. Eating heartily is the surest way a guest can compliment the host on a meal. However, to avoid being given more food than desired, a small portion may be left on the plate. Because of the importance that Filipinos attach to personal and family honor, one should not criticize anyone. Filipinos may criticize each other, but they do not appreciate an outsider's criticism.

Personal Appearance: As elsewhere in the world, clothing trends have changed in the Philippines. A few years ago, everyday work clothing for men consisted of shorts and a T-shirt. Today, shorts have been replaced by denim jeans or suits. Women typically dress in western

---

*****Culturgrams** are briefings to aid understanding of, feeling for, and communication with other people. Culturgrams are condensations of the best information available. Your insights will be appreciated. If you have refining suggestions, please contact Brigham Young University David M. Kennedy Center for International Studies, Publication Services, 280 HRCB, Provo, Utah 84602 (801) 378-6528. Copyright © 1986. All rights reserved. Printed in the USA.

clothing; however, shorts are not appropriate attire for women in public. In rural areas, near ankle-length, wraparound skirts are worn with blouses. The national costume for men is an elaborately embroidered shirt that hangs out over the pants, called a *barong*. For women, it is a full-length dress with a scooped neckline and butterfly sleeves, called a *terno*. Both are worn only for formal affairs. Business attire for men is a less elaborate, white or pastel-colored *barong* with dress slacks and western dress for women.

THE PEOPLE

General Attitudes: Filipinos have been influenced by the Chinese, Malayan, Moslem, Spanish, and American cultures. Sensitivity is considered an important character trait to Filipinos. Insincerity is easily detected by them and can ruin a relationship. Individualism is less important than loyalty to one's family, relatives, and friends. Interdependence is more important than independence. Making social relationships run smoothly is seen as being more important than expressing personal views. A Filipino may even consider frankness and outspokenness to be rude and uncultured. Accepting a favor obliges a Filipino to repay with a greater favor, although never with money. This feeling of obligation is strictly binding for Filipinos, but not for foreigners. Bringing shame to an individual reflects on his family and is avoided at all costs. Innovation, change, and competition are often looked upon as gambles because failure would bring shame or upset the balance of social relationships. Change in religion is discouraged, and when one does convert to another religion, it may be seen as a sign of ingratitude to parents. Fatalism is a common attitude toward life, characterized by the typical expression *Bahala na*, which roughly translated means "Accept what comes and bear it with hope and patience." Success may also be attributed to fate rather than effort.

Population: The population of the Philippines is about 54.8 million and is growing at the high rate of 2.5% annually (0.9% in U.S.). The population has doubled since 1946. The people are predominantly of Malayan descent: 91.5% Christian Malay and 4% Muslim Malay. Also, 1.5% of the population is Chinese. Negritos, a short, dark-skinned people, inhabit the uplands of the islands around the Sulu Sea. The Igorot and Ifugao live in the mountains of northern Luzon. The population density is 357 people per square mile (58 in U.S.).

Language: Eighty-seven dialects are spoken throughout the 7,107 islands. The 3 major dialects are Ilocano (northern Luzon), Tagalog (central and southern Luzon), and Cebuano (southern islands). For a time in the 1960s and 1970s, there was a popular movement to establish a national language called Pilipino. Because of its basis mainly in Tagalog, Pilipino has never gained full acceptance by speakers of other dialects. With so many dialects in the country, English has been and continues to be the unifying language. English is the language of the public schools from the fourth grade through college. The Philippines has the third largest English-speaking population in the world.

Religion: The Philippines is unique among Asian countries because it is the only nation that is predominantly Christian: 85% of the population are Roman Catholic, 6% belong to the Philippine Independent (or Aglipayan) Church, and 3% are Protestant. The Muslim population, called Moros, make up about 4% of the population and live mainly in the southern islands. Over the years there has been constant friction between the fiercely independent Moros and the Philippine government. In remote areas, people are still influenced by traditional folk beliefs. Other minority religions also have adherents.

LIFESTYLE

The Family: The average family size in the Philippines is 5.9 people — one of the largest in the world (3.1 in U.S.). Professionally and otherwise, Filipino women generally enjoy equality with men. In the cities, women work in government, business, and industry. In rural areas, they work alongside their husbands in the rice fields. Women also manage the household, family finances, and care for children. A mother's advice to her son is taken very seriously. Family ties are very important to Filipinos and often influence many aspects of their lives. Depending on the degree of closeness, Filipino family members tend to feel free to call on one another for financial assistance. The borrower is expected to help other family members when he is in a position to do so.

Marriage: Until a generation or two ago, nearly all marriages were arranged by the parents. Today, in both rural and urban areas, parents continue to exert strong influence in the choice of a mate. Couples are expected to marry and begin a family as soon as they are financially secure. It is the obligation of the groom and his family to pay for the wedding ceremony and feast. Although discouraged by the government, the family of the bride may also pay a dowry to the groom.

Diet: Rice is the staple food in the Filipino diet. The main source of protein is fish, accompanied by a variety of vegetables and tropical fruit. A typical meal might consist of boiled rice, fried fish, a vegetable, and fruit for dessert.

Recreation: People spend their leisure time socializing with relatives and neighbors or going to movies; the Philippines is the fourth largest producer of films in the world. *Mahjong* (a Chinese card game played with tiles), cockfights, horse racing, and gambling are very popular. Basketball is a favorite sport throughout the country. Sports are often played on Sunday because most people work or attend school 6 days a week.

Holidays: Holidays include New Year's Day (January 1), Holy Thursday and Good Friday (dates variable), Bataan Day (April 9), Labor Day (May 1), Independence Day (June 12), Philippine-American Friendship Day (July 4), All Saints Day (November 1), National Heroes Day (November 30), Christmas Day (December 25), and Rizal Day (December 30).

THE NATION

Land and Climate: The Philippines is made up of some 7,107 islands. The total land area is approximately equal to the state of Arizona. However, the coastline is twice the length of the United States' coastline. Approximately 53% of the land is covered by forests and 30% is arable. The climate ranges from warm to hot. The rainy season extends from June to October. Typhoons are likely from June to November, but may occur during any season. Coats are almost never worn by Filipinos except in Baguio City from November to February.

History and Government: The first Western contact made in the Philippines was made by Magellan in 1521, who claimed the area in the name of the king of Spain. China, Japan, and other groups tried unsuccessfully to take over the Philippines, but Spain maintained its control for nearly 400 years. Jose Rizal, writer and patriot, helped inspire a revolt against Spain in 1896. War was declared between Spain and the United States in 1898. Spain turned the islands over to the United States in 1899. Internal strife continued until 1901, when American control formally began. The Japanese invaded in 1941, and the Philippines fell under Japanese control until the end of World War II. On July 4, 1946, the Philippines became an independent republic. In 1977, President Ferdinand Marcos declared the Philippines to be under martial law, and he ruled by decree until 1986, when he was removed from power. The 1983 assassination of Benigno S. Aquino, Jr., Marcos's chief political opponent, led to Marcos's downfall in early 1986. In a dramatic and peaceful transition of power, Senator Aquino's widow, Corazon C. Aquino, became the country's first woman president. Since then her government has faced strong opposition from both communist insurgents and Marcos loyalists. In February of 1987, a new constitution was approved, providing for a republican form of government including a presidency, two houses of congress, and a judiciary. The official capital is Quezon City, named after Manuel Quezon, the first president of the Philippines after the country became a U.S. commonwealth in 1935.

Economy: The average gross national product (GNP) per capita in the Philippines is about $790 annually ($14,300 in U.S.). Though the economy is still based on agriculture, lumber, and fishing, the percentage of people employed in industry has climbed to nearly 50% in the past few years. The main agricultural products are sugar, rice, corn, coconut, bananas, abaca, and tobacco.

The Philippines is also a major world producer of minerals, including gold and copper. Recently, offshore oil exploration has discovered some modest petroleum deposits. The standard monetary unit is the *peso*. Inflation is typically higher than in the U.S.

Education: In the Philippines, education is highly valued. Almost 40% of the nation's budget is spent on education. The literacy rate is about 88%, one of the highest in East Asia and the Pacific.

Transportation: As the economy improves, more and more middle-class Filipinos in metropolitan areas buy their own cars. In turn, major highways are improving and a north-south freeway system is developing on the main island of Luzon. In most areas, a majority of the people still use public transportation: bus systems and *jeepneys* (minibuses styled like jeeps). An elevated public mass-transit rail system in metropolitan Manila was completed in 1984. In the provinces, roads and highways are very narrow and are frequently washed away by torrential rains. Ferries and banca boats constitute the most important means of inter-island travel. Airlines, however, are becoming increasingly important, with several flights daily to and from Manila and other major cities. Tourists may also travel the main islands in air-conditioned tourist buses.

Health: The medical services offered in Manila are quite reliable. The water supply in Manila is generally considered safe to drink, but visitors should not drink untreated or unboiled water. Because of the climate, mosquitos are a nuisance. High-potency mosquito repellants are recommended for visitors. For further medical information, contact International Health Consultants, PO Box 34582, Bethesda, MD 20817.

For Further Information

Because space is so limited in this *Culturgram* and needs are so varied, no suggested readings are included. We recommend a visit to your local library or bookstore. Check *Books in Print* and various cataloging systems for country-specific titles. Review *Encyclopedia Britannica* or similar comprehensive summaries. The U.S. government publishes *Country Profiles* which many libraries subscribe to. Computer searches (DIALOG, SDC, BRS, ISI) are now available at most major libraries. Contact the Philipine Embassy, 1617 Massachusetts Ave., N.W., Washington, D.C. 20036, or the Phillippine Ministry of Tourism, 3460 Wilshire Boulevard, Suite 1212, Los Angeles, CA 90010 or 556 Fifth Ave., New York, NY 10036. The U.S. Embassy in the Phillipines is located at 1201 Roxas Blvd., Manila, Phillipines.

How to Use This Culturgram

Quickly read the whole text as an overview. Then circle or give priority numbers to specific questions you have or ideas you want to pursue. Use the *Culturgram* as a guide to check on regional differences and current situations.

Maps

Culturgram maps are meant only as simple geographical orientations. Boundary representations are not necessarily authoritative. Different sources also vary spelling, transliterations, and accents.

Rev. 1/88

CULTURGRAM*

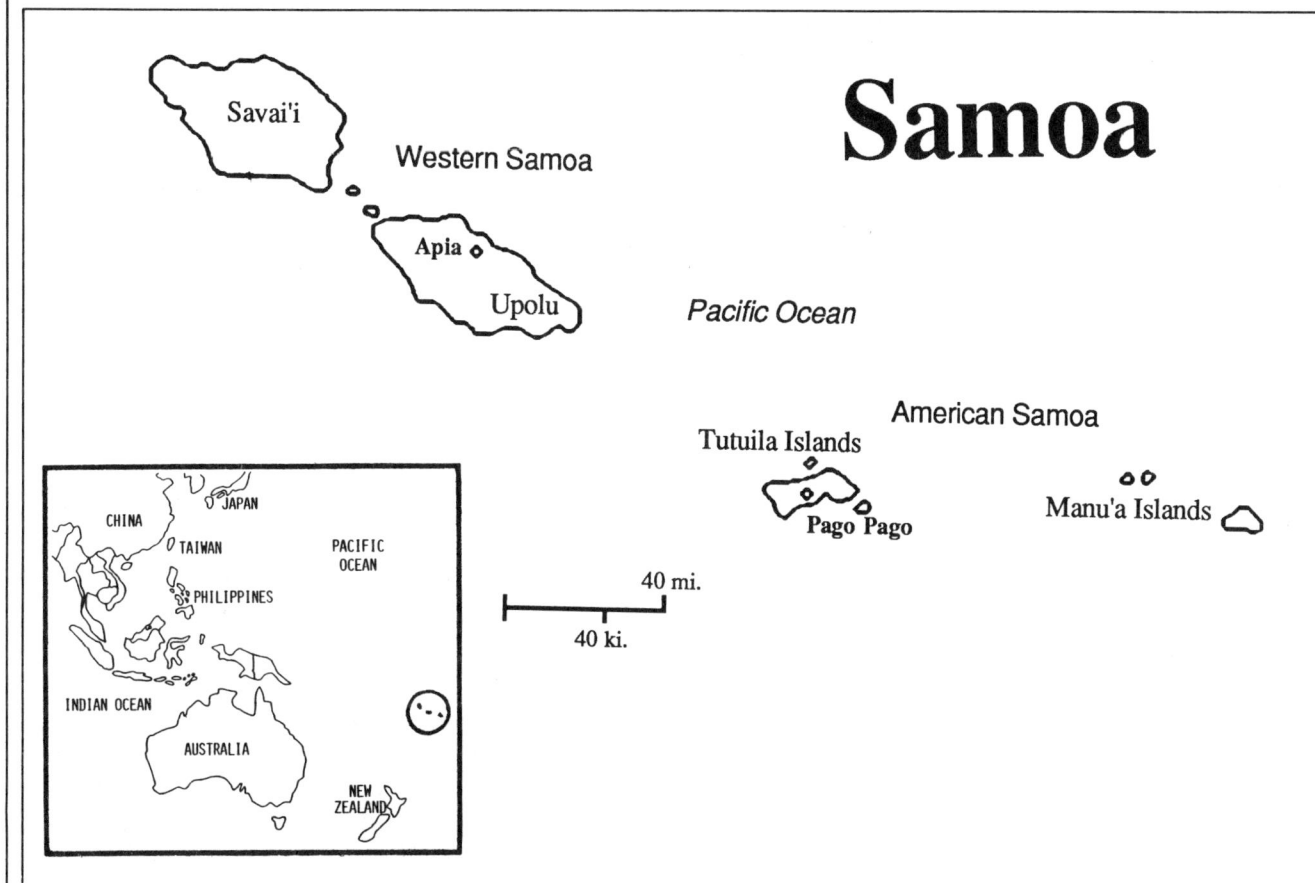

Samoa

Note: Because of the similarities of the two cultures, the Independent State of Western Samoa and American Samoa (a U.S. territory) have been combined in this Culturgram.

CUSTOMS AND COURTESIES

Greetings: Samoans prize eloquent speech. For this reason, a formal greeting such as *susu mai* or *afio mai* (meaning "listen" or "come") should be offered before beginning conversation. Use of these greetings indicates special respect.

Visiting: Visitors are not invited to enter a Samoan home until the host has laid out mats for the visitors to sit on. In more modern homes, chairs are used instead of floor mats. Visitors are then welcomed by the head of the house. It is customary to leave shoes outside and to sit cross-legged on mats. Whenever a guest enters a home, speeches of welcome are delivered. The guest should make an appropriate response to the formal greeting. Guests are expected to sit where the host indicates (generally where the host lays the mat). Guests should not point their legs toward the center of the room. It is also considered impolite to stretch one's legs in the presence of others. If a guest must stretch his or her legs because they are tired from sitting cross-legged, turn sideways and stretch them to the side. One should not prop legs up when sitting. Samoans believe that whatever a person has is at the complete disposal of all others. The attitude of sharing is manifested by the importance of gift giving. After receiving a gift, one should express appreciation for it and sometimes present a gift in return.

*****Culturgrams** are briefings to aid understanding of, feeling for, and communication with other people. Culturgrams are condensations of the best information available. Your insights will be appreciated. If you have refining suggestions, please contact Brigham Young University David M. Kennedy Center for International Studies, Publication Services, 280 HRCB, Provo, Utah 84602 (801) 378-6528. Copyright © 1986. All rights reserved. Printed in the USA.

Eating: Most Samoan foods are eaten with the fingers. However, in most cases, visitors will be provided with utensils. During a meal, a bowl of water will often be provided for washing hands. Guests may request this before the meal if it is not offered. Visitors should feel at ease when eating and take only those foods that appeal to them. If offered food when not hungry, it is polite for the guest to eat a small amount to show appreciation to the host. The host would be disappointed and hurt if the guest refused all offers. It is not appropriate to express distaste for certain foods. Compliments are always appreciated. Water in hotels is clean and drinkable. Other water should be boiled before drinking.

Personal Appearance: Although some men and women wear western-style clothing, most Samoans wear traditional Samoan attire. Men wear a *lava-lava* (wraparound skirt) with a shirt. Samoan custom forbids women to wear pants or slacks, except when participating in athletic events. They usually wear a *puletasi* (long dress). On Sunday, almost all of the people wear white. Samoans also feel that a smile is an important part of their personal appearance.

THE PEOPLE

General Attitudes: Samoans have a strong sense of what is called *fa' a Samoa*, or the Samoan way. This generally means a slow-paced, carefree way of life. They also have a leadership structure called the *matai*, or chief system. The *matai* is the head of the extended family, and is selected by the members. From birth, Samoans learn and experience the nature of this hierarchal order. The *matai* system is the basis of the Samoan political system, family life, economic livelihood, and social life. Samoans have a speech-centered culture. There are many unique ways of communicating a thought, an expectation, a wish, or a command. This is done, at times, in an indirect way, and words such as the polite yes may mean no to a Samoan. However, what visitors say is often taken quite literally. Respect for adults and superiors should be exhibited when possible. Common American gesturing is usually not appropriate. Swaying from side to side indicates contempt or angry behavior. Samoans often will answer the way they think the person listening expects them to. It is usually felt to be far worse to disagree with someone in authority, or to not give the anticipated reply, than it is to not do what has been agreed upon.

Population: The population of Samoa is 197,000, with 163,000 living in Western Samoa and 34,000 living in American Samoa. The population-density rate is 141 people per square mile in Western Samoa and over 400 people per square mile in American Samoa (58 in U.S.). The population is growing at a rate of 0.9% annually (same as U.S.). Most Samoans are of Polynesian descent. Approximately 10% are of mixed Samoan and European parentage. There are also a few hundred Europeans, Chinese, and other Pacific Islanders.

Language: Most of the people speak Samoan, a Polynesian language which is spoken with pride. English is also an official language and is widely used.

Religion: Almost all Samoans are Christians. Approximately one-half of the people are associated with the London Missionary Society, or Congregation Christian Church in Samoa. The remainder belong to various churches: Methodists, Catholics, Church of Jesus Christ of Latter-day Saints (Mormons), Seventh-day Adventists, and others.

LIFESTYLE

The Family: A typical Samoan village is made up of a series of families. A family member is anyone who is related to any one *matai* by birth, marriage, or adoption. All of the matai of a village form the *fono*, or council, and govern the affairs of the village. Each *matai* is responsible for the labor, activities, well-being, feeding, and housing of his family. There is a strong obligation on the part of family members to share their sustenance with the extended family and, to some extent, with the entire village. Land is held in trusteeship in the name of the *matai*. The large, extended families normally have between 20 and 30 members. Young children are taught not to bother adults and are usually under the supervision of the older children. Any adults may freely scold children. If the offense is serious enough, a child may be hit or formally shamed. Discipline within a home is generally strict. Children are taught not to rebel against authority.

Diet: The basic food crops in Samoa are bananas, breadfruit, and *taro*. Pork, chicken, and fish are often a part of Samoan meals, especially during feasts.

Recreation: Samoans love to dance and to play their own version of cricket. Boating events, volleyball, rugby, and basketball are also popular. Music and singing are also popular recreational activities.

THE NATION

Land and Climate: Independent Western Samoa, with Apia as its capital, is comprised of 2 large islands and several smaller islands. Its total land area is just less than the state of Rhode Island. Approximately 65% of the land is covered by forests. American Samoa, a U.S. territory, is much smaller—about the same size as Washington D.C. Pago Pago is the capital. Throughout Samoa the climate is tropical and humid, but southeast trade winds often make temperatures pleasantly mild. Temperatures change little, seldom rising above 85° F. or falling below 75° F. Most rainfall occurs from October to March.

History and Government: What little is known about Samoa's early history comes from oral history. No written records were kept until the 1800s. The first Europeans to sight the islands were the Dutch in 1772. Missionaries from the London Missionary Society began colonizing the islands in 1830, and as a result the Samoans were quickly converted to Christianity. The Samoan Islands were ruled by chieftains until the 1860s, when they came under the control of the British, American, and German consuls. Eastern Samoa was later annexed by the United States, and Western Samoa, by Germany. Following World War I, Western Samoa came under the direction of New Zealand. Western Samoa was finally given independence on January 1, 1962. Today, a special treaty relationship is maintained with New Zealand. It became a member of the British Commonwealth of Nations in 1970 and joined the United Nations in 1976. Western Samoa is now an independent constitutional monarchy with a parliament and a prime minister. Malietoa Tanumafili II has been the largely ceremonial chief of state since 1963. American Samoa is headed by a governor and has been administered by the United States Department of the Interior since 1951. In 1977, the islanders elected their first Samoan-born governor, Peter T. Coleman. The current governor is A. P. Lutali.

Economy: Agriculture and fishing are the mainstays of Western Samoa's economy. Approximately 90% of the people in Western Samoa are employed in agriculture. Copra, cocoa, bananas, taro, and yams are the major products. Industrially, timber, forestry, and tourism are important to the economy. The average annual gross national product (GNP) per capita is about $770 ($14,300 in U.S.). The monetary unit is the *tala*. American Samoa's economy has been strengthened by the United States. Because of recent growth in industry, Samoans are greatly dependent on food exports from Western Samoa and Tonga. Canned tuna is the only major export of American Samoa. Tourism, fishing, and handicrafts also employ many people. In American Samoa, per capita income is considerably higher than Western Samoa. The monetary unit in American Samoa is the U.S. dollar.

Education: In Western Samoa education is essentially free and compulsory between the ages of 7 and 15. Inadequate finances and facilities limit the availability and quality of education. The literacy rate is between 85 and 90%. Education is also free and compulsory in American Samoa. Some students go abroad for university education, mainly to the United States and New Zealand. The literacy rate is also 90%. Educated people are held in high esteem.

Transportation and Communication: Public transportation is now widespread throughout Samoa. Only 1% of the people own an automobile. Inter-island boat transportation is available. The major islands are now connected by air transport. Telephones are common in most of American Samoa, and also in Apia, Western Samoa. In Western Samoa, telegrams are the most reliable form of overseas communication. Local newspapers are available. Television and radio are also popular.

Health: Hospital facilities and medical care are readily available, especially in American Samoa. For further information, contact International Health Consultants, PO Box 34582, Bethesda, MD 20817.

For Further Information

Because space is so limited in this *Culturgram* and needs are so varied, no suggested readings are included. We recommend a visit to your local library or bookstore. Check *Books in Print* and various cataloging systems for country-specific titles. Review *Encyclopedia Britannica* or similar comprehensive summaries. The U.S. government publishes *Country Profiles* which many libraries subscribe to. Computer searches (DIALOG, SDC, BRS, ISI) are now available at most major libraries. Contact Western Samoa Embassy, 820 Second Ave., Room 303, New York, NY 10017, or the Pacific Island Tourism Development Council, PO Box 2359, Honolulu, HI 96813.

How to Use This Culturgram

Quickly read the whole text as an overview. Then circle or give priority numbers to specific questions you have or ideas you want to pursue. Use the *Culturgram* as a guide to check on regional differences and current situations.

Maps

Culturgram maps are meant only as simple geographical orientations. Boundary representations are not necessarily authoritative. Different sources also vary spelling, transliterations, and accents.

Rev. 1/88

CULTURGRAM*

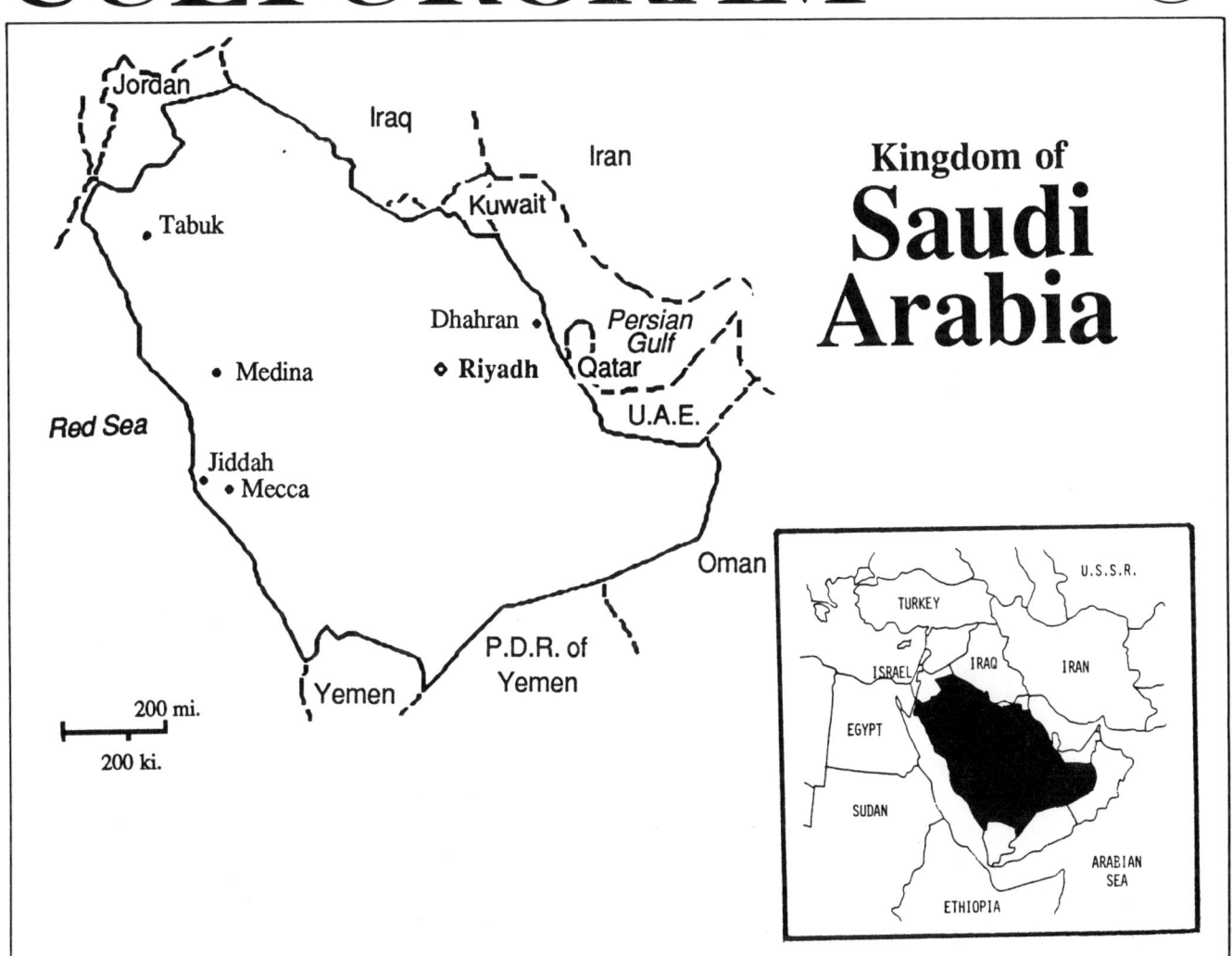

Kingdom of Saudi Arabia

CUSTOMS AND COURTESIES

Greetings: There are several forms of greeting in Saudi Arabia. The most common is a handshake with the right hand and the phrase *Assalaamu alaykum* (Peace be upon you). Frequently males will follow up by extending the left hand to each other's right shoulder and kiss the right and left cheeks. The greeting used depends on the individuals' relationship to each other and their status in Saudi Arabian society. When accompanied by a veiled woman, the man will normally not introduce her, nor should one expect to shake hands with her.

Visiting: Invitations to a Saudi Arabian home are often given to a man alone. If his wife is invited, she may be separated and sent to eat with the other women. It is not appropriate to bring a gift for the woman of the house. Gifts should be given and received with the right hand. Tea or coffee is served at all meetings. It is best to put a hand over the cup or tilt it several times and say *"bes"* (enough) to indicate when one has had enough. Drinking of alcoholic beverages is prohibited and it is best to refrain from smoking unless your host does so. Coffee is served and incense is passed around at the end of a gathering as a signal that it is time to leave. Toward the end of a meeting, Saudi Arabians may lose interest and prefer to redirect the conversation to nonbusiness matters.

---

*Culturgrams are briefings to aid understanding of, feeling for, and communication with other people. Culturgrams are condensations of the best information available. Your insights will be appreciated. If you have refining suggestions, please contact Brigham Young University David M. Kennedy Center for International Studies, Publication Services, 280 HRCB, Provo, Utah 84602 (801) 378-6528. Copyright © 1986. All rights reserved. Printed in the USA.

Eating: Western dining etiquette is observed only in more Westernized circles. Food is typically eaten with the hands. Finger food must be eaten with the right hand only. However, bread may be torn with the left hand. The Saudi Arabians delight in preparing an abundance of food for their guests and it is acceptable to take a second serving. Though hosts often strongly urge their guests to eat more, one may graciously decline. In restaurants, the bill is presented at the table and can be paid to either the waiter or the cashier.

Gestures: It is impolite to point at Saudi Arabians or signal them with the hand. One should also avoid using the left hand for gesturing or handling items in the presence of Saudi Arabians. It is advisable to avoid pointing the soles of your shoes towards Saudi Arabians as it is an insult. Crossing your legs in the company of some Saudi Arabians may be taken as a sign of disrespect.

Personal Appearance: Saudi Arabian men and women still wear traditional Arab dress. The men wear the *ghutra* (head cloth) and *thobe* (white flowing robes). The women wear the veil and *abaya* (black robe that covers from head to foot, often over long dresses tailored from beautiful, imported fabrics.) One should not ask the Saudi Arabians to remove their head coverings. Visitors should dress conservatively, and women should especially avoid wearing shorts, short sleeves, low necklines, and tight-fitting clothing. Otherwise women may be subjected to misconceptions that could lead to embarrassment or harrassment.

THE PEOPLE

General Attitudes: Life in Saudi Arabia is relaxed and slow paced, just the opposite of the rushed American lifestyle. Saudi Arabians like to establish trust and confidence with the people they deal with before proceeding with any business at hand. They are very conscious of personal and family honor and can be easily offended by any perceived insult of that honor. Saudi Arabians are generous and hospitable, and greatly concerned with the welfare of their guests.

Population: The population of Saudi Arabia is currently 11,152,000, and is growing at a high rate of 3.3%. Approximately 75% of the total labor force (3 million) are foreign workers, mainly from Yemen, Egypt, and Palestine. Other nationalities include Indians, Pakistanis, Koreans, and Americans. The Saudis consider this large foreign population to be a serious threat to future stability. The indigenous population is comprised of homogeneous nomadic tribes. The population-density rate is only about 12 people per square mile (58 in U.S.).

Language: Arabic is the official language of the kingdom. It is the language of the Koran (Islamic scripture) and is also considered to be the language of God. English is spoken in some urban markets and is widely spoken in business and educated circles.

Religion: Islam is the only legally and officially recognized religion. Arabia is the birthplace of the revered prophet Mohammad, and Saudi Arabia is the home of Islam's 2 most important shrines: Mecca and Medina. Non-Muslims are not admitted into these sacred cities. The Koran is the basis for daily life, and Islamic law and tradition form the constitution of the Kingdom. Muslims believe that Moses, Abraham, and Jesus are also prophets, but see no need for an atonement and do not accept Jesus as the Son of God. Saudi Arabians are not allowed to join Christian churches. Foreigners are allowed freedom of religion but proselyting is illegal.

LIFESTYLE

The Family: Although the Saudi Arabian family is traditionally a strong, male-dominated unit, women do exercise considerable influence within the home. Most families live as extended families, but more nuclear families are moving to the city and living in single-family homes. Sons generally live in a neighborhood close to their father's home. Separation of male and female is a way of life in Saudi Arabia. Rules governing the actions of women are based on Saudi Arabian law and custom, and are designed to respect and protect a woman's femininity. A woman's behavior reflects on her family's honor and reputation. Women are not allowed to interact with men outside of their family and are forbidden to drive a car or bicycle. Many of these laws also apply to female visitors.

Dating and Marriage: Marriages are often arranged, but a growing minority of young men and women are being allowed to choose their mates. Currently, non-Saudi wives of Saudi Arabian men need a special permit to enter and reside in the country. A traditional Saudi Arabian wedding is an Islamic civil ceremony followed by separate parties for the men and women. Traditionally, men pay dowries for their brides, with the money being used to help the new couple establish their first home. Although Islamic law allows a man to have up to 4 wives, most Saudi Arabian men have only 1 wife.

Social and Economic Levels: Since the 1930s, a major goal of the Saudi regime has been to centralize governmental power. To this end, the formerly nomadic tribes have been encouraged to settle in the cities and reorient themselves to a centralized society and economy. The government subsidizes housing projects with oil revenues, and provides land and the equivalent of a $90,000 no-interest loan to any Saudi Arabian desiring to build. Apartments in Western-style apartment buildings are expensive and in short supply.

Business Hours: The work week runs from Saturday to Wednesday, with Thursday and Friday being the weekend. Friday is the Muslim day of rest and worship. Government offices are open from 9 a.m. to 2 p.m., while non-government shops are open from 8 a.m. to noon, and again from 4 p.m. to 8:30 p.m. During Ramadan, working hours are adjusted and many offices are closed by noon.

Diet: Saudi dishes are composed mainly of rice with lamb or chicken, and are mildly spicy. Saudi Arabians serve coffee or tea before all their meals. Buttermilk and camel's milk are also popular beverages. The Koran forbids the consumption of pork and alcoholic beverages.

Recreation: Soccer is the national sport, but only men are permitted to play or watch at the stadium. Saudi Arabian men also enjoy horse and camel races, hunting and hawking. Women enjoy visiting with other women, collecting jewelry, and caring for their own and extended family members' children.

Holidays: The Islamic calendar is based on the lunar month of 29 1/2 days, making the year 10 to 11 days shorter than the Western year. For this reason, holidays vary from year to year, with the exception of one holiday, National Day, which is celebrated on September 23. The calendar begins at the year of the Hegira (flight of Mohammad from Mecca to Medina) in the seventh century A.D. During the month of Ramadan, all Muslims abstain from food, drink, and smoking during the daylight hours. Visitors are required by law to observe the fast of Ramadan while in public.

THE NATION

Land and Climate: Saudi Arabia is the twelfth largest country in the world. It is one-fourth the size of the U.S. and comprises 1.4% of the world land total. Saudi Arabia is a vast arid plain of sand and rock, with rugged mountains in the west. Rainfall is slight, and only 1% of the land can be cultivated. Another 1% of the land is forest, and the remaining 98% is desert. Most cities are built on the coast or in the oases that dot the face of the desert.

History and Government: Arabia has a rich and colorful history. Starting in the 7th century A.D., the Prophet Mohammad proclaimed the message of Islam from the centers of Mecca and Medina. Islam soon spread as far as North Africa and central Asia. The history of present-day Saudi Arabia begins in 1902, when Abdulaziz ibn Saud recaptured his ancestoral home in Riyadh. After 30 years of fighting, Abdulaziz united the major rival factions and declared himself king of Saudi Arabia. After World War II, the vast oil reserves of the kingdom were opened, and Abdulaziz began to use the oil revenue to speed the process of modernization. This process has been carried onward by the succeeding Kings Saud, Faisal, and Khalid. Saudi Arabia is an absolute monarchy and is governed by the Saudi family, descendants of Abdulaziz. The leaders of the family appoint the king. Islamic laws and practices form the basis for modern Saudi law.

Economy: Saudi Arabia has one of the strongest economies in the world. The gross national product (GNP) per capita is nearly $10,335 ($14,300 in U.S.). Although only 3% of the population is involved in oil related industries, oil is the most important part of the economy. Saudi Arabia has the world's largest petroleum reserves (one-fourth of the world total) and the fifth largest natural gas reserves. It is the second largest petroleum producer and the third largest energy producer in the world. Oil accounts for 99% of the country's exports, giving the country the world's most favorable balance of trade. ARAMCO (Arab American Oil Co.) is the major energy-producing organization, and came completely under Saudi Arabian control in 1980. Revenue from the oil is rapidly being invested in modernization and in expanding the industrial base. Because of the inhospitable climate and terrain, the nation must import the majority of its food, but dates, grains, and livestock are produced. The unit of currency is the *riyal*, which is considered to be an internationally solid currency. The annual inflation rate is typically over 25%.

Education: The government finances education through the university level. Saudi Arabia spends a larger percentage of its GNP on education than any other country in the world. Although enrollment in the past has been low, the trend is reversing. Men and women attend separate schools, but more women are getting university degrees and entering the work force. Generous support is provided for vocational training in order to decrease the amount of skilled workers that must be imported from abroad. The literacy rate is estimated at 50%.

Transportation and Communications: The Kingdom is continually expanding its system of roads and telephones. The most convenient mode of transportation between cities, however, is the airplane. Daily flights link up to 20 cities in the kingdom. Travel in the city is best done by taxi or bus. The telephone system, when completed, will be one of the most modern in the world. International telephone, telegraph, and telex services are currently available.

Health: Although standards of health are not yet up to par with the West, the country is progressing rapidly. Medical facilities are improving, and many doctors have been trained in the U.S. Drinking water may need to be boiled or filtered in some places, and fruits and vegetables should be washed and peeled. For further medical information, contact International Health Consultants, PO Box 34582, Bethesda, MD 20817.

For Further Information

Because space is so limited in this *Culturgram* and needs are so varied, no suggested readings are included. We recommend a visit to your local library or bookstore. Check *Books in Print* and various cataloging systems for country-specific titles. Review *Encyclopedia Britannica* or similar comprehensive summaries. The U.S. government publishes *Country Profiles* which many libraries subscribe to. Computer searches (DIALOG, SDC, BRS, ISI) are now available at most major libraries. Contact the Embassy of Saudi Arabia, 610 New Hampshire Ave. NW, Washington, D.C. 20048, or the Saudi Arabia Tourist Information, 866 UN Plaza, New York, NY 10017.

How to Use This Culturgram

Quickly read the whole text as an overview. Then circle or give priority numbers to specific questions you have or ideas you want to pursue. Use the *Culturgram* as a guide to check on regional differences and current situations.

Maps

Culturgram maps are meant only as simple geographical orientations. Boundary representations are not necessarily authoritative. Different sources also vary spelling, transliterations, and accents.

Rev. 1/88

CULTURGRAM*

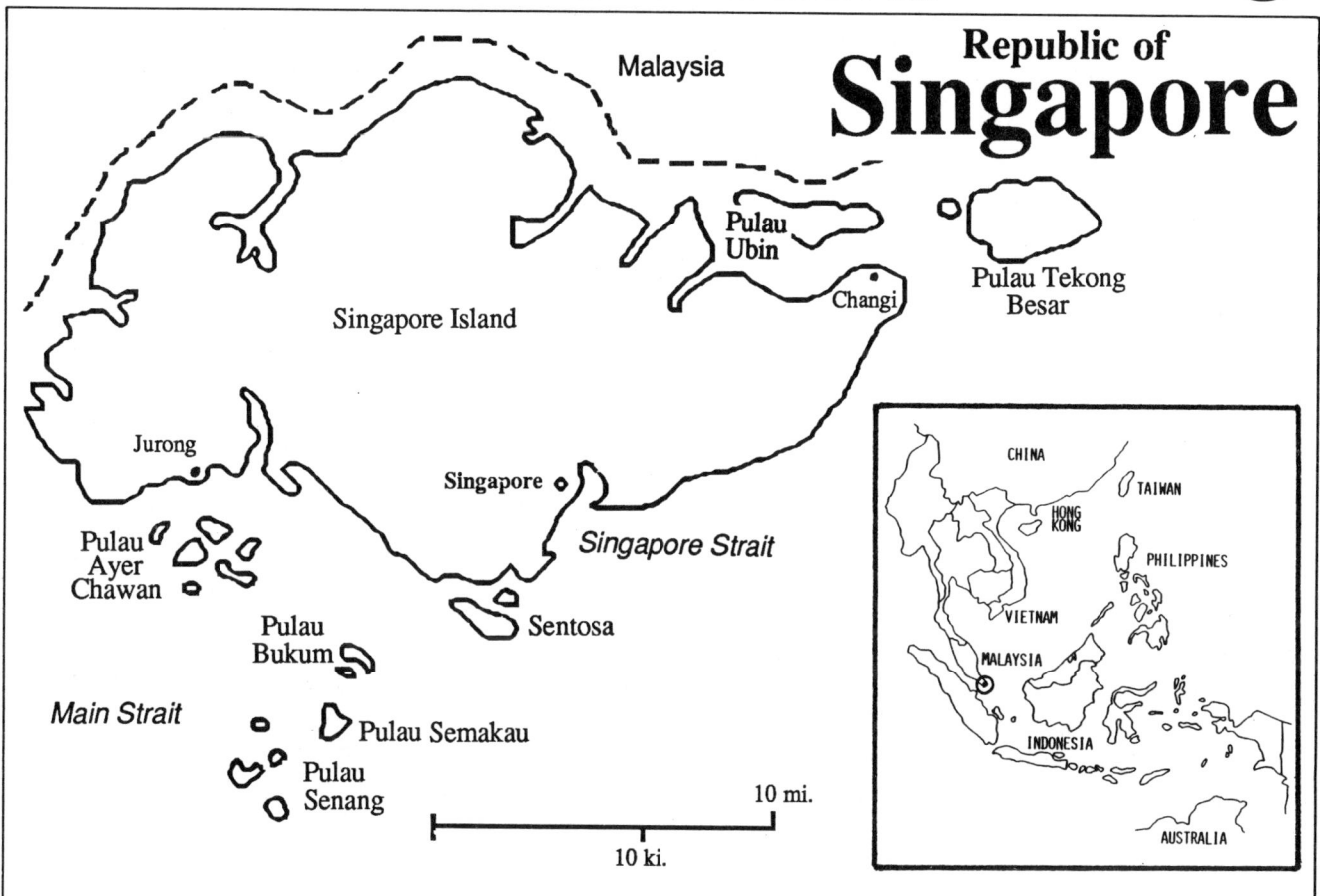

Republic of Singapore

CUSTOMS AND COURTESIES

Greetings: Singapore has been called "Instant Asia" because of the great diversity of cultures and peoples living together there. Such cultural diversity offers the visitor, in the compass of a small 14 by 26 mile island, experience with 3 of the major cultures of Asia—Chinese, Malay, and Indian. Although specific customs and courtesies usually depend on the nationality and age group one is associating with, there are some guidelines that generally apply. As a result of British influence, Singapore is quite modern. However, the customs of ethnic groups are also followed, so greetings often vary. The handshake is the most common gesture of greeting, with the addition of a slight bow to Chinese and older people. Great respect is paid to the elderly and visitors should also show respect to them. For example, on buses it is polite to give one's seat to an elderly person, male or female, before a younger woman.

Visiting: Westerners are expected to be punctual. Shoes are removed before entering most religious buildings (temples and mosques) and sometimes before entering a home. Compliments are appreciated, but usually denied for modesty's sake. Gifts are not opened at the time they are received. One should never make jokes about food that is being served.

*****Culturgrams** are briefings to aid understanding of, feeling for, and communication with other people. Culturgrams are condensations of the best information available. Your insights will be appreciated. If you have refining suggestions, please contact Brigham Young University David M. Kennedy Center for International Studies, Publication Services, 280 HRCB, Provo, Utah 84602 (801) 378-6528. Copyright © 1986. All rights reserved. Printed in the USA.

Gestures: Touching another's head is impolite. When crossing the legs, one knee should be directly over the other knee; the foot or sole should not be pointed at anyone. Also, feet should not be used to move objects. Hitting the fist into the cupped hand is inappropriate. Beckoning is done with the palm down instead of up. Finger gestures (OK sign, pointing etc.) are considered rude. Never beckon using only one finger. A slight bow when entering, leaving, or passing a group of people shows courtesy.

THE PEOPLE

General Attitudes: The multi-racial makeup of the country has in the past led to some racial conflict. However, the government has been remarkably successful in promoting racial harmony and national unity. Most Singaporean youth identify themselves as Singaporeans first and as Chinese, Malay, or Indian second. The work ethic has been strongly advocated and Singaporeans have a reputation as an industrious people. There is a strong anti-communist sentiment throughout the country.

Population: Singapore's population is about 2.5 million. The population-growth rate is 1.2% (0.9% in U.S.) and is gradually decreasing. The population density is 10,000 people per square mile (58 in U.S.), making it the fourth most densely populated country in the world. One hundred percent of the people live in urban areas (73% in U.S.). Approximately 76% of the people are of Chinese descent, 15% of Malay descent, 7% of Indian descent, and the remaining 2% comprise other ethnic groups. Presently, half the population is under 25 years of age.

Language: The multiplicity of languages reflects the racial diversity of Singapore. English, Mandarin (Chinese), Malay, and Tamil are the 4 official languages of the country. Malay is the national language, as designated in the Constitution. However, all Singaporeans are expected to learn English. English is the most widely used language in science, technology, commerce, and tourism. Mandarin has been established as a required second language for most citizens. The language situation is complicated by the fact that many Chinese do not speak Mandarin as their native tongue; they speak Hokkien, Teochew, Cantonese, or one of a half-dozen other Chinese dialects. In this environment, most Singaporeans become at least bilingual; many speak 3 to 5 languages. The government has adopted a policy of encouraging the use of Mandarin, Malay, or Tamil to sustain traditional cultures and values while learning English for utilitarian purposes. English is also the language of the administration in the government.

Religion: Singaporeans enjoy freedom of worship. (However, some religious groups have been interpreted as being anti-government and are not allowed to organize.) Approximately 40% of the people are Buddhist (mostly Chinese), 30% secular (a growing percentage), 15% Moslem (mostly Malays), 10% Christian (Europeans, Eurasians, and a few Chinese and Indians), and 7% Hindu (Indians). Buddhist and Hindu temples, Moslem mosques, and Christian churches are found throughout the country, along with 2 Jewish synagogues. The government is strictly secular, favoring no religion over another.

LIFESTYLE

The Family: Traditionally, the Chinese, Malay, and Indian peoples have encouraged large families; however, with the limited space and resources of a very small country, the government of Singapore has established a vigorous family planning program. Using the slogan "Two children are enough," the government has built a family planning program that has been a model for many developing countries throughout the world. Still, the average family size in Singapore is about 5 people (3.1 in U.S.). The family system is strong and cooperation, loyalty, respect for elders, and unity are highly valued in families of all races.

Dating and Marriage: Dating begins at age 17 or 18. Parents (especially Chinese) often discourage dating, feeling that youth should concentrate on their studies. A few Hindu, Malay, and Chinese families still believe in arranging their children's marriages, but this is no longer common practice. The individuals involved make their own choices but usually consult their families. It is against the law for couples to live together without being married.

Social and Economic Levels: The average personal income is one of the highest in Southeast Asia. Houses, however, are generally small and crowded—2 rooms per house and nearly 3 people per room. Approximately 60% of the people live in Housing Development Board high-rise buildings. Because of the limited space, homes are very expensive. Generally, foreigners are not permitted to buy land or a house in Singapore. Approximately 30% of the people have telephones and nearly 7% own an automobile. Only 6% of the population live in absolute poverty—the third lowest rate in the world.

Diet: Rice is the dietary staple, with fish as the main source of protein. Some highly spiced foods are also enjoyed. Nearly all the island's food supply must be imported. Restaurants that serve American and European cuisine are widely available.

Business Hours: Shops are open from 8:30 a.m. to 4:30 p.m. Monday through Friday and from 8:30 a.m. to 12:30 p.m. on Saturdays. If a business remains open on Sunday, it is required by law to close on another day.

Recreation: Singaporeans enjoy many of the same sports enjoyed in the United States. The most popular sports are soccer, badminton, basketball, baseball, tennis, and golf. Naturally, water sports are also favorites.

Holidays: National holidays include New Year's Day (January 1), Hari Raya Haji (January, February, or March), and Chinese New Year (2 days in either January or February). Government offices close only for Chinese New Year, but many shops remain closed for a full week. Other holidays are Good Friday (March or April), Labor Day (May 1), Vesak Day (May), National Day (August 9), Deepavali, or the Hindu ceremony of lights (October or November), Hari Raya Puasa and Christmas (December 25). There are a number of other religious festivals that are not classified as public holidays but particular groups celebrate them privately. The dates of most holidays vary depending on the lunar or Chinese calendars.

THE NATION

Land and Climate: Singapore is about the size of the city of Chicago (224 square miles). It is only one-sixth the size of Rhode Island, the smallest state in the United States. Except for the central plateau, most of the island is low-lying and originally consisted of swamps and jungles. Eighty-five percent of the jungle is cleared, and there is very little wildlife. Land-fill operations are enlarging the island by several feet per week. The capital city, Singapore, occupies land that was reclaimed from the sea through land-fill operations. Singapore's climate is unchanging. Temperatures are between 78 and 82° F. year-round and humidity is very high. Night breezes are common and typhoons are also frequent during the rainy season (June to September).

History and Government: Singapore, strategically located on the western edge of the Pacific Ocean, was a thriving port (Temasek) in the great 14th century Buddhist empire that ruled the area. Singapore was notorious as a hideout for pirates until it came under British rule in 1824. The now-thriving trade city was created out of a mangrove swamp largely by the far-seeing leadership of Sir Stamford Raffles who first landed there in 1819. Singapore joined the Federation of Malaysia in 1963 but became an independent republic on August 9, 1965. Singapore's prime minister, Lee Kuan Yew, is very popular among the people. His approach is practical, emphasizing economy and progressive programs rather than ideology. The government is stable and popular. All parliamentary seats are held by elected representatives of the People's Action Party. As a measure against local and foreign Communist influences, the press is government-licensed.

Economy: Although Singapore is the smallest nation in Southeast Asia, its economy is one of the most prosperous. The people have the highest standard of living in East Asia after Japan. Gross national product (GNP) per capita is $6,395 annually ($14,300 in U.S.) and is growing at a yearly rate of 10.2%. Since 1970, Singapore has averaged nearly 10% growth every year (currently 7.9%). Commerce is the foundation of the economy. Singapore is the fourth largest port in the world and has the fourth largest trade volume per capita. Much of the country's trade consists of receiving exports from other countries and then re-exporting them. Petroleum refining is the largest industry in Singapore, and the city has become the hub of petroleum exploration efforts in Southeast Asia. In recent years the city has also become a financial and banking center for the region. Though the island is small, tourism also ranks high, supporting the economy with an influx of foreign currency. Other industries include rubber production, electronics, and oil drilling equipment production. Only 3% of the gross national product comes from fishing and agriculture. Unemployment and inflation are typically lower than in the United States. The currency, the Singapore dollar, is the tenth strongest in the world.

Education: Education is highly valued. Free education is available for Singaporean children from the age of 6 to 14. The literacy rate has recently risen to 84%. In over 80% of the primary schools, English is the language of instruction. Bilingualism is often emphasized. Many students also go on to pursue degrees in universities abroad. Most higher-education degrees from abroad are valued in Singapore.

Transportation and Communication: Singapore is served by international airlines and is linked to Thailand and Malaysia by road and rail. Singapore has the third most roads per square mile in the world. Both cars and gasoline are very expensive in Singapore, about twice the cost in the United States. Telecommunications and telephone service are modern and comprehensive. Radio and television systems are operated by the government. Newspapers are privately owned and are published in English, Chinese, Indian and Malay.

Health: Medical facilities and services are excellent. A high standard of health is attributed to the development of good housing, modern sanitation and a general concern for sound hygienic practices among the people and on the part of the government. Life expectancy among Singaporeans is about 71 years (74 in U.S.). The government promotes extensive tree planting and the streets are kept clean, partly because there is a $500 fine for littering. Singapore is often referred to as the cleanest city in Asia. For further medical information contact International Health Consultants, PO Box 34582, Bethesda, MD 20817.

For Further Information

Because space is so limited in this *Culturgram* and needs are so varied, no suggested readings are included. We recommend a visit to your local library or bookstore. Check *Books in Print* and various cataloging systems for country-specific titles. Review *Encyclopedia Britannica* or similar comprehensive summaries. The U.S. government publishes *Country Profiles* which many libraries subscribe to. Computer searches (DIALOG, SDC, BRS, ISI) are now available at most major libraries. Contact the Embassy of Singapore, 1824 R Street, NW, Washington, D.C. 20009, or the Singapore Tourist Promotion Board, 251 Post St., San Francisco, CA 94108.

How to Use This Culturgram

Quickly read the whole text as an overview. Then circle or give priority numbers to specific questions you have or ideas you want to pursue. Use the *Culturgram* as a guide to check on regional differences and current situations.

Maps

Culturgram maps are meant only as simple geographical orientations. Boundary representations are not necessarily authoritative. Different sources also vary spelling, transliterations, and accents.

Rev. 1/88

CULTURGRAM*

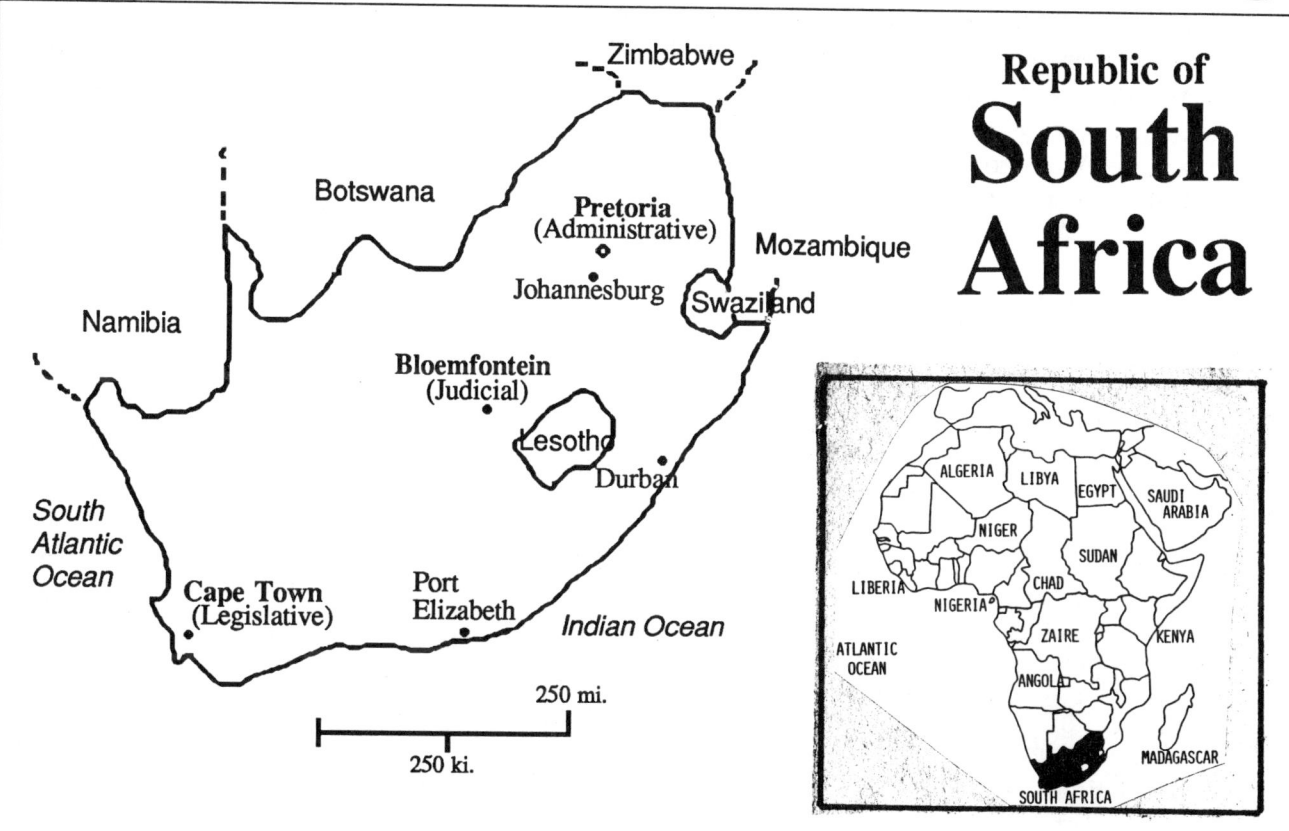

Republic of South Africa

CUSTOMS AND COURTESIES

Greetings: Because of ethnic diversity, many different greetings are used in South Africa. Visitors will hear the usual English greetings, "hello" or "good morning." Afrikaners and most Coloured people will say *goeie more*. The Zulu greet each other with *sakubona*, the Xhosa with *molo*, and the Sotho or Tswana with *Dumela*. Acquaintances commonly wave from a distance. First names are used only among close friends. Loud talking is not considered appropriate.

Visiting: Most South Africans (all ethnic groups) are very hospitable to guests. They enjoy discussing topics similar to those discussed by Americans. Politics is a favorite topic of conversation, but blacks must use discretion because of restrictions placed on them. Black Americans, Japanese, and Chinese are accorded "honorary white" status for the duration of their stay — entitling them to the standard privileges and facilities reserved for whites. Foreign visitors must obtain permits to visit large black townships which are found outside of major cities. South Africans are sensitive about negative criticism but welcome objective comments.

Eating: The continental style of eating with the knife in the right hand and the fork in the left is generally observed. In rural areas people eat with spoons or with the fingers. In restaurants, water is not generally served unless requested. Eating on the street, in most cases, is not acceptable.

Personal Appearance: South Africans are generally more formal in dress than are people in the United States. A shirt and tie are common attire for men. Men may also wear shorts with knee socks rather than trousers. Women generally wear comfortable dresses or other modest attire.

---

*Culturgrams are briefings to aid understanding of, feeling for, and communication with other people. Culturgrams are condensations of the best information available. Your insights will be appreciated. If you have refining suggestions, please contact Brigham Young University David M. Kennedy Center for International Studies, Publication Services, 280 HRCB, Provo, Utah 84602 (801) 378-6528. Copyright © 1986. All rights reserved. Printed in the USA.

Gestures: When yawning, one should cover the mouth. The "victory" sign, two fingers up with palm towards one's self, is not appropriate. One should also avoid making a fist with the thumb between the index and middle fingers. Spitting in public is inappropriate. Gesturing to someone, especially blacks, with the left hand should be avoided.

Traveling: When traveling by bus, one must have the correct change for the ticket when boarding. Taxis are expensive but can be located at designated pickup spots or summoned by telephone. Trains are a common form of transportation in larger cities and suburbs. Tickets are purchased at the station. Trains usually run behind schedule.

THE PEOPLE

General Attitudes: South Africans consider themselves open-minded, sturdy, and independent. Hospitality is an old tradition. Generally, South Africans are easy going. The moral standards in South Africa are generally high and it is desirable to be young and athletic. South Africans are strongly nationalistic and may resent outright criticism, particularly of their racial policy. Some animosities still exist from the Boer War between the Afrikaners and the English. Some people also still feel that the whites are superior to the black Africans, the Coloureds (people of mixed origin), and the Indians, as represented by the country's *apartheid* (racial separation) policies and practices.

Population: The population of South Africa is about 32 million people. It is growing at a rate of 2.4% annually (0.9% in U.S.). The black-African growth rate is somewhat higher than the rate for whites. About one-half of the population live in the cities. The population-density rate is 55 people per square mile (58 in U.S.). South Africa is one of the least ethnically homogeneous countries in the world. The people can be divided into 4 main groups. Black South Africans constitute about 72% of the population. Blacks can be further classified into 9 different ethnic groups, each with a distinct culture, language, historical background, and national identity. The Zulu, Xhosa, and Sotho are the largest groups. The next largest is the white South Africans, who constitute 16% of the population. They are divided between the English-speaking descendants of English, Irish, and Scottish settlers and the Afrikaans-speaking descendants of Dutch, German, and French colonials. They maintain control of the government and the army. The "Coloureds," mixed descendants of whites, Hottentots (Africans), and slaves imported from the Dutch East Indies during South Africa's colonial period, make up another distinct group (9% of the population). Indians are the fourth group, comprising about 3% of the total population. Throughout most of South Africa, the 4 groups are segregated by law in employment, housing, and education. White minority rule has been relinquished in the countries of Venda, Ciskei, Transkei, and Bophuthatswana. However, these new nations are not recognized by any country other than South Africa.

Language: Languages spoken in South Africa are as diverse as the ethnic groups. Among the blacks, there are four main language groups, 23 sub-groups, and numerous dialects. White South Africans speak either Afrikaans (a derivative of Dutch), English, or both. Afrikaans and English are the official languages of the country. Afrikaans is spoken by two-thirds of the white population and by nearly all of the Coloureds. Indians speak their native East Indian tongues. Most of the population of South Africa are bilingual. English is spoken by all in the large cities. Current government policies require black children to be taught primarily in their native language.

Religion: Approximately 60% of the blacks and most of the whites and Coloureds are Christians. The white, Afrikaans-speaking population belong predominantly to the Dutch Reformed Church. For these people, religion plays an important role in everyday life. Other principal Christian faiths are Anglican, Methodist, and Presbyterian. Although they may be Christian, many blacks also continue to observe tribal customs. Several African "charismatic" churches, combining Christian and traditional African rituals, have many adherents. Most of the Indians are Hindus.

LIFESTYLE

The Family: White family life is similar to that of American and European families. The family usually lives as a nuclear unit. Black families, however, have been weakened by the policy of apartheid. Black men and women must often work away from home, men in the mines and women as servants. Black parents hope the best for their children, but education and economic opportunities are limited and far inferior to those of whites. "Resettlement" programs for blacks have also restricted normal family life. Elderly persons or persons of some social stature are sometimes referred to as "uncle" and "aunt" as a token of respect. Children are usually reserved; discipline is strict.

Social and Economic Levels: The standard of living among the whites is among the highest in the world. They enjoy good housing and often own cars. They constitute only 30% of the work force, but earn 64% of the national income. Blacks and other non-white South Africans do not enjoy the same standard of living. Many live far below the poverty level and do not have running water and electricity. Despite the high growth rate of non-white income, the gap between whites and non-whites remains significant and is actually increasing in some areas.

Diet: For whites, meals are similar to those of Americans. Breakfast usually consists of fruit juice, eggs, and hot cereal with milk. During the winter, porridge is common. The midday meal is light, generally a fruit or vegetable salad with sandwiches or soup. Dinner, usually eaten at 6 or 7 p.m., is the main meal. It consists of meat with potatoes or rice. Green vegetables and pumpkins are also popular. Wine, tea, and coffee are common beverages. The diet of rural Africans is almost exclusively made up of *mealie* meal (corn meal porridge, sometimes cooked with vegetables and meat). Most urban Africans can afford only tea and bread for breakfast.

Recreation: The climate invites outdoor sports participation. Soccer, rugby, and beach activities are enjoyed. Those who can afford equipment or club memberships also enjoy cricket, squash, lawn bowling, horse and car racing, golf, field hockey, and tennis. South Africans are ostracized from international competitions because of their racial policies. Legislation pertaining to the segregation of hotels, restaurants, clubs, and similar facilities has been abolished. The discretion of owners has resulted in increasing numbers of these gathering places becoming completely multi-racial. Traditional dances performed by Johannesburg miners attract large audiences.

Holidays: Holidays celebrated nationally are New Year's Day, Good Friday, Easter Monday, Ascension Day, Republic Day (May 31), Settlers' Day (first Monday in September), Kruger Day (October 10), Day of the Covenant (December 16), Christmas Day, and Day of Goodwill, or Boxing Day (December 26).

THE NATION

Land and Climate: South Africa is larger than the states of Texas, New Mexico, and Oklahoma combined. It is a large interior plateau rimmed by a narrow coastal belt. Altitudes reach 5000 feet. Its main rivers are the Orange-Vaal and the Limpopo. The climate is subtropical. Winter rains prevail from May to September, but much of the country is semi-arid. Water conservation is very important. Generally, there is little humidity except in the Natal Province along the coast, which is very humid in the summer, yet comfortable in the winter. The government reserves 85% of the land for whites. The remaining 15% is designated as African "homelands." All black Africans officially belong to one of the homelands regardless of where they live.

History and Government: Hottentots, Bushmen, and other Africans lived in southern Africa for thousands of years, although little is known of their history. In 1652, the Dutch East India Company established a provisions station at Cape Town, led by Jan Van Riebeeck. French Huguenot refugees and Germans joined the Dutch colony in 1688. These people became known as Boers. Britain gained formal possession of the Cape Colony in 1814 through the Napoleonic wars. Dissatisfaction with British rule led many Boers to migrate to the interior in the Great Trek of 1835–48. Their migration led to war with the Zulus and other black African tribes. The Boers defeated the Zulus in 1838. After the discovery of gold and diamonds in the Boer territories in the late 19th century, Britain annexed parts of the area. Tension between the Boers and the British erupted into the Boer War (1899–1902), in which the Boers were defeated. Britain combined the 2 British colonies, Cape and Natal, with the Boer republics of the Orange Free-state and Transvaal to create the Union of South Africa in 1910. In 1961 the country gained independence from Britain and became a republic. That same year, the it withdrew from the British Commonwealth because of criticism of its racial policies. Since the 1960s, South Africa has been the scene of much political turmoil over its apartheid policies. In 1974, the United Nations suspended South Africa's voting privileges because of civil rights violations. The UN Security Council ordered a worldwide embargo of military supplies to South Africa in 1977 — the first such action ever taken by the UN against a member nation. The South African government granted sovereignty to four black homelands: Transkei in 1976, Bophuthatswana in 1977, Venda in 1979, and Ciskei in 1981. The president of the republic is elected by an electoral college consisting of the members of the House of Assembly. Only white South Africans can vote in national elections. Coloureds and Indians are represented in the Parliament and the Cabinet. Blacks participate in elections for homeland and municipal governments but are not represented nationally. Objection to the policy of apartheid is increasing, both internationally and domestically. Many Blacks have died in recent years due to racial violence, tribal conflict, and political rivalry.

Economy: South Africa is the richest nation in Africa. Average annual gross national product (GNP) per capita is approximately $2,500 ($14,300 in U.S.). The economy is currently declining at a yearly rate of 3%. Over 30% of the people are employed in agriculture. Main crops include corn, wool, wheat, sugarcane, tobacco, citrus fruits, and dairy products. South Africa is self-sufficient in foodstuffs. Industry is very important to the South African economy. Many valuable minerals are found in the vast areas of the country. South Africa is the largest gold producer in the world, producing nearly three-quarters of the world total. It ranks second in uranium, and third in diamonds. Coal is also in plentiful supply. Important industries include automobile assembly, metalworking, machinery, textiles, iron and steel, chemicals, and fertilizers. The unit of currency is the *rand*, a controlled floating currency.

Education: Public education is segregated according to race. Schooling is compulsory for all white children between the ages of 7 and 16. Where accommodations permit, attendance is compulsory for Coloureds and Indians between the ages of 7 and 14. School attendance is compulsory for only the first four years for blacks. The government has, however, greatly increased the budgetary allocation for black education in the last 10 years and set compulsory education on a level equal to the whites as a goal. Over 21% of the blacks are attending school in South Africa, compared with an average of only 10% in other African nations. There are 14 universities in South Africa: 10 for whites, 1 for Indians, 1 for Coloureds, and 7 for blacks. The University of South Africa is the world's largest correspondence university. Literacy rates are estimated as follows: whites 99%, Coloureds 60%, blacks 50%, and Indians 85%.

Transportation and Communications: Railroads carry freight and passengers. South African Airways serves all major cities of the Republic and some overseas destinations. The air services are the best on the continent. The press is highly advanced. Television is available throughout most of the country, one station broadcasting in Nquini and Sotho, and another alternating between English and Afrikaans in early and late evenings. There are 20 radio stations broadcasting in 24 languages, reaching 98% of the population. Most radio and television services are provided by the government-regulated South African Broadcasting Corporation, with limited competition from several radio stations.

Health: All medical services are socialized. Medical facilities are excellent for whites, but inadequate for blacks. The ratio of doctors for whites is 1 to 400. For rural Africans it is 1 to 40,000. Malnutrition and communicable diseases are still found in South Africa, and the infant-mortality rate among rural blacks is one of the highest in the world. For further medical information contact International Health Consultants, PO Box 34582, Bethesda, MD 20817.

For Further Information

Because space is so limited in this *Culturgram* and needs are so varied, no suggested readings are included. We recommend a visit to your local library or bookstore. Check Books in Print and various cataloging systems for country-specific titles. Review *Encyclopedia Britannica* or similar comprehensive summaries. The U.S. government publishes *Country Profiles* which many libraries subscribe to. Computer searches (DIALOG, SDC, BRS, ISI) are now available at most major libraries. Contact the South African Embassy, 3051 Massachusetts Ave., Washington, D.C. 20008., or the South African Tourist Board, 747 Third Ave., 20th Floor, New York, NY 10017.

Rev.1/88

CULTURGRAM*

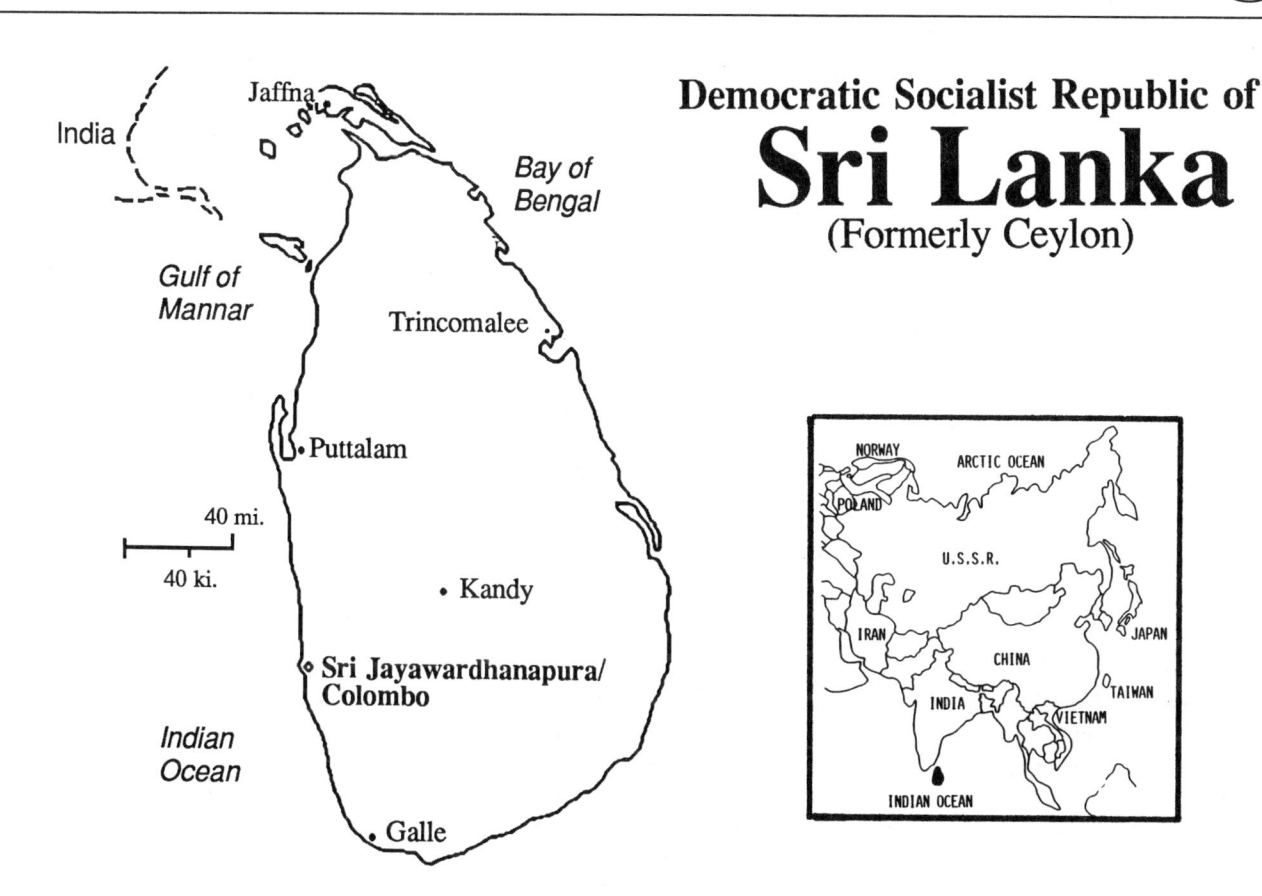

Democratic Socialist Republic of
Sri Lanka
(Formerly Ceylon)

CUSTOMS AND COURTESIES

Greetings: Forms of greeting vary from ethnic group to ethnic group, and from caste to caste. The traditional greeting of placing one's palms together under the chin and bowing slightly is widely practiced in Sri Lanka. In Sinhala, the language of the majority, the common verbal greeting is *Ayubowan*, pronounced (ah-you-BOH-one). Because Sri Lanka has had a long exposure to Britain, the western handshake and common Anglo-Saxon greetings are also acceptable. Titles are very important to Sri Lankans, and it is proper to address acquaintances by their titles.

Eating: The different religions of the country play a large role in determining what should and should not be eaten. Sri Lankans of all religious groups seek to avoid those things that would cause spiritual pollution. Because food enters into the body, it is considered a prime source of potential pollution. Sri Lankans are careful about the types of food they eat. Those that adhere strictly to Buddhist doctrines do not eat flesh of any kind. Some Buddhists, however, include fish or eggs in their diet. Hindus do not eat beef or pork, and Muslims do not eat pork. Visitors to Sri Lanka should be aware of these religious constraints on food.

THE PEOPLE

General Attitudes: Sri Lankans are an exceptionally bright people with relatively open attitudes. There are, however, shades of differences between various ethnic, religious, and social groups. Although caste played a significant role in the relations between all of the peoples in the past, today Sri Lankans will generally associate freely with members of other castes. Although some manual skills and crafts are associated with certain castes, division of labor by caste is fast becoming a

---

*Culturgrams are briefings to aid understanding of, feeling for, and communication with other people. Culturgrams are condensations of the best information available. Your insights will be appreciated. If you have refining suggestions, please contact Brigham Young University David M. Kennedy Center for International Studies, Publication Services, 280 HRCB, Provo, Utah 84602 (801) 378-6528. Copyright © 1986. All rights reserved. Printed in the USA.

thing of the past. Because of the desirability of advanced technology, education in western technology and science is sought by many.

Population: The population of Sri Lanka is approximately 15.6 million, and is growing at a rate of 1.8% annually (0.9% in U.S.). The population density is about 550 people per square mile (58 in U.S.), but nearly 1400 per square mile on arable land. Approximately one-fourth of the population live in urban areas. The main ethnic groups are the Sinhalese, descendants of the first Indo-Aryan settlers of Sri Lanka (74% of the population); the Tamils, descendents of the Southern Indian settlers (18%); and the Islamic Moors (7%). The remaining 1% is composed of Malays, the Burghers (descendents of Dutch colonists), and the Veddhas, a small remnant of the island's original inhabitants. The Tamil minority is divided between Sri Lankan Tamils who have dwelt on the island for centuries, and Indian Tamils who were imported by the British in the 19th century to work on tea plantations. Until recently, the Indian Tamils did not enjoy the rights of citizenship. A compromise with India returned half of the Indian Tamils to India and granted the remaining Indians full rights of citizenship. Charges of Sinhalese discrimination against the Tamils and demands for an autonomous Tamil state in northern and eastern Sri Lanka create tension between the 2 groups and periodically lead to outbreaks of violence.

Language: Sinhalese, a modern Aryan language that can be traced back to Sanskrit and Pali, is the official language of Sri Lanka. Both Sinhalese and Tamil, a Dravidian language which is also spoken in south India, are national languages. The constitution guarantees both groups the right to use their own native tongue. English is spoken by about 12% of the people, mainly within more educated circles and in the government. Approximately 2% of the people speak all 3 languages.

Religion: Since the introduction of Buddhism by the Indian Prince Mahinda in the third century B.C., Sri Lanka has been a stronghold of the Theravada branch of Buddhism. Nearly 70% of the people are Buddhist, primarily the Sinhalese majority, and Buddhism is the religion supported by the government. Freedom of religion is allowed, however. Approximately 15% are Hindu, mainly the Tamil. Their worship is centered around the Hindu god Shiva. Also, about 8% are Muslim, and 8% are Christian. A recent reawakening of a Sinhalese nationalistic Buddhist movement and restrictions on Christian missionary activities have led to a decline in Christian converts among the Sinhalese.

LIFESTYLE

The Family: Traditionally, the caste systems of each of the ethnic groups in Sri Lanka have governed the family system and the relationships between relatives. The family is the central social unit in all Sri Lankan societies. In the family, the man is dominant; traditionally men will eat first, followed by the women and children. Although the husband is dominant, the wife manages the affairs of the household and exerts a great deal of influence on all family matters. Elders are deeply respected, and younger family members will generally yield to their advice and counsel.

Dating and Marriage: Although individual choice of marriage is found among more westernized circles, traditional practices in arranging marriages still prevail in Sri Lanka. Marriage outside of caste traditionally has religious taboos associated with it, and males and females of the same generation within caste and family are designated as either marriageable or unmarriageable in relation to each other. This tradition continues to fade as Sri Lanka becomes more modernized and westernized. Sexual purity is an essential part of the marriage contract on the part of the female. Marriage between members of different ethnic groups is socially unacceptable.

Social and Economic Levels: Compared to western levels, Sri Lanka has a very low level of economic development. Twenty-two percent of the population live in absolute poverty, and few homes enjoy modern conveniences. Despite this, Sri Lankans are proud of the progress their country is making. Compared to people of other less-developed countries, Sri Lankans enjoys a high quality of life.

Diet: Rice is the staple in the Sri Lankan diet and is the basic food for all meals. The government subsidy for rice sold to the poor is one of the most volatile political issues in the country. Many varieties of fruits and vegetables are available to supplement the diet. Sri Lankans typically consume little meat. Many different curry powders are used in cooking. These vary from mild to extremely spicy. Sri Lankans consume a large amount of pulse (peas and beans) and nuts. Tea, served with most meals and as a refreshment, is popular in Sri Lanka. Wealthier families enjoy supplementing their diets with European cuisine.

Recreation: The people of Sri Lanka enjoy many sports introduced by the British, including soccer, rugby, and cricket. Tennis, badminton, and horse racing are also popular. Attending western and Sri Lankan movies are favorite pastimes. Sri Lanka has a long tradition in the dramatic arts, and the people enjoy traditional live and puppet theater.

Holidays: Official Sri Lankan holidays include Buddhist, Hindu, Muslim, and Christian festivals, such as Vesak, Thaipongal, Ramadan, and Good Friday respectively. There are also cultural holidays, such as the Sinhalese and Tamil New Year, which is in April. The Buddhist calendar is based on the phases of the moon and, therefore, every full moon (Poya day) is a holiday.

THE NATION

Land and Climate: Sri Lanka, formerly called Ceylon, is a teardrop shaped island located south of the Indian subcontinent. It is slightly larger in total land area than the state of West Virginia. Approximately 25% of the land is under cultivation and 44% is covered by forests. The northern end of the island, inhabited by the Tamil minority, is flat and requires irrigation to cultivate crops. The southern and central regions are mountainous, and are inhabited by the Sinhalese majority. Tea, rubber, and coconut plantations are located in the central mountains. Sri Lanka has a generally uniform tropical climate, with temperatures averaging 80° F. year round. The island is in the path of seasonal monsoon rains, and yearly rainfall averages from 40 inches in the north to over 200 inches in the south. Many Europeans, finding the climate and the economy attractive, retire in Sri Lanka.

History and Government: The first inhabitants of Sri Lanka, the Veddhas, have largely been assimilated into society; and no record of their history remains. Around 500 B.C., an Indo-Aryan group, led by the semi-legendary Prince Vijaya, migrated to Sri Lanka and formed a small kingdom. The present-day Sinhalese descended from this group. In 307 B.C., the Indian Prince Mahinda, son of the great Buddhist King Asoka, introduced Buddhism to the Sinhalese population. After the demise of Buddhism in India, Sri Lanka became the stronghold of Buddhism in South Asia. South Indian Tamils also came to the island at an early date and have kept some cultural and religious ties with the state of Tamil Nadu in India. A second migration of Tamils occurred in the 19th century as the British imported Indian laborers to work the tea plantations. For 450 years (until 1948), Sri Lanka was under the influence of European powers—the Portuguese from 1505 to 1656, the Dutch from 1656 to 1766, and finally the British from 1766 to 1948. The Kandyan Kingdom was the final independent kingdom on the island, and was colonized by the British early in the 19th century. The island was named Ceylon by the British, and became a British colony. In 1948, the island peacefully obtained freedom from British rule and since then, through several elections, a freely-elected democratic government has been maintained. In 1971, there was an uprising by mostly unemployed, educated young people, but the uprising was quelled and order maintained. In 1972, partially in response to the previous year's unrest, a new constitution was approved. In that document, the name of the country was changed from Ceylon to the Republic of Sri Lanka, meaning "resplendent island." In 1978, the country became the Democratic Socialist Republic of Sri Lanka, and the system was changed to an elected presidential system. On April 29, 1982, the capital of Sri Lanka returned to Colombo (Sri Jayawardhanapura), which was the capital of the country at the time of Portuguese arrival in the 16th century.

Economy: Sri Lanka's economy is hindered in growth because of the island's few natural resources and only a small industrial capacity, and thus must import many commodities. Average gross national product (GNP) per capita is only $380 annually, one of the smallest amounts in the world ($14,300 in U.S.). Approximately 53% of the people are employed in agriculture, but explosive population growth has made it necessary to import food to meet the demands of the population. Major agricultural products include rice, rubber (Sri Lanka is the fourth largest producer in the world), tea, and coconuts. Recent decline in the price of these commodities has further depressed the Sri Lankan economy. The processing of rubber, tea, and other food products, along with petroleum production, are the main industries in Sri Lanka. Tourism plays a large role in raising income for the island. The country is plagued by high unemployment and extensive underemployment. Inflation is typically higher than in the U.S.

Education: Public education is free and compulsory in the primary and secondary levels, and Sri Lanka boasts one of the highest literacy rates in South Asia (85%). Although the government is stressing the development of vocational skills, traditional caste restrictions and the lingering of British values lead many students to continue their studies in the liberal arts. Unemployment among liberal arts graduates has been high and a serious problem in the past. More women in skilled positions are entering the work force each year.

Transportation and Communication: Buses and taxis are plentiful in urban areas. Buses are often extremely crowded. Most cities are linked by paved roads and rail, and most roads are passable year round. Few Sri Lankans own a car. There are many newspapers, printed in Sinhalese, Tamil, and English, and the press is generally free to express individual opinions. Radio and television broadcasts are available in all of the above major languages.

Health: Sri Lanka experiences the problems of most developing nations, and lacks adequate health and sanitation facilities. Sri Lanka's infant-mortality rate and maternal-mortality rate are among the highest in the world. Most existing facilities are located in the larger urban areas. Water is usually unsanitary, and should be boiled before use. Ice and dairy products should be avoided because they are often a source of stomach disorders to visitors. The best medical facilities are found in the city of Colombo.

For Further Information

Because space is so limited in this *Culturgram* and needs are so varied, no suggested readings are included. We recommend a visit to your local library or bookstore. Check *Books in Print* and various cataloging systems for country-specific titles. Review *Encyclopedia Britannica* or similar comprehensive summaries. The U.S. government publishes *Country Profiles* which many libraries subscribe to. Computer searches (DIALOG, SDC, BRS, ISI) are now available at most major libraries. Contact the Embassy of Sri Lanka, 2148 Wyoming Ave.,N.W., Washington, D.C. 20008, or the Sri Lanka Tourist Board, 609 Fifth Ave., Room 714, New York, NY 10017. The U.S. Embassy in Sri Lanka is located at 210 Galle Road, Colombo 3; P.O. Box 106, Sri Lanka.

How to Use This Culturgram

Quickly read the whole text as an overview. Then circle or give priority numbers to specific questions you have or ideas you want to pursue. Use the *Culturgram* as a guide to check on regional differences and current situations.

Maps

Culturgram maps are meant only as simple geographical orientations. Boundary representations are not necessarily authoritative. Different sources also vary spelling, transliterations, and accents.

Rev. 1/88

CULTURGRAM*

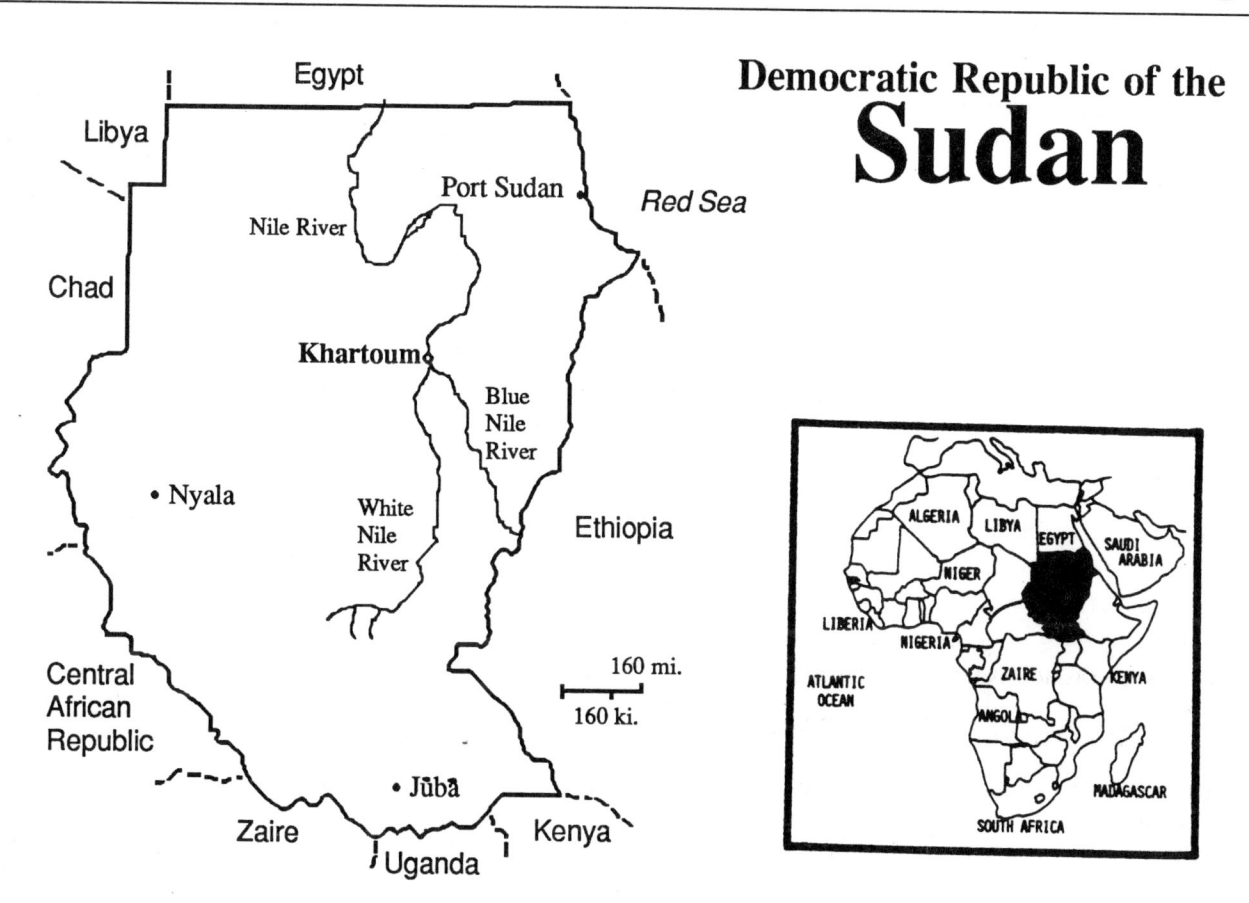

Democratic Republic of the Sudan

CUSTOMS AND COURTESIES

Note: There is a sharp distinction between the customs of the Arab and Arabized peoples of the northern and central Sudan, and those of the black African peoples of the southern Sudan. This Culturgram deals only with the Arabic- and Nubian-speaking peoples of the north.

Greetings: Hospitality is a Sudanese custom shared with the rest of the Arabic-speaking world. The northern Sudanese are a formal and traditional people, yet very cordial in their greetings of friends as well as strangers. A firm but gentle handshake with a member of the same sex is always in order, and friends frequently embrace. Men do not publicly shake hands or otherwise touch women unless a hand is extended by the woman. The usual verbal greeting is *Salaam ʿalaykum* (peace be upon you) or *Ahlan wa-sahlan* (welcome!), followed by *Kayf Haalak* (how are you?).

Visiting: The Sudanese home is the owner's private domain, and one does not usually visit without an explicit invitation. Such an invitation may be considered a distinct honor, and it is quite in order for a visitor to take a small gift (but never alcohol) as a token of appreciation. Guests are usually offered coffee, tea, or juice, perhaps with some kind of food. Refreshments should not be refused, since this expression of hospitality is very important to all educated Sudanese. Conversation should always be kept on a social level, even if one is involved in business dealings with the host. One should not ask about the women of the household nor discuss personal topics.

---

*Culturgrams are briefings to aid understanding of, feeling for, and communication with other people. Culturgrams are condensations of the best information available. Your insights will be appreciated. If you have refining suggestions, please contact Brigham Young University David M. Kennedy Center for International Studies, Publication Services, 280 HRCB, Provo, Utah 84602 (801) 378-6528. Copyright © 1986. All rights reserved. Printed in the USA.

Eating: A meal in the Sudan is a social occasion to be enjoyed. Although western-style restaurants and foods are located in Khartoum, the majority of Sudanese eat local dishes according to their own customs. One normally sits on the floor, and food is eaten with the fingers of the right hand. Most Sudanese have one large meal a day.

Personal Appearance: In Khartoum, some local businessmen dress western style. This is not frequent, however, outside of urban environments. It is very rare to see a woman in western dress. The nomadic people of the desert wear heavy robes to protect them from the heat and blowing sand. Visitors are advised to wear conservative clothing. Shorts, halter tops, or any other abbreviated attire is not publicly acceptable.

Gestures: In common with other Near Eastern countries, use of the left hand should be limited. Guests should not accept or give things to others with that hand; they may use either both hands or the right hand alone. Pointing with the finger is considered rude and should be avoided. As in many other cultures, when sitting in the presence of others it is offensive to allow the bottoms of one's feet (or shoes) to be seen.

THE PEOPLE

General Attitudes: For all the seeming outward formality of life, the northern Sudanese are surprisingly vocal and expressive. They are an individualistic people given to expressing their opinions openly, though it is almost always in a polite and considerate manner. They are also a fatalistic people and believe strongly in putting up with the unpredictabilities of everyday life. Westerners should not be alarmed at what seems to be an attitude of general disinterest. The Sudanese habit of quietly appraising a situation does not imply a lack of concern, nor does it preclude future action. Sudanese people are pragmatists at heart.

Population: The Sudan has a population of 22 million. The Arabized peoples inhabiting the northern and central parts of the country account for approximately 50%. A Nubian minority (8%) is concentrated around the Nile in northern Sudan. The Dinka, Funj, Nuer, Shilluk, and other peoples of southern Sudan are speakers of Nilo-Saharan languages and have customs quite distinct from those of the northern Arabic-speaking majority. The population-growth rate is 2.7% per year, with about 45% of the population under the age of 15. Approximately 25% of the people are city dwellers. The capital, Khartoum, has a population of over 2 million. The populations of all Sudanese cities, notably Juba and Kosti, have grown rapidly in the last 10 years.

Language: While Arabic is the official language of the entire country, it is the primary language only in the northern and central regions. English is the acknowledged principal language of the south, but Nilo-Saharan languages (Dinka, Nuer) are also spoken, as are over 135 other languages. Nubian languages are still spoken by small bilingual minorities around the Nile in the north.

Religion: Approximately 73% of the people are Sunni Moslem. The remainder follow traditional tribal religions.

LIFESTYLE

The Family: The Sudanese family is a strongly male-oriented, patriarchal, extended family. Three generations of males and their spouses and children usually live in the same household. This pattern is the norm throughout the Sudan, but is less dominant in Khartoum, where smaller western-style families are found. The home is a cohesive, private place, in which much of one's life goes on and to which one can always return for support. Though it is male-dominated, the home is managed by the women of the family. Women's roles are quite different from those of men, but are not considered subservient.

Dating and Marriage: Western-style dating does not occur in the Sudan. Marriages represent the joining of 2 families, and consequently their arrangement is a matter of concern to all members of both families. Such arrangements, however, are rarely made without the approval of the potential mates. Marriages tend to endure well.

Social Levels: Sudanese society is highly stratified. In addition to an underprivileged lower class, there is also a substantial middle class (both in the cities and the rural regions), and a small upper class. Governmental positions are usually filled by members of the upper class. The Islamic institution of *zakat* (tithing to help support the needy) offsets major economic disabilities to a surprising extent. Some significant differences—social as well as economic—are still apparent between various segments of the population. The vast cultural differences that exist between the Arabic speakers of the north and non-Arabic speakers of the south is a great social challenge. Although attempts are made to handle problems equitably, a great deal remains to be done before the southern Sudanese will be socially and economically equal with the north.

Diet: Sudanese foods are typically Near Eastern. Lamb, goat, and fowl are the usual meats, and pasta-like dishes are also popular. Other common foods include pancake-like breads made of sorghum or millet flour and spicy soups with meat or eggs. Regional dishes, often highly spiced, are typical in the south.

Work: The workplace is also a distinct entity in Sudanese life. It is largely controlled by the business class, and access to any segment of the business world can be made only through the use of intermediaries. The Sudanese government is the nation's largest employer.

Holidays: While the official calendar is the western (Gregorian) calendar, daily life is regulated by the Islamic lunar calendar. Moslem Holy Days are important, especially Ramadan, the month of fasting. The Moslem Sabbath, Friday, is observed by most people. National holidays include New Year's (January 1), Unity Day (March 3), and May Revolution Day (May 23). Dates vary for religious holidays.

THE NATION

Land and Climate: The Sudan is the largest country in Africa and is almost one-third the size of the continental U.S. Most of the Sudan is large plain, bounded to the west by the mountains of the Nile and Congo River watersheds and to the east by the hills along the Red Sea. The dominant features of the country are the vast deserts and, as in Egypt to the north, the Nile River. Temperatures are high throughout the year, often reaching well over 100° F. in Khartoum. Large dust and sand storms are also common in the north. Rain is rare except in the massive swamps of the far south (the Sudd), where the rainy season lasts for 8 to 9 months.

History and Government: The Sudan has a long and interesting history. Contacts between Egypt and Nubia, the Sudan's northern area, date to several millennia B.C. In Biblical times, the area was known as Cush. A Nubian dynasty conquered and ruled Egypt until about 340 AD. During the early years of the Christian era, the Sudan was part of the Christian Kingdom of Aksum, centered in Ethiopia. When the Arabs successfully invaded Egypt in the 600s A.D. a treaty with Nubia forbade Nubian settlement in Egypt as well as Moslem settlement in the Sudan. The area remained Christian until the 15th century, when it fell under Egyptian domination. Nevertheless, the Sudan remained semi-autonomous. In 1881, Muhammed Ahmed proclaimed himself *al-Mahdi* (the guide), and led a successful revolt against Egypt. In 1898, however, Egypt regained control of the region with the help of the British. In 1953, the people voted for complete independence from Egypt. On January 1, 1956, the Sudan became a separate nation. Until 1986,

Sudan was a single-party republic. In 1972, the 3 southern provinces (largely non-Arab and non-Moslem), were given regional autonomy. This action temporarily relieved the tensions between the north and the south caused by sharp cultural and social differences. In a military coup 1985 Abdul Ramhmanin overthrew the government. One year later, as he had promised, elections were held to elect representatives for a national assembly, which in turn would write Sudan's new constitution. Since 1982 Sudan has also been participating in a civil war, waged between the government the Sudanese People's Liberation Army from the south of the country.

Economy: The mainstay of the Sudan's economy is agriculture, involving more than 77% of the active labor force. Grains are the primary crops, while cotton, groundnuts, and sesame seed are the major exports. Sudan is the principal producer of gum arabic, supplying 90% of the world total, and is the world's fifth largest producer of peanuts. An inadequate transportation system and the high cost of moving agricultural products over great distances are major hindrances to economic development. Per capita income in the Sudan is approximately $347 ($14,300 in U.S.). Approximately one fifth of the sudanese population suffer from famine.

Education: Nine years of education is compulsory. The literacy rate is approximately 20% in the Arabic-speaking sections of the country. Approximately 50% of school-age children in northern and central Sudan are enrolled in school. The University of Khartoum is an adequate four-year and graduate university, but present facilities on all levels of education do not meet the needs of the country.

Health: Boiled water is usually provided by major hotels. Dairy products should be avoided. Visitors should make sure that all food is well cooked and served hot. All fruits and vegetables should be washed and peeled before they are eaten. Average Sudanese life expectancy is low (43 years), and health facilities are limited. Parasitic diseases are endemic, particularly in the central and southern parts of the country. A large influx of refugees from both Chad and Ethiopia in recent years has increased the problem of adequate medical care. For further information contact International Health Consultants, P.O. Box 34582, Bethesda, MD 20817.

For Further Information

Because space is so limited in this *Culturgram* and needs are so varied, no suggested readings are included. We recommend a visit to your local library or bookstore. Check *Books in Print* and various cataloging systems for country-specific titles. Review *Encyclopedia Britannica* or similar comprehensive summaries. The U.S. government publishes *Country Profiles* which many libraries subscribe to. Computer searches (DIALOG, SDC, BRS, ISI) are now available at most major libraries. Contact the Embassy of the Sudan, 2210 Massachusetts Avenue, NW, Washington, D.C. 20008, or the Tourism and Hotels Corportaion, P.O. Box 7104, Khartoum, Sudan.

How to Use This Culturgram

Quickly read the whole text as an overview. Then circle or give priority numbers to specific questions you have or ideas you want to pursue. Use the *Culturgram* as a guide to check on regional differences and current situations.

Maps

Culturgram maps are meant only as simple geographical orientations. Boundary representations are not necessarily authoritative. Different sources also vary spelling, transliterations, and accents.

Rev. 1/88

CULTURGRAM*

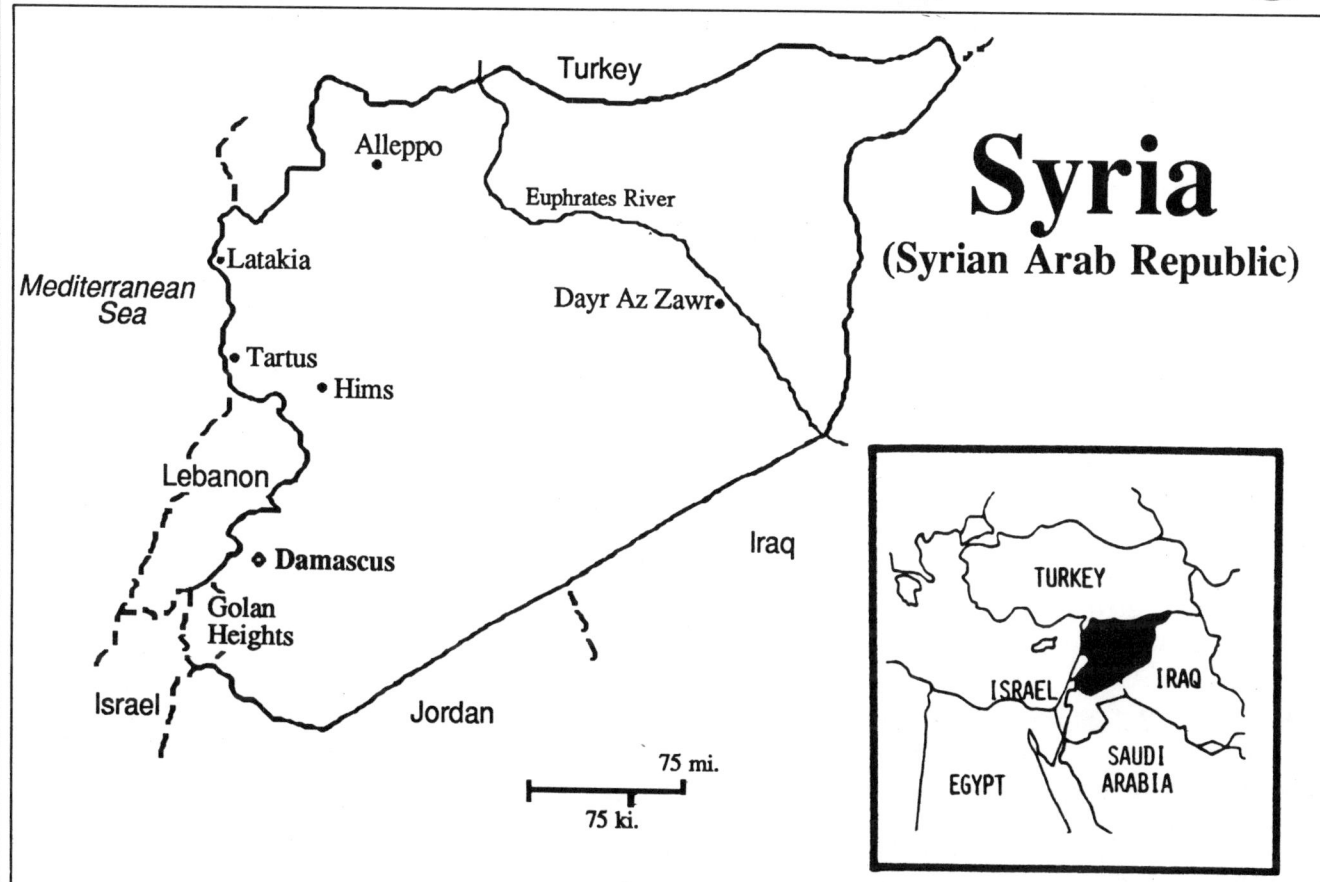

Syria
(Syrian Arab Republic)

CUSTOMS AND COURTESIES

Greetings: Syrians are very hospitable. They welcome people with an outstretched hand to shake while saying *Marhaba* (Hello) and *Keef Haalak* (How are you?) to inquire after one's health. Men may embrace each other in greeting (depending on the degree of their relationship or friendship) and women exchange kisses on either cheek.

Visiting: Syrians are more reserved than westerners in inviting non-family members to their homes. They may invite business and professional acquaintances home for tea in the afternoon, but generally they will meet guests for a drink in the early evening or host them at private clubs or restaurants for lunch or dinner. In restaurants, the host will pay for the whole group. Visiting hours are in the late afternoon or following supper. While most residences provide ashtrays and matches for smoking, it is polite to request permission to smoke. Visits should be for pleasure, not opportunities to talk business or to give bad news to the host.

Eating: Syrian cuisine is famous for its variety and expertise. A number of dishes will be offered; some to be eaten as finger food, some to be eaten western style. Syrians usually decline offers of food twice out of politeness before accepting the third time. Hosts generally offer food or drink 3 times. Therefore, to decline an offer of food or drink, one must refuse 3 times.

Gestures: Avoid pointing at or directing Syrians with the hand; this is considered rude. Resting a foot on the knee in such a way that the sole of the foot is pointed at another person is also offensive. Women should be especially modest in crossing their legs while sitting.

Personal Appearance: Urban Syrians generally dress in western styles, although one will often see people dressed in traditional clothing. Syrian dress often reflects religious mores.

*Culturgrams are briefings to aid understanding of, feeling for, and communication with other people. Culturgrams are condensations of the best information available. Your insights will be appreciated. If you have refining suggestions, please contact Brigham Young University David M. Kennedy Center for International Studies, Publication Services, 280 HRCB, Provo, Utah 84602 (801) 378-6528. Copyright © 1986. All rights reserved. Printed in the USA.

Bedouin women traditionally wear long dresses and the men wear *jalabas* (long robe) and a *keffiyah* (head covering). In the last few years, veiling has become more common among urban Muslim women, though it is not expected of foreigners. Women often dress in a modest western-style coat or heavy dress, dark stockings and shoes. Women may cover their hair with a scarf, or may use the scarf—usually black—to cover the whole head, tucking it into the collar. For visitors, western-style suits or conservative shirts and slacks will suffice for men. Women should dress modestly, cover their shoulders and upper arms, and not wear overly tight skirts or pants. Women may wear pants on the street.

THE PEOPLE

General Attitudes: Educated Syrians are cosmopolitan, traveled, multilingual, and intellectually astute. They are also conservative, dignified, and very proud of Syria and their national heritage.

Population: The population of Syria numbers approximately 11 million, of which the majority is Arab. Minorities include Kurds, Armenians, Turks, Circassian Russians and Assyrians (Syriac speakers). There are also over a quarter of a million Palestinian refugees. Damascus, the southern trade center, has over 1.5 million inhabitants, and Aleppo, the focal point of the northern trade routes, has a population of 1 million. The population-growth rate is 2.7% per year (0.9% in U.S.).

Language: Arabic is the national language and is used for all occasions. In addition, most educated men and women are trained in French and, more recently, English. Street and business signs are usually in Arabic (some are also in French) and getting around is sometimes difficult for visitors without a guide or some advance directions.

Religion: Religion plays a major role in Syrian life and politics. Islam is the major religion (about 80-85% of the population), and 80-85% of Syrian Muslims are Sunni. Other Islamic groups include Shiites, Alawites, and Druze. Christians account for about 15% of the total population. The major Christian groups are Greek Orthodox, Armenian Orthodox, Syrian Orthodox, Syrian Catholic, Maronites, and other small groups including Roman Catholics and Protestants. A few thousand Jews live in Damascus and Aleppo.

LIFESTYLE

The Family: The family is the basic unit of society and the center of an individual's life. All activities revolve around family members and family life, and any achievement by a family member advances the entire family. The father is the undisputed leader of the family. Both paternal and maternal relatives are part of the everyday life of all family members. Most social activities are organized by and for family members. The children mainly socialize with cousins, aunts, and uncles. Although the nuclear family is becoming more common—given contemporary housing and work-required moves to other locales—one still finds extended family households.

Dating and Marriage: Although dating is becoming more common in the westernized parts of Syria, it is still restricted to cousins and close friends. University students have more freedom to organize social events, but most associations follow previous family acquaintance. Although students are sometimes free to choose a spouse, they will be careful to choose one the family approves of and to seek family consent. In more traditional sectors of society, dating is not common and families play a dominant role in selecting marital partners.

Business Hours: Banking and government office hours are from 8 a.m. to 1 p.m. Stores, private businesses, and doctors' offices generally open in the morning and close around 1 p.m. They open again in the late afternoon, around 5 or 6 o'clock, for 2 hours.

Social and Economic Levels: Syria, which was overwhelmingly rural before World War II, is now 55% urban. The urban population is well distributed throughout 7 cities. Current work on dams and irrigation systems near the Euphrates is designed to further encourage this migration. Since the socialist policies of the Baath party were instigated, Syria has undergone a shift in elite structure. A growing middle class of Baath party functionaries and merchants has grown in importance and wealth, while the government has distributed the land of the traditional elite to the peasants that farm it.

Diet: Syrian cuisine is varied and delicious. *Mezza* (a table full of appetizers) is often served at restaurants or clubs. It will include pastes made of chickpeas and eggplant, dishes of meats mixed with spices and wheat (either raw or grilled), pickles, olives, and bread. Syrian sweets are world famous. Islamic law forbids eating pork and drinking alcohol.

Recreation: Soccer is the major sport and is followed avidly. Basketball has also gained great popularity in recent years, especially among school boys. Water sports are popular in the coastal cities. Visiting family and friends, or socializing with them in a private club, is a common pastime. Many middle-class families own video machines and enjoy watching films or television with their families. Syrians seldom go out to movies.

Holidays: The major Syrian holidays are the Muslim and Christian religious holidays: Christmas, Easter, New Years, Eid al-Adha (Feast of Sacrifice), Eid al-Fitr (Feast following Ramadan), and Ashura (the Shiite Day of Atonement). Armenian Orthodox Christmas is observed January 6. The Muslim holidays are based on the Islamic lunar calendar and vary from year to year. The ninth month of the Islamic year is Ramadan. Throughout this month Muslims abstain from food, drink, and tobacco from dawn to dusk, then visit friends and relatives in the evening. During Ramadan, special attention is paid to the needs of the poor, and business hours are shortened.

THE NATION

Land and Climate: Syria is basically divided into two regions: the coastal region with a narrow range of mountains, and the much larger eastern region with some mountains and large deserts. The climatic range is great. Summers are hot and dry; winters are cold, with snow in the north. In area, Syria measures 71,498 square miles (185,180 sq. km.), roughly the combined size of Indiana and Illinois. The proximity of the mountain ranges to the coast guarantees Syria adequate rainfall in the west, but the area around Damascus is primarily desert. This desert extends some 500 miles before ending at the Euphrates River. The northern part of the country has fertile agricultural land and is well cultivated.

History: Syria is an ancient land with a rich cultural heritage. The world's first alphabet was invented in Syria by the Phoenicians. Aleppo is the oldest continuously inhabited city in the world and Damascus is the oldest continuously inhabited capital in the world. In its early history, Syria dominated an enormous commercial and political network. Syria was conquered by Alexander the Great, ruled by his successors (the Seleucids), and then brought into the Roman Empire. Christianity was strong in Syria until the time of the Muslim conquest in 635 A.D. The first Muslim empire, the Umayyad, ruled the expanding Islamic lands until 750. Damascus continued as a major Muslim trade and political center until the twentieth century, when the Treaty of Versailles made Syria a French mandate. Syria gained independence in 1946. Economic and political pressures on the new state led to unrest, and a series of military-led coup d'etats followed. In 1970, the Defense Minister, Hafez al-Assad, took power. He is still the president of Syria.

Government: Since 1958, the Baath (Resurrection) Party with its ideology of liberty, unity, and socialism, has been the only political party allowed to function in the state. Accordingly, it controls all the ministries, the army, and the state apparatus under the leadership of President Assad. The emphasis on unity within the Arab nation has led Syria to champion the cause of the Palestinians, making it a major opponent of Israel. Syria has fought wars with Israel in 1948, 1967, and 1973. The Syrian nation has also maintained an active interest in the Lebanese conflicts of the past decade, as their populations are closely related. Syria has said it will not tolerate an anti-Syrian force to be in control of Lebanon.

Economy: The Syrian economy has been based on agriculture for millenia. Today, agriculture employs about 50% of the labor force. Current emphasis is on industrial output, while still working to keep agricultural productivity high. Under the Baath Party's socialist stance, the government controls all industry, except small private businesses. It operates the oil refinery, the large electricity plants, the railways, and various manufacturing plants. Extensive land reform has been effected. Syria's chief exports are raw cotton, woolens, and textiles. Textile manufacturing is Syria's largest industry. Per capita gross national product (GNP) is approximately $1,780 ($14,300 in U.S.).

Education: Syrian schools include public (tuition-free), religious, and secular private schools. In addition, several schools are operated by the United Nations for Palestinian refugee children. The bulk of the students (over 90%) are in public schools. The literacy rate in Syria is around 53%. Over 90% of young boys and almost 70% of young girls begin primary schools, but the attrition rate is high, especially in rural areas. There are 3 universities at Damascus, Aleppo, and Latakia, plus the Institute of Petroleum and Chemical Engineering at Homs.

Transportation and Communications: Syria's location has long made it a communications center for the region. Syria has 2 major ports, Tartus and Latakia, and Damascus and Aleppo each have an international airport. Three separate railways serve the country and lead to adjoining nations. A good system of paved roads links all parts of the country. For most trips within the country, buses provide the easiest and most efficient mode of travel. To assure seats, it is advisable to book tickets 24 hours ahead of time. Service taxis run along set routes and pick up passengers until the taxi is full. They also run between cities. When traveling throughout Syria, visitors should be aware of the various security checkpoints. It is wise to take them seriously, move slowly, and obey policemen. Telephone service is good both within Syria and to international connections.

Health: Boiled water must be used for ice cubes, brushing teeth, etc., and is provided by major hotels. Be sure that all food is well cooked and served hot. All fruit and vegetables should be peeled before they are eaten. Dairy products are of unreliable quality and should be avoided. Syria boasts a number of excellent doctors trained in medical programs in the United States and Europe. Hospital care is best in major cities. The university teaching hospitals are also recommended. For further health and medical information, contact International Health Consultants, PO Box 34582, Bethesda, MD 20817.

For Further Information

Because space is so limited in this *Culturgram* and needs are so varied, no suggested readings are included. We recommend a visit to your local library or bookstore. Check *Books in Print* and various cataloging systems for country-specific titles. Review *Encyclopedia Britannica* or similar comprehensive summaries. The U.S. government publishes *Country Profiles* which many libraries subscribe to. Computer searches (DIALOG, SDC, BRS, ISI) are now available at most major libraries. Contact the Embassy of Syria, 2215 Wyoming Ave., NW, Washington, D.C. 20008, or the Ministry of Tourism, Abi Faras Al-Hamadani St., Damascus, Syria. The U.S. Embassy in Syria is located at Abu Rumaneh, Al Mansur St. No. 2, Damascus, P.O. Box 29, Syria.

How to Use This Culturgram

Quickly read the whole text as an overview. Then circle or give priority numbers to specific questions you have or ideas you want to pursue. Use the *Culturgram* as a guide to check on regional differences and current situations.

Maps

Culturgram maps are meant only as simple geographical orientations. Boundary representations are not necessarily authoritative. Different sources also vary spelling, transliterations, and accents.

Rev. 1/88

CULTURGRAM*

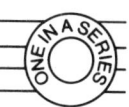

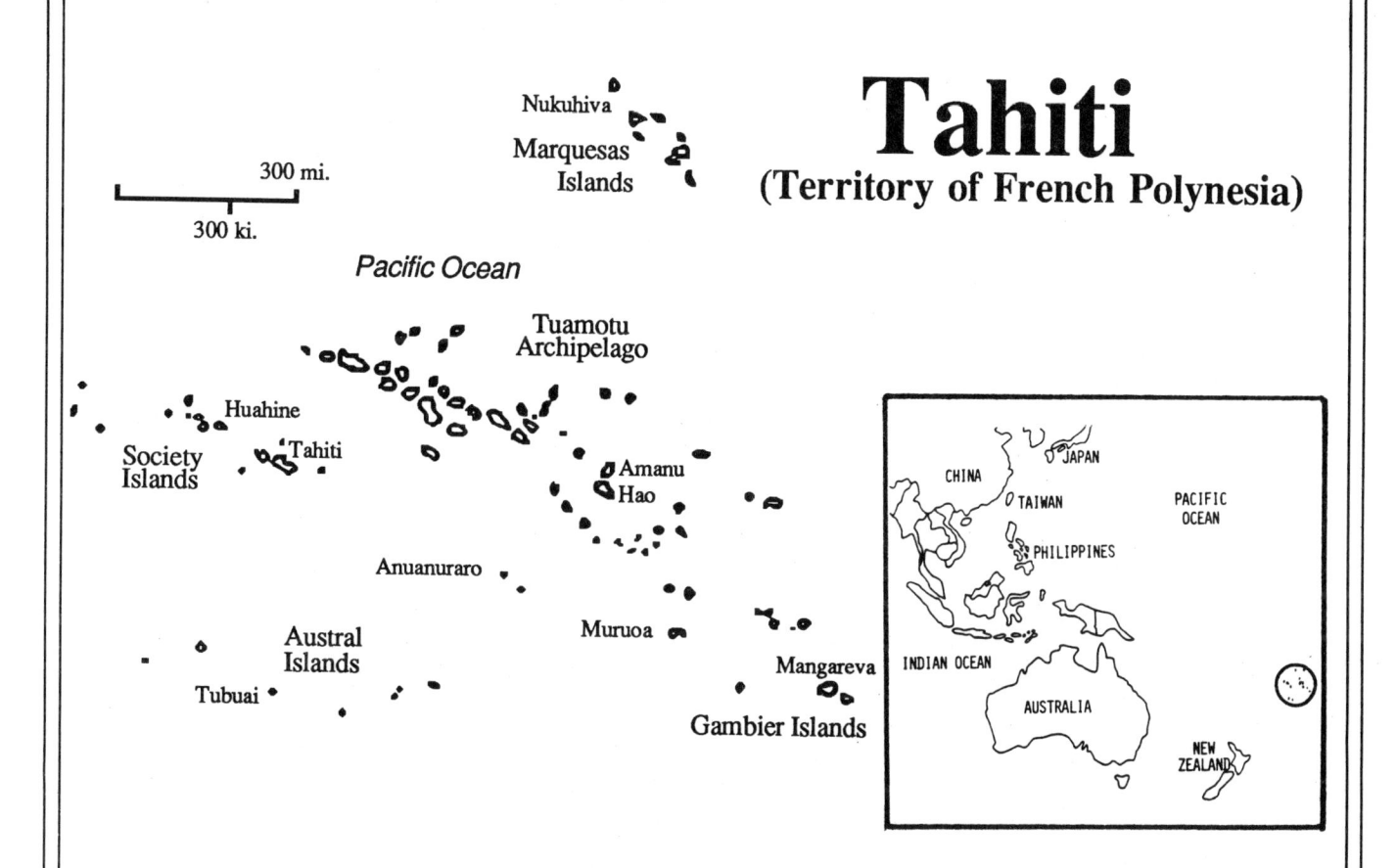

Tahiti
(Territory of French Polynesia)

CUSTOMS AND COURTESIES

Greetings: French Polynesia, although influenced by French culture, has maintained many of its own traditional customs. The French in French Polynesia practice traditional European customs and courtesies. Most people shake hands when they meet. If a French Polynesian's hand is dirty, a wrist, elbow, or even shoulder will be extended. The people are very disappointed if a visitor does not take time to shake hands with everyone in a gathering of about 30 people or fewer. Tahitian and French women usually kiss each other on the cheeks when greeting each other formally or after a long separation.

Visiting: French Polynesians have a real *joie de vivre,* or joy of life. They are relaxed, natural, and invariably try to make their guests comfortable. A favorite maxim is, "If you act like old friends when you first meet, you will soon feel that you are." A guest should express sincere interest in the host's family and home, but should be careful not to single out any one item of decor; otherwise the host may feel obligated to give the item to the guest as a gift. It is customary to remove one's shoes before entering a home.

Eating: French Polynesia enjoys a great variety of culinary choice, with excellent French and Chinese cuisine in addition to the traditional native foods. Western dishes are also readily available. Etiquette varies greatly depending on the food and the family. "Observe and do likewise" is a good

---

*****Culturgrams** are briefings to aid understanding of, feeling for, and communication with other people. Culturgrams are condensations of the best information available. Your insights will be appreciated. If you have refining suggestions, please contact Brigham Young University David M. Kennedy Center for International Studies, Publication Services, 280 HRCB, Provo, Utah 84602 (801) 378-6528. Copyright © 1986. All rights reserved. Printed in the USA.

rule to follow. Traditional Tahitian foods are eaten with the fingers, while Chinese food is eaten with chopsticks. Utensils are always supplied on request. It is considered impolite to refuse food or to make excuse for not eating. One should not eat everything on the plate just to be polite, as this is a signal to the host to serve another helping. Sometimes, guests are invited to eat while the host family watches. Although this may seem embarrassing, the guest should eat and show appreciation. In a restaurant, tipping is not encouraged.

Personal Appearance: Cool, informal clothes are worn throughout the year. Clothes should be neat and clean, as French Polynesians are keenly aware of cleanliness. Footwear for both men and women is usually a pair of thongs or sandals without stockings or hose. Dresses of *pareu* cloth are worn at home and at the beach. Women usually wear dresses instead of shorts.

THE PEOPLE

General Attitudes: French Polynesians highly value personal relations and are warm and receptive, although they may seem a bit reticent until they become better acquainted. They enjoy life, and try to live as simply and as happily as possible. European influence, however, is increasing the pace of life. To many, time is not important. This becomes more evident as one travels further from the capital city of Papeete.

Population: About 166,000 people live on the 130 islands of French Polynesia, the majority on the island of Tahiti. Close to 65,000 live in and around the capital city of Papeete. The population is growing at an average annual rate of 2.3% (0.9% in U.S.). There are few pure-blooded Polynesians. Most of the populace is a mixture of Chinese or European and native Polynesian. About 78% of the people are of Polynesian decent, 12% Chinese (Hakka), and 10% French.

Language: French is the official language in the territory. It is used exclusively in the schools, and is spoken widely in Tahiti. Tahitian, however, remains the language of the majority and is spoken at home and especially on the outer islands. The Chinese community speaks the Hakka dialect. English is not widely spoken, although anyone involved in the tourism industry speaks French and some English. Each of the different island groups has its own language or dialect; some are very similar to Tahitian, while others are completely different.

Religion: The Tahitian people no longer worship the many gods of nature, as they once did, but are still influenced by traditional beliefs. Missionaries from the English London Missionary Society of the Evangelical Church arrived just before the turn of the eighteenth century, and other Christian missionaries soon followed. Currently, 55% of the people are Protestant, 30% are Catholic, 6% are Latter-day Saints (Mormon), and 2% are Adventists. Tahitians are strongly religious people.

LIFESTYLE

The Family: Traditionally, Tahitian families were large, usually with many children and several generations living under the same roof. It is still common for couples to live with the husband's or wife's parents for a time after marriage, but increased contact with western culture is leading to more nuclear families. In the Polynesian culture children are precious, and their upbringing is often shared by grandparents or other sets of adoptive parents (*faamu*). This system of informal adoption remains active today and makes family relations very complex.

Dating and Marriage: In most Polynesian cultures, the girls are more closely supervised than the boys. "Dating," as defined by western standards, is generally not seen in French Polynesia, except among the French adolescents. Tahitians usually go together in groups to dance, sing, talk, or participate in sports. Marriages are traditionally influenced by the families, but there are no longer any class distinctions in Tahiti. Western influences have led to greater freedom in choosing a spouse. Marriages are a festive time of feasting and merrymaking.

Social and Economic Levels: Although the average income in French Polynesia is lower than that of western countries, the middle-class income meets the needs of the people. The upper class is composed of French, Chinese, and a few mixed Tahitians, who have the economic power. Government employees, teachers, and others who are paid high salaries by the French government make up the middle-class. The working class is composed of the laborers, farmers, fishermen, etc. The cost of living has risen considerably in the last few years, but the minimum wage has also increased proportionally. On the outer islands, the average house is a 1 or 2 room fiberboard, tin-roofed structure with a separate cooking house and bath facilities. Neatness is important in the house and yard. Economic status is often determined by one's knowledge of the French language.

Diet: Tahitians have been influenced by French society and generally eat 3 meals a day: a light breakfast of bread and a hot drink, a large meal at noon, and a light supper. The Tahitian diet is composed of bread, fish, sweet potatoes, breadfruit, taro, potatoes, rice, and local fruits and vegetables. The basic diet of people in urban areas includes many western food products and meats.

Business Hours: Government offices are open from 7:30 a.m. to 3:30 p.m. Most stores are open from 7:30 to 11:30 a.m. and from 2:00 p.m. to 5:30 p.m. Chinese shops are often open from 5:30 a.m. to 10 p.m., 7 days a week. Most other shops are closed on Sundays, although Sunday morning is the most important day at the Papeete market, where locals come to sell their food products, crafts, and flowers.

Recreation: Recreation is of prime importance in the lives of French Polynesians. Sports, television, movies, and dances are the most popular forms of recreation. Soccer is the national sport. Boxing, volleyball, basketball, cycling, and water sports (especially wind-surfing and canoeing) are other favorites.

Holidays: National holidays are New Year's Day (January 1), Easter Monday (March or April), Labor Day (May 1), Ascension Thursday (May), Pentecost Monday (May or June), National Bastille Day (July 14), Assumption of Virgin Mary (August 15), Toussaint or Memorial Day (November 1), Veteran's Day (November 11). Bastille Day, the French National Holiday, is celebrated during the second 2 weeks of July and is known as the *Tiurai* (meaning July). This is considered the most spectacular celebration of the year and is a good time for a tourist to visit Tahiti (but a difficult time to accomplish any business). The celebrations include parades, athletic competitions, dancing, and cultural events.

THE NATION

Land and Climate: French Polynesia consists of about 130 islands, divided into 5 main island groups for administrative purposes: the Winward Islands (including Tahiti), the Leeward Islands, the Tuamotus and Gambier Islands, the Marquesas Islands, and the Australs, or Tubuai, Islands. The Winward and Leeward islands combined are often referred to as the Society Islands. The total land area is slightly larger than the state of Rhode Island. The Society Islands are a blend of volcanic peaks and lush tropical forests. White, sandy beaches surround each island, as does a coral reef, providing quiet lagoons. The Marquesas are much the same, but do not have beaches. The Tuamotus and Gambiers are low-lying atolls; their highest elevation is no more than 3 to 7 feet. The climate is warm (75 to 85° F.) and humid (75 to 85%) year round. Trade winds blow constantly, however, and combat the effects of the humidity. The rainy season is from November to February, and the most comfortable time of the year is from May to September.

History and Government: Tahiti became a French protectorate in 1842 when the French government helped Queen Pomare II gather the 9 districts of the island under her authority. The other groups of islands gradually came under French domain before the turn of the 19th century. The islands later became a territory in 1880. Internal self-rule was obtained in 1977. The government includes a French-appointed governor with absolute veto power, a locally elected deputy governor, and a locally elected Territorial Assembly.

Economy: The average gross national product (GNP) per capita in French Polynesia is about $6,400 annually ($14,300 in U.S.). The economy is strongly tied to tourism and the C.E.P. (Centre Experimental du Pacifique), France's nuclear testing program. The C.E.P. alone accounts for 30% of the GNP. Agriculture is also very important to the economy. Coconut (copra) is the most important crop and accounts for 80% of the territory's exports. Also, mother-of-pearls account for 14% of the exports. Other major products include vanilla, coffee, and phosphates. France continues to be the territory's largest trading partner. In recent years, Tahiti has become world renowned as a vacation and resort area. To encourage tourism, new facilities are being constructed each year. The monetary unit is the French Pacific *franc*.

Education: The French government has established primary, secondary, and vocational schools on the islands that comply to the standards of education in France. School is compulsory from age 6 to 14 and is free. Private schools are heavily subsidized by the government and follow the public-school curriculum. Adult education programs are popular and are also free. Some high-school graduates receive scholarships to study in France or to further their training at advanced vocational schools in Tahiti. Almost all young people can read and write.

Transportation: Motorbikes and cars are the most common forms of transportation. Buses are numerous and fairly regular on the Society Islands. Local airlines and shipping lines service most of the islands. Locals often travel by boat, but this is not recommended for tourists. Taxis service the hotels and airports, but are relatively expensive.

Health: Medical services are heavily subsidized by the government for the local population. Medical facilities and personnel are good, and only major medical problems must be treated in New Zealand, France, or the United States. Health evacuations from the outer islands are carried out efficiently by the military. For further medical information, contact International Health Consultants, PO Box 34582, Bethesda, MD 20817.

For Further Information

Because space is so limited in this *Culturgram* and needs are so varied, no suggested readings are included. We recommend a visit to your local library or bookstore. Check *Books in Print* and various cataloging systems for country-specific titles. Review *Encyclopedia Britannica* or similar comprehensive summaries. The U.S. government publishes *Country Profiles* which many libraries subscribe to. Computer searches (DIALOG, SDC, BRS, ISI) are now available at most major libraries. Contact the French Embassy, 4101 Reservoir Road NW, Washington D.C. 20007, or the Tahiti Tourist Promotion Board, 2330 Westwood Blvd. #200, Los Angeles, CA 90064.

How to Use This Culturgram

Quickly read the whole text as an overview. Then circle or give priority numbers to specific questions you have or ideas you want to pursue. Use the *Culturgram* as a guide to check on regional differences and current situations.

Maps

Culturgram maps are meant only as simple geographical orientations. Boundary representations are not necessarily authoritative. Different sources also vary spelling, transliterations, and accents.

Rev. 1/88

CULTURGRAM*

Taiwan
(Republic of China)

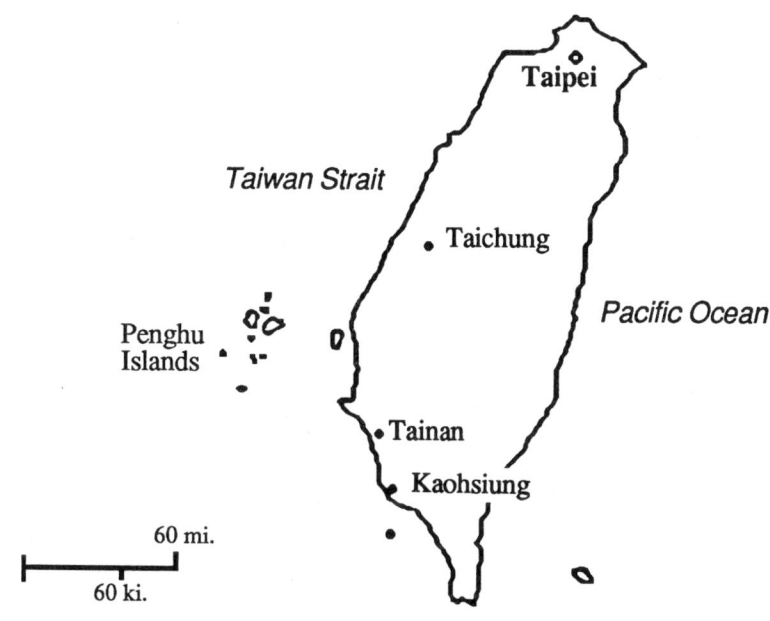

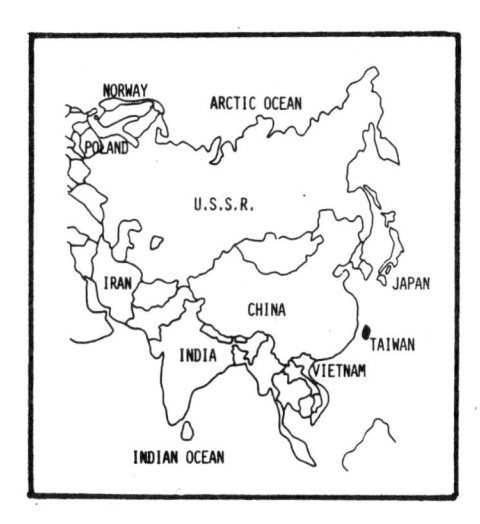

CUSTOMS AND COURTESIES

Greetings: A nod of one's head is considered appropriate when meeting someone for the first time, but for acquaintances and close friends, a handshake is most common. A slight bow shows special respect, but should not be exaggerated. In Chinese names, the one-syllable family name always comes first and the two-syllable given name second. When addressing a person, the family name and title are used rather than the first name; only in rare cases are first names used. Thus, Yu Tai-fa should be addressed as Mr. Yu. It is common to ask young people about their schoolwork when greeting them. The elderly appreciate a question about their health. Asking someone if they have eaten shows concern and is a common greeting.

Visiting: Shoes are usually removed before entering a home and slippers are worn inside. The elderly are always recognized and greeted first. Guests are likely to receive tea, candy, fruit, juice or a soft drink. Dinner conversation often centers on the meal—how it was prepared, what the ingredients were, and where they were obtained. Upon leaving, the host will usually escort the guest a considerable distance from the home. To this the guest should politely give token resistance, returning thanks for the special hospitality. When visiting a family it is appropriate to bring a small gift, such as fruit, especially around New Year's time. Both hands should be used when exchanging a gift or other object. Gifts are usually not opened in the presence of the giver. Sincere compliments are appreciated. However, modesty is expressed by politely denying them. Compliments

---

*Culturgrams are briefings to aid understanding of, feeling for, and communication with other people. Culturgrams are condensations of the best information available. Your insights will be appreciated. If you have refining suggestions, please contact Brigham Young University David M. Kennedy Center for International Studies, Publication Services, 280 HRCB, Provo, Utah 84602 (801) 378-6528. Copyright © 1986. All rights reserved. Printed in the USA.

about a particular object may make the host feel obligated to give the object to the guest as a gift.

Eating: Chopsticks and a soup spoon are the common eating utensils in Taiwan. Food is placed in the center of the table. The host usually chooses the food for the guests and serves it to them. Guests are expected to eat what is offered them, if possible. It is considered impolite not to finish all the rice in the bowl and it is perfectly acceptable to ask for a refill. When eating rice, it is proper to hold the bowl near the mouth. Bones, seeds, etc., are placed on the table or on a plate provided for them, but not in the rice bowl or on the plate one is eating from. Guests should lay their chopsticks neatly on the table when they have finished eating. At a restaurant, the Chinese host always expects to pay. The guest may also politely offer to pay but should not insist. Business is not usually discussed while eating. If a toothpick is used, the mouth should be covered. Napkins are not common, so it is wise to carry a handkerchief. Food should not be eaten on the street. Water should be boiled or otherwise prepared for drinking. The Chinese have a heritage of fine cuisine, including Peking duck, Szchuan vegetables, and New Year's rice cakes.

Gestures: The open hand should be used for pointing rather than the index finger. Beckoning to people is done with the palm facing down instead of up. It is common for young lady friends to hold hands, but putting one's arm around the shoulders of another may be considered inappropriate. Shaking one hand from side to side with the palm forward means no. People do not use their feet to move objects such as chairs or doors. While sitting down, the hands are usually placed in one's lap, and the legs should not be jiggled. Women may cross their legs. Winking is impolite.

THE PEOPLE

General Attitudes: Frankness or abruptness, especially in offering criticism of any kind, should be avoided. People in Taiwan are generally reserved, quiet, refined, and friendly. They respect a person who is friendly and who carefully avoids hurting the feelings of others. Loud, untactful, or boisterous behavior is usually regarded as being in very poor taste. The Confucian ethic of proper social and family relationships form the foundation of Chinese society. The schools and government foster the tradition of respect for and obedience to parents. Moral standards are very high. Traditionally, men and women do not show affection in public. Long hair for men and immodest dress are not common. An individual's actions reflect upon his whole family.

Population: The population of Taiwan is over 19 million, and is growing at an annual rate of 1.3% (0.9% growth rate in U.S.). Approximately 84% of the population are Taiwanese, 14% are mainland Chinese, and 2% are aborigines. Over 60% of the people live in urban areas. The population density of 1,127 people per square mile is one of the highest in the world (58 in U.S.).

Language: The official language in Taiwan is the Mandarin dialect of Chinese. However, a majority of the people also speak Taiwanese. The Hakka dialect is also spoken. Many older people speak Japanese.

Religion: Most people are Buddhist, Confucianist, Taoist, or a combination of these and other beliefs. Approximately 7.5% of the population are Christian, while less than 1% are Muslim. Photographs should not be taken inside Buddhist temples.

LIFESTYLE

The Family: Families in Taiwan are generally quite large and it is not uncommon for grandparents and other relatives to live together. Affection is usually not displayed in a traditional western manner, but families have a deep-rooted unity and a feeling of obligation to each other. Family members will agree rather than cause disunity in the family.

Dating: Dating is limited and depends largely on social and economic status. For those who do date, movies, dining, and socializing are the most popular activities.

Business Hours: A six-day, 48 hour workweek is common. A traditional break from noon to 2:00 p.m. is now being discouraged. Smaller shops are usually open from early morning until late at night.

Diet: Rice is eaten with every meal. Soup, seafoods, pork, chicken, vegetables, and fruit are most commonly eaten. Most foods, including vegetables, are fried. Tea is served often. Meals are taken seriously and seldom missed.

Recreation: The most popular forms of recreation are movies, picnics, and hiking. Basketball, ping pong, volleyball, baseball, badminton, tennis, and soccer are popular sports. Taiwan's little league baseball teams have been world champions several years. There are no professional sports teams in Taiwan.

Holidays: People in Taiwan follow the Lunar calendar, which begins with New Year's Day (late January or February). Other holidays include Youth Day (March 29), Chiang Kai-Shek's Death (April 5), Confucious' Birthday or Teacher's Day (September 28), National Day (October 10), Restoration Day (October 25), Chiang Kai-Shek's Birthday (October 31), Dr. Sun Yat-sen's Birthday (November 12), and Constitution Day (December 25). Chinese New Year, the biggest holiday of the year, is celebrated in February.

THE NATION

Land and Climate: Taiwan is about the size of the states of Massachusetts and Connecticut combined. It is located about 100 miles off the coast of China. The Pescadores Islands (Matsu, and Quemoy) are also controlled by Taiwan. In the north, the warm, humid summer season lasts from May to October. January and February can be very cold and rainy. Southern Taiwan is warmer and less humid, much like southern California. It can get very cold in the south, but for a shorter period of time. Typhoons often occur from June to October. Temperatures average about 75° F. in the south.

History and Government: Chinese immigration to Taiwan began as early as the T'ang dynasty (618-907). In 1628, the Dutch took control of the island. In 1683, the Manchus of mainland China conquered the island, and made Taiwan a province of China. The island was ceded to Japan following the Sino-Japanese War of 1895 and was under Japanese control until 1945. In 1949, the advancing communist forces of Mao Tse-tung forced President Chiang Kai-shek's Nationalist government and nearly 2 million soldiers to flee from the mainland to Taiwan. Since that time, the Nationalist government of Taiwan has considered itself to be the legal government of all of China. Communist China's plans to invade the island were blocked in 1950 when President Harry S. Truman sent the U.S. Seventh Fleet to patrol the Taiwan Strait. In 1955, the U.S. signed an agreement to protect Taiwan in case of attack from mainland China. In 1971, the People's Republic of China (mainland China) was admitted to the United Nations in Taiwan's place, despite U.S. objections. President Richard Nixon declared that U.S.-Taiwan relations would be maintained. On January 1, 1979, the United States normalized relations with the People's Republic of China. As a result, the 1955 mutual defense pact with Taiwan was terminated and official diplomatic relations between the United States and Taiwan have been severed. However, relations continue on an unofficial basis through the American Institute. In 1981, Taiwan adopted a policy of maximum patience in seeking to discourage the U.S. from further strengthening its ties with mainland China. Today, the Republic of China on Taiwan is virtually a one-party government ruled by the Kuomintang (KMT) political party, with Chiang Ching-kuo (son of Chiang Kai-shek) as president since 1978. Because Taiwan is technically still at war with the Chinese communists on the mainland, all men are obligated to serve in the armed forces for 2 or 3 years. Taiwan has been ranked as the tenth strongest military power in the world, and second in number of soldiers per capita.

Economy: Taiwan's economy is one of the fastest growing economies in the world and one of the strongest in Asia. Currently, the gross national product (GNP) per capita is about $2,985 annually ($14,300 in U.S.), over 3 times mainland China's annual GNP per capita. The economy is growing at a rate of 8% annually. Taiwan's labor force is growing at a rate of 5% annually, the fastest in the world. Since 1962, foreign trade has increased dramatically. Major industries include electronics, textiles, chemicals, fertilizer, cement, plastics, aircraft, sugar milling, and shipbuilding. Major agricultural products include poultry, hogs, rice, sugarcane, tea, fruits, and vegetables. Also forestry, mining, and tourism are important to the economy. Even though arable land is limited, agriculture in Taiwan has been extremely efficient.

Education: Education is free and compulsory up to age 15. Universities are few and are difficult to enter. Students work very hard to prepare for the college entrance examinations given each July. Taiwan's literacy rate is over 90%.

Transportation: Many people own cars, but bicycles, motorcycles, buses, and taxis are the principal forms of transportation. Trains are used for traveling longer distances. Taiwan's public transportation systems are among the best in Asia.

Health: For specific medical information, contact International Health Consultants, PO Box 34582, Bethesda, MD 20817.

For Further Information

Because space is so limited in this *Culturgram* and needs are so varied, no suggested readings are included. We recommend a visit to your local library or bookstore. Check *Books in Print* and various cataloging systems for country-specific titles. Review *Encyclopedia Britannica* or similar comprehensive summaries. The U.S. government publishes *Country Profiles* which many libraries subscribe to. Computer searches (DIALOG, SDC, BRS, ISI) are now available at most major libraries. Contact the Republic of China Tourism Bureau, 1 World Trade Center, Suite 8855, New York, NY 10048.

How to Use This Culturgram

Quickly read the whole text as an overview. Then circle or give priority numbers to specific questions you have or ideas you want to pursue. Use the *Culturgram* as a guide to check on regional differences and current situations.

Maps

Culturgram maps are meant only as simple geographical orientations. Boundary representations are not necessarily authoritative. Different sources also vary spelling, transliterations, and accents.

Rev. 1/88

CULTURGRAM*

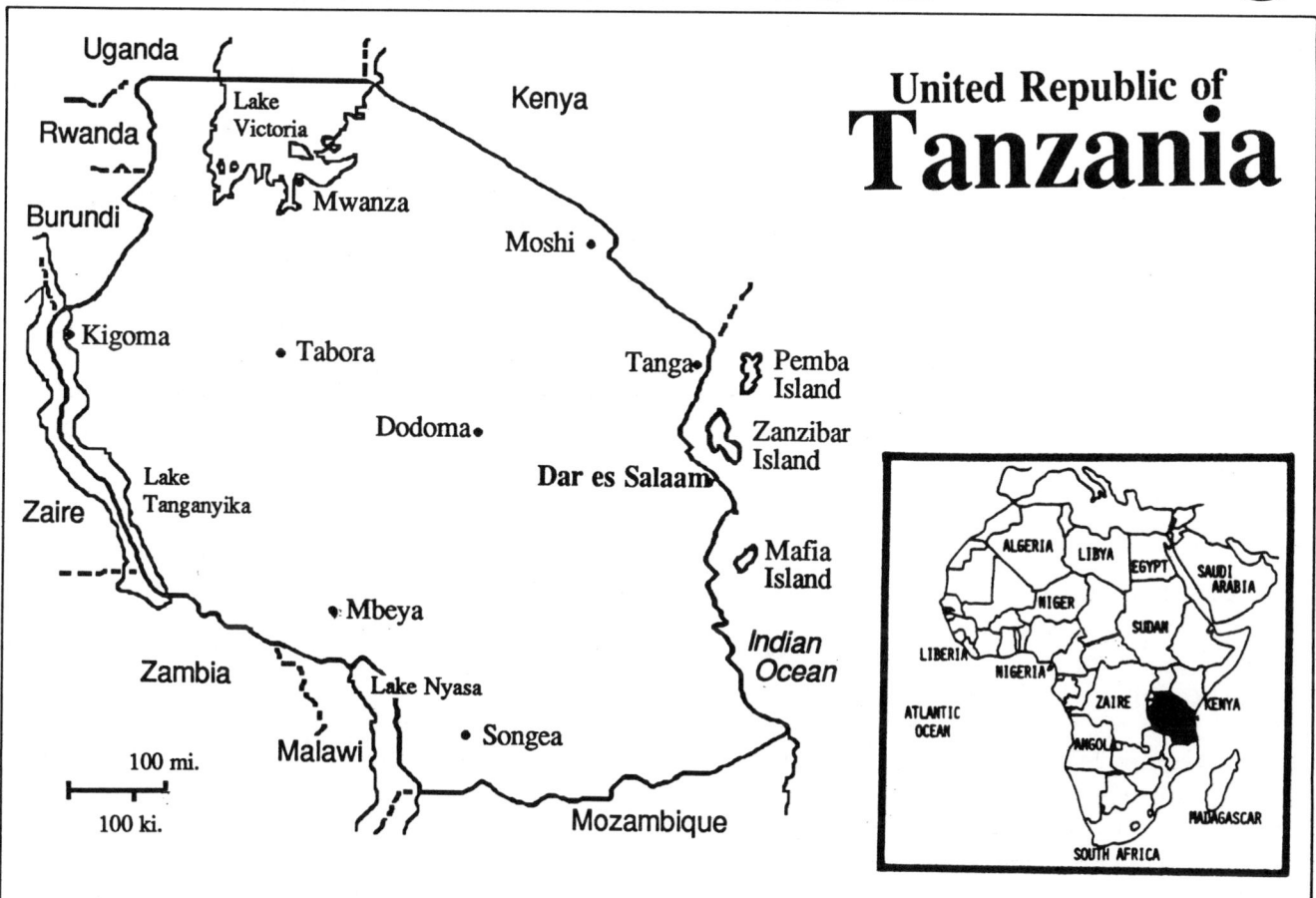

United Republic of Tanzania

CUSTOMS AND COURTESIES

Note: Tanzania is the home of more than 130 different ethnic groups, each with its own customs and traditions. This Culturgram broadly describes the culture of the Swahili-speaking coastal population, which is politically and culturally dominant.

Greetings: The most common verbal greeting is *Jambo*, usually followed by a handshake. Men do not publicly shake hands with women in Tanzania, but foreigners are usually exempt from this rule.

Visiting: Small gifts are customary when visiting a Tanzanian home for the first time. Flowers, however, are best left to express condolences.

Eating: An unexpected visit to a Tanzanian home at meal time requires that the guest be invited in and fed, so visiting times should be carefully chosen. Tanzanians normally eat with the fingers, and follow the general Moslem custom (even among non-Moslems) of using the right hand only. In most cases, socializing is reserved for after the meal.

Personal Appearance: Urban Tanzanians usually wear western-style clothes. Visitors are expected to dress conservatively. Shorts should be avoided except in very clearly defined work or play situations.

---

*Culturgrams are briefings to aid understanding of, feeling for, and communication with other people. Culturgrams are condensations of the best information available. Your insights will be appreciated. If you have refining suggestions, please contact Brigham Young University David M. Kennedy Center for International Studies, Publication Services, 280 HRCB, Provo, Utah 84602 (801) 378-6528. Copyright © 1986. All rights reserved. Printed in the USA.

Gestures: Most European gestures are acceptable. Do not, however, gesture with or use the left hand when giving or receiving anything from another person. Avoid the verbal gesture of tch-tch: it is considered insulting.

THE PEOPLE

General Attitudes: Regardless of tribal affiliation, Tanzanian social systems are traditionally group-oriented. The individual is expected to put himself second to group welfare. Consequently, Tanzanians are extremely polite and generous people both in private, and, particularly, in public. It is considered very impolite to pass a person (except of course in a large crowd), without showing some sign of recognition, be it only a smile. Tanzanians do not use obscene language of any kind, even mildly. Any kind of verbal abuse or upbraiding, especially in public, is a cardinal sin reflecting on the other person's entire upbringing and background. Nevertheless, westerners frequently perceive Tanzanians (and East Africans in general) to be abrupt and occasionally impolite. This is largely because the words "please" and "thank you" are not native to the Bantu languages; the Swahili equivalents, *tafadhali* and *asante*, respectively, have been borrowed from Arabic. Requests are often made without a "please," and help may be accepted without a "thank you." This is not impolite, but simply a cultural habit. Tanzanians appreciate personal efforts, but show their thanks in other ways.

Population: Tanzania has approximately 22 million inhabitants, with a population density of 42 persons per square mile (58 in U.S.). The growth rate is 3.2% per year. Less than 10% of the people live in cities, which are rare except along the coast. Over 98% of the people are native African in origin; by far the largest percentage consists of 33 Bantu-speaking tribes. There are also Nilotic tribes (3), Khoisan tribes (2), and Afro-Asiatic tribes (2). The Nyamwezi-Sukuma (12.6% of the population), is the largest group and the only one of the more than 130 ethnic groups which has more than 1 million members. The capital, Dar es Salaam, has a population approaching 1 million. Dodoma, located in the center of Tanzania, has been designated to become the new capital by 1990. The island of Zanzibar has a population of over 600,000.

Language: It was in the coastal regions of what are today Tanzania and Kenya that the Bantu trade-language called Swahili (Kiswahili) had its origins. Over the centuries, this initially artificial medium has become a vibrant and highly cultured tongue and is the primary official language of the country. Most speakers of the more than 40 other languages in Tanzania also speak Swahili. English is a second official language and is widely heard in urban coastal areas.

Religion: The coastal peoples are largely Moslem (30%) or Christian (30%). Most rural Tanzanians adhere to traditional tribal religions (40%).

LIFESTYLE

The Family: The basis of Tanzanian socialism is Ujamaa, or familyhood. The nation's extended families have been encouraged to act as economic as well as family units. Families are traditionally large, usually including either the father's brothers and their families (in the north) or the mother's sisters and their families (in the south), as well as one's birth family. Urban families are often smaller and less cohesive than those residing in rural areas.

Marriage: Marriage in the early 20s is normal. While individual preference in mates is permitted, cross-cousin marriage (with the mother's brother's child or the father's sister's child) is encouraged, particularly in rural environments. The husband's family normally gives a dowry to the bride's family.

Social Classes: Particularly on Zanzibar, social class distinctions were formerly extensive and based primarily on race. Since the revolution of 1964, racial classes have largely vanished. Now social position depends on education and political status.

Diet: Tanzanian staples are grains, fruits, and vegetables. The most common meats are chicken, goat, and lamb. A very popular food is *kitumbura*, a fried bread common to much of East Africa.

Recreation: Soccer, track and field, and boxing are popular sports in Tanzania. Big game hunting is permissible under certain restrictions and only during certain times of the year. Tanzania has been known for its world-class runners. Water sports are popular along the coast.

Holidays: Tanzania celebrates various civic and religious holidays, including New Year's Day, Zanzibar Revolution Day (January 12), Easter, Union Day (April 26), International Worker's Day (May 1), Saba Saba Day (July 7), Independence Day (December 9), and Christmas. Islamic religious holidays follow the Moslem lunar calendar and vary in date from year to year.

THE NATION

Land and Climate: The United Republic of Tanzania consists of mainland Tanganyika and the islands of Zanzibar and Pemba. Tanganyika (about the size of Texas) is a land of great variation. Most of the country is either low-lying coastal plain, upland plain (the Serengeti), or plateau. Tanzania contains the highest point in Africa, on the top of Mt. Kilimanjaro (19,340 ft.), as well as the lowest point, on the floor of Lake Tanganyika (1,174 ft. below sea level). The equatorial climate (90° F. on the coast) is tempered by inland altitudes (68° F.). Rains fall primarily from March to May and October to December, with seasonal variation from north to south. The tse-tse fly infests nearly two-thirds of the mainland, precluding any widespread practice of animal husbandry. Zanzibar and Pemba are low coral islands, with a combined area about the size of Delaware.

History and Government: Finds at Olduvai Gorge indicate that Tanzania has been inhabited for at least a million years. In the 8th century A.D., Arab traders from southern Arabia began to explore and settle the coast, founding the important city of Kilwa. Over many generations these foreign adventurers mixed with the local Bantu population to produce both the Swahili language and the modern peoples of the coastal regions. During the 1400-1700s, the Portuguese and Arabic overlords from Oman and Muscat developed a series of populous and powerful trading cities and sultanates—particularly on the islands of Zanzibar and Pemba. The Sultanate of Zanzibar controlled both the islands and the mainland coast with a firm hand until the mid-1800s. In 1886, Tanganyika became a German protectorate. Zanzibar retained its independence, but lost some control to the British in Kenya. In 1920, Tanganyika fell under British rule. In 1961, Tanganyika was granted independence, followed in 1963 by a fully independent Zanzibar. In 1964, the two nations merged to form Tanzania. Due to the farsightedness of President Julius Nyerere, this union has been very successful. The country has become a socialist republic, governed by a President, Cabinet, and National Assembly. A carefully designed series of constitutional checks and balances makes it virtually impossible for any single interest group to gain control. The stated goal of the government is the creation of a true socialist state.

Economy: Agriculture dominates the Tanzanian economy, employing over 80% of the labor force and contributing about 48% of the GNP. Per capita income is $210 ($14,300 in U.S.). The economy has been either stagnant or in decline during the last few years. Major exports include sisal, cloves, coffee, cotton, and diamonds. Tanzania is the world's tenth largest producer of diamonds. The economy of Zanzibar is based primarily on cloves. Together, Zanzibar and Pemba are the world's principal suppliers of this spice. Tanzanian industries include agricultural processing, oil refining, and textile production. Tanzania's major trading partners are West Germany, Great Britain, and the United States.

Education: Tanzania's literacy rate is 79%. School is taught in Swahili, and English is taught as a second language. About 50% of school-age children attend school. The University of Dar es Salaam is the national university, and places emphasis on training for community service rather than strictly academic pursuits.

Transportation and Communications: The transportation system is only moderately developed. There are 2 newspapers and 5 telephones per 1,000 people. Taxis are available in the cities; fares should be agreed upon in advance. Buses are generally overcrowded. Traffic moves on the left.

Health: In rural areas malaria, sleeping sickness, and a wide variety of intestinal parasitic diseases are common. Boiled water must be used for ice cubes, brushing teeth, etc., and is provided by major hotels. Make sure all food is well cooked and served hot, and all fruits and vegetables are peeled before eating. Medical help can be found in Dar es Salaam, but evacuation to Nairobi is recommended for serious medical attention. With very few physicians (one per 16,000 people), the need for expanded health care is great. For further medical information, contact International Health Consultants, PO Box 34582, Bethesda, MD 20817.

For Further Information

Because space is so limited in this *Culturgram* and needs are so varied, no suggested readings are included. We recommend a visit to your local library or bookstore. Check *Books in Print* and various cataloging systems for country-specific titles. Review *Encyclopedia Britannica* or similar comprehensive summaries. The U.S. government publishes *Country Profiles* which many libraries subscribe to. Computer searches (DIALOG, SDC, BRS, ISI) are now available at most major libraries. Contact the Embassy of Tanzania, 2129 R Street, NW, Washington, D.C. 20008, or the Tanzania Tourist Corp., 205 East 42nd St., Suite 1300, New York, NY 10017. The U.S. Embassy in Tanzania is located at 36 Laibon Road (off Bagamoyo Road), Dar es Salaam, (P.O. Box 9123), Tanzania.

How to Use This Culturgram

Quickly read the whole text as an overview. Then circle or give priority numbers to specific questions you have or ideas you want to pursue. Use the *Culturgram* as a guide to check on regional differences and current situations.

Maps

Culturgram maps are meant only as simple geographical orientations. Boundary representations are not necessarily authoritative. Different sources also vary spelling, transliterations, and accents.

Rev. 1/88

CULTURGRAM*

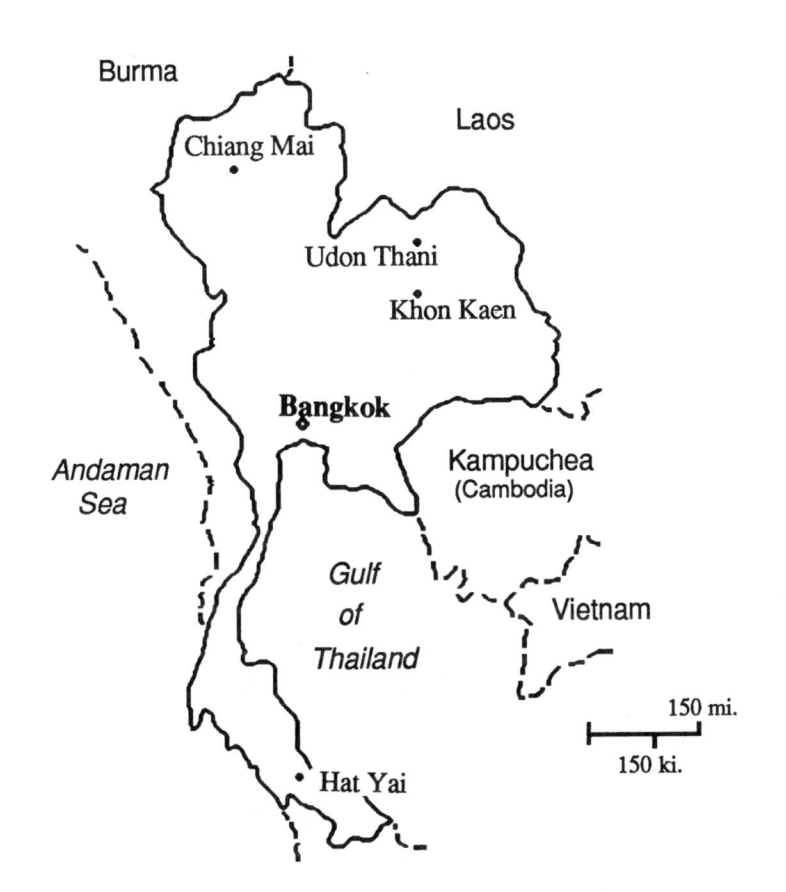

Kingdom of Thailand

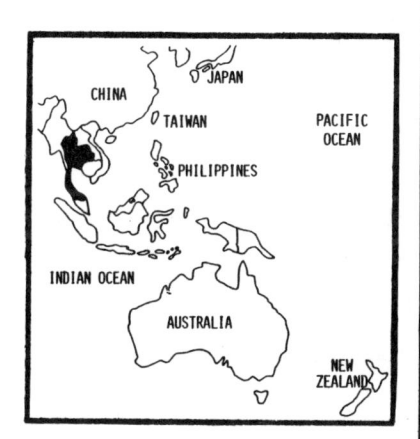

CUSTOMS AND COURTESIES

Greetings: Thais generally do not shake hands except in more westernized social groups. The traditional and most common Thai greeting is called the *wai* (rhymes with eye). The *wai* is made by placing both hands together in a prayer position at the chest and bowing slightly. The higher the hands are placed, the more respect is shown. One should not raise the tip of the fingers above eye level. Among adults, failure to return a *wai* greeting is like refusing to shake hands in the West. The *wai* gesture can mean "hello," "thank you," or "I'm sorry." When receiving a gift, one is expected to *wai*. Thais address one another by their first names, reserving the last names for very formal occasions, as in writing. In formal circles, visitors can use Mr., Mrs., or Miss before the last name.

Visiting: It is customary to remove one's shoes when entering a Buddhist temple or a private home. Because Thai tradition says that a spirit resides in the doorsill of a home, guests should avoid stepping on doorsills. It is courteous to sit on the floor if your host does. Guests should show genuine interest in the host and his family. It is not necessary to bring a gift when visiting a home. Visitors should not compliment the host too excessively on items of decor, or the host may feel obligated to give the item as a gift.

Eating: Thais use forks and spoons at the dining table. The spoon is held in the right hand and the fork in the left. The fork is used to push food onto the spoon. Thais do not normally use knives because food is served in small pieces. In the northern and northeastern areas of Thailand, the people eat a steamed, sticky rice with their fingers instead of utensils. Chopsticks are used in

*__Culturgrams__ are briefings to aid understanding of, feeling for, and communication with other people. Culturgrams are condensations of the best information available. Your insights will be appreciated. If you have refining suggestions, please contact Brigham Young University David M. Kennedy Center for International Studies, Publication Services, 280 HRCB, Provo, Utah 84602 (801) 378-6528. Copyright © 1986. All rights reserved. Printed in the USA.

Chinese homes and restaurants. The host normally serves the guests a second helping and insists that the visitors eat as much as they desire. Food is placed in the middle of the table and is not passed from person to person. When finished, one should place the spoon and fork together on the plate and leave a small amount of food to show that one has had enough. In restaurants, tips are usually unnecessary, but sometimes a 5 to 10% tip is given to waitresses.

Gestures: A person's head is considered sacred and one should neither touch another's head nor pass an object over it. The bottoms of the feet are the lowest part of the body and should never be pointed in the direction of another person. People avoid stamping their feet, touching people with them, or using them to move or point at objects. It is usually considered offensive to cross the legs while sitting, especially in the presence of an older person. Placing one's arm over the back of the chair in which another person is sitting is offensive. Men and women generally do not touch or show any affection in public. Good friends of the same sex, however, will sometimes hold hands. Women must never touch a Buddhist monk or offer to shake hands. It is advisable to show respect for religious statues and other religious articles.

Shopping: Thailand's cities have both large department stores and small privately owned shops. The department stores are more expensive and carry many fashionable items. Prices in these stores are not negotiable. Small shops along the streets carry anything from car parts to beautiful silk dresses, including many items found in the larger stores. Prices in these stores are not set, but bargaining should be done in good taste, understanding that shop owners make very little profit.

Traveling: Customarily, Thais give their seats on buses or trains to little children, old people, women, or Buddhist monks. The last row of seats on the bus is reserved for the monks.

THE PEOPLE

General Attitudes: Thailand means "land of the free," and the Thais are proud of the fact that their country has never been under foreign rule. They now consider the communists in Laos, Kampuchea (Cambodia), and Vietnam to be their biggest threat. The King and Queen are the most respected and honored persons in Thailand, and a Thai would be offended by any joke or ill reference to them. In fact, very strict laws govern the way people may refer to the royalty. Individuals are subject to arrest, and even deportation, for saying or writing anything deemed offensive to the royal family. Traditionally, success was measured by a person's religious and nationalistic attitudes. Now the trend is toward wealth and education. Wealth is generally looked on as a reflection of virtue. The Thais have much respect for those who unselfishly help others and who lead virtuous lives. The Thai expression, *Mai Pen Rai* (never mind), characterizes their general feeling toward life—it should be enjoyed, and problems and setbacks shouldn't be taken too seriously. Thais are generally content with what they are and what they have. Another name for Thailand is "the land of smiles." Thais are a reserved people and usually consider criticism of others to be in poor taste. A sense of humor, laughter, and a pleasant, smiling attitude are regarded highly . On the other hand, a lack of reserve such as speaking loudly or showing anger in public is offensive and may cause one to lose a Thai's respect.

Population: The population of Thailand is approximately 52.7 million and is growing at a rate of 1.9% annually (0.9% in U.S.). Only about 14% of the people live directly in the cities. The population-density rate is 210 people per square mile (58 in U.S.). About 75% of the people are Thais, 14% are Chinese, and 11% belong to other minorities. Thailand is currently experiencing a large influx of refugees from Laos, Kampuchea, and Vietnam.

Language: Thai is the official language, but each of the regions of the country have their own dialect. Chinese and Malay are also spoken by significant minorities. English is spoken as a second language by many of the highly educated.

Religion: Although Thailand guarantees religious freedom for all, 95.5% of the people are Buddhist. More Buddhists live in Thailand than in any other country in the world. Buddhism deeply affects Thai life, as shown by the many temples (*wats*) that dominate Thai communities. Traditionally, all young men were expected to become Buddhist monks for at least 3 months of their lives, during which time they study and practice Buddhism. This practice is not enforced as strictly as it once was. Four percent of the people are Muslim. The remainder are Confucianist or Christian.

LIFESTYLE

The Family: Thai families are very close, and many generations may live in the same household. The oldest male is usually the patriarch of the family. All members abide by the elders' decisions, and children often obey parents' advice even after reaching adulthood. This custom, however, is changing as the country becomes increasingly modernized. Thais have a great respect for their parents. In a farmer's family, everyone works on the farm together, including the grandparents (if they are not too old). Generally, the grandmother stays at home to care for the children. The average family size in Thailand is 5.8 people (3.1 in U.S.).

Dating and Marriage: Girls generally lead a more sheltered life than boys in Thailand. Traditionally a young man who wants to marry a girl must make himself agreeable to her whole family. He then sends his parents to them to make known his wishes. If the marriage is agreed on, a date is set for the wedding. Western-style dating has recently become popular in the large cities.

Work: The average workweek in Thailand is 48 hours, one of the longest in the world. Most businesses are open Monday through Friday from 8:30 a.m. to 4:30 p.m, although some shops stay open until 6 p.m. Smaller shops are open on Saturday and Sunday and some stay open until 10 p.m.

Recreation: The most popular sports in Thailand are soccer, table tennis, badminton, and volleyball. *Takro* (a sport played by trying to keep a wicker ball in the air without using the hands) and kite fighting are also favorite sports. Various martial arts are also enjoyed by Thai youth.

Holidays: National holidays include New Years (December 31-January 1), Thai New Year (Song Kran, April 13), Queen's Day (August 12), Loy Krathong (1st full moon in November), Chulalongkorn Day, honoring the "Beloved Monarch", 1868-1910, who abolished slavery and brought about many other needed reforms in Thai laws and customs (October 23), Birthday of the King (December 5).

Diet: Rice is the staple of the Thai diet. Thai food is usually spicy and may consist of rice, vegetables, fruits, fish, and eggs. Curries and pepper sauces are also popular. Typical meats include beef, chicken, and pork. Thailand also boasts a wide variety of tropical fruit year-round.

THE NATION

Land and Climate: Thailand is slightly larger in land area than the state of Texas. The major cities are Bangkok (the capital, with 6 million people), Chiang Mai, Korat, Ubon Ratchatani, and Udorn Dhani. The hot, dry season is from March to May and the rainy season, with high temperatures is from June to October. The cool season is from November to February, with temperatures averaging in the low 80s. Thailand is green year-round, with many flowers and tropical fruit trees.

History and Government: Approximately 1000 years ago, the Thais migrated from southern China to the present area of Thailand and established the Kingdom of Sukothai in the 1200s. After long conflicts with the Khmers of Cambodia and the Burmese, the Thais were able to solidify control of the area. In the 1800s, King Mongkut was able to keep the Kingdom of Siam free from European domination. His son, King Chulalongkorn, abolished slavery and brought about many reforms. A bloodless coup in 1932 created a constitutional monarchy. Siam became Thailand in 1939. During World War II, the Japanese occupied Thailand. The United States played a major role in keeping Thailand free after World War II. Recent history has been marked by a long series of military coups. The present king is Bhumibol Adulyadej.

Economy: Agriculture is the backbone of the nation's economy. Approximately 76% of the people are employed in farming. Thailand is the third largest rubber producer and the fifth largest rice producer in the world. Other major agricultural products include sugar, corn, and tapioca. Nine percent of the people are employed in the industrial sector. Agricultural processing, textiles, wood and wood products, cement, and mining are important industries. Thailand is the world's second largest producer of tin and the third largest producer of tungsten. Average gross national product (GNP) per capita is $790 annually ($14,300 in U.S.). Approximately 20% of the people live in absolute poverty. The economy is growing at the unusually high rate of 5.8% each year. The monetary unit is the *baht*.

Education: After 1 to 3 years of kindergarten, children are required to complete six years of school, but high costs and insufficient facilities make this difficult. Tuition for the public and private secondary schools is paid by the student's family. Universities are mostly government operated and entrance is by examination. There is stiff competition for the limited number of places available in universities. Boys from distant parts of the country have more opportunities to go to the city and study at colleges and universities than girls do because they can live in the many temples there. Girls can live only in hostels and boarding houses. Marriage is discouraged and sometimes prohibited while attending college. The literacy rate is about 84%.

Transportation: Most larger cities are connected by rail, highways, and air service. Local transportation is by bus, taxi, *samlor* (3-wheeled taxi), and *silor* (4-wheeled mini cab). Less than 1% of the people own cars. The canals of Bangkok, called the *klongs*, are often used for transportation. One can see children going to school and adults going to work by way of boat along the *klongs*. Boats can also be seen carrying food and flowers to open-air markets. Recently, however, many of the canals have been filled in and paved. On special occasions the King travels the waterway in his royal barge propelled by 70 oarsmen in bright red uniforms.

Health: Unless one is accustomed to the water in Thailand, only bottled or boiled water should be consumed. Health services are limited, especially in the rural areas. Many good physicians can be found in Bangkok. The government is attempting to modernize health care, but progress is slow. For further medical information, contact International Health Consultants, PO Box 34582, Bethesda, MD 20817.

For Further Information

Because space is so limited in this *Culturgram* and needs are so varied, no suggested readings are included. We recommend a visit to your local library or bookstore. Check *Books in Print* and various cataloging systems for country-specific titles. Review *Encyclopedia Britannica* or similar comprehensive summaries. The U.S. government publishes *Country Profiles* which many libraries subscribe to. Computer searches (DIALOG, SDC, BRS, ISI) are now available at most major libraries. Contact the Embassy of Thailand, 2300 Kalorama Road, Washington, D.C. 20008, or Tourist Authority of Thailand, 5 World Trade Center, Suite 2449, New York, NY 10048.

How to Use This Culturgram

Quickly read the whole text as an overview. Then circle or give priority numbers to specific questions you have or ideas you want to pursue. Use the *Culturgram* as a guide to check on regional differences and current situations.

Maps

Culturgram maps are meant only as simple geographical orientations. Boundary representations are not necessarily authoritative. Different sources also vary spelling, transliterations, and accents.

Rev. 1/88

CULTURGRAM*

Kingdom of Tonga

Niuafo'ou Tafahi Niuatoputapu

South Pacific Ocean

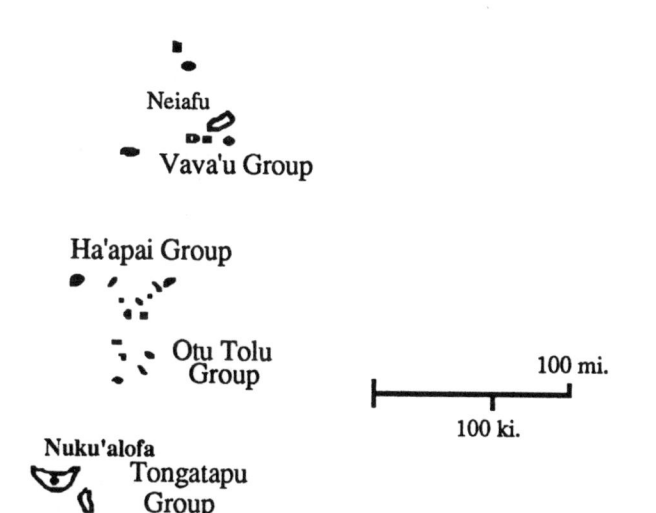

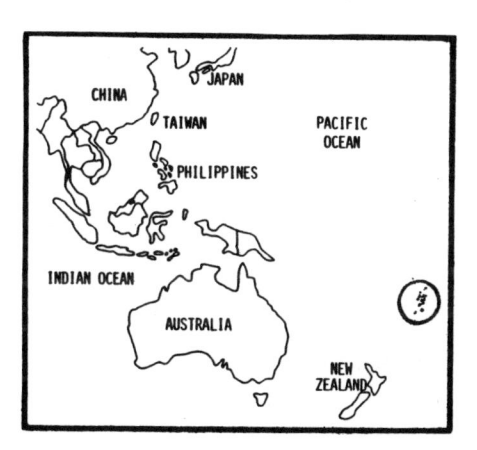

Neiafu
Vava'u Group

Ha'apai Group

Otu Tolu Group

100 mi.
100 ki.

Nuku'alofa
Tongatapu Group

CUSTOMS AND COURTESIES

Greetings: It is appropriate to greet people either with a handshake, or with a spoken greeting. Tongans customarily call those with whom they are familiar by their given names. To indicate respect, titles and family names are used together.

Visiting: If a family feels the house is not adequately furnished or cleaned, they may be reluctant to invite a visitor in. If invited in, the visitor is often directed to the best seat in the house. Children are kept out of the way as much as possible. The family will always try to give visitors the conveniences they are used to, but if a visitor can sit on floor mats, the family will enjoy and appreciate it. Men sit cross-legged on the floor. Women sit with both legs bent backward to one side, regardless of dress. A brief complimentary speech from guests before leaving is a high honor to the family. Tongans generally enjoy receiving compliments but have difficulty giving personal compliments. Visitors should be cautious in praising objects in a home; the host may give the item as a gift. Gifts are appropriate tokens of appreciation but are expected only from close friends. Flowers are not regarded as gifts. Customarily, Tongans do not open wrapped gifts in front of the one giving the gift.

Eating: The visitor usually eats with only a few selected members of the family. Children are sent away or eat in a different place. Although Tongans usually do not converse during meals, they do enjoy visitors who talk to them, especially about their home countries and

---

*****Culturgrams** are briefings to aid understanding of, feeling for, and communication with other people. Culturgrams are condensations of the best information available. Your insights will be appreciated. If you have refining suggestions, please contact Brigham Young University David M. Kennedy Center for International Studies, Publication Services, 280 HRCB, Provo, Utah 84602 (801) 378-6528. Copyright © 1986. All rights reserved. Printed in the USA.

travel experiences. Visitors, however, should be careful not to boast. Eating utensils are often used, but Tongans prefer to eat with their hands. Standing while eating and drinking is not appropriate, even though one may see it done by others.

Personal Appearance: Modesty is very important. Most females would not wear short skirts or low-necked dresses. By law, men above the age of 16 must wear shirts in public places. Many men do not even take off their shirts in their own homes. For many generations, men wore *valas* (calf length pieces of material wrapped around the waist); a *ta'ovala* (not a cloth, but a piece of fine material made from leaves, and worn around the waist, tied with a piece of coconut-fiber rope); and open-necked shirts. In recent years a tie and coat, shoes and socks have been added. Today trousers are more common, but *vala*, *ta'ovala* and tie are still required when associating with nobility. Sunglasses are worn as jewelry. Long hair for men is not considered appropriate. Pants are not considered appropriate for women.

Gestures: Raising the eyebrows is a gesture meaning "yes" or "I agree." It is not appropriate to call anyone other than children by using hand motions. A downward wave of the arm is a gesture to "come here." A forward and upward wave is a gesture to "go" or "goodbye."

Shopping: Merchandise is sold as priced, without bargaining, except for local produce in the marketplace. Most goods are kept behind the counter, and shoppers ask to see what they are interested in. Packages are often wrapped in newspapers. Tipping in restaurants is not required, but visitors may do so. All payments are in cash, unless an account has been established.

THE PEOPLE

General Attitudes: The Tongan way of life is easy-going; whatever does not get done today can be done tomorrow. Many women sit most of the day weaving baskets and mats and sell them inexpensively. The Tongans are well known for their generosity, almost to a fault. They prefer to converse from a distance and especially enjoy hearing adventure stories of the sea or the reef, legends of island people, or analogies with their ways of farming. The use of body gestures or visual aids to express ideas help a great deal in communicating. Crossing the legs is indicative of good breeding and etiquette, although non-Tongans are usually not expected to behave in this fashion. Guests should always be modest in public.

Population: The three main island groups of Tongatapu, Vava'u, and Ha'apai, and the island of 'Eua are inhabited by approximately 107,000 Tongans. The growth rate is 1.9% annually. Approximately 66% of the people live on the island of Tongatapu, the largest island, covering 99 square miles. The population-density rate in Tonga is about 362 people per square mile (58 in U.S.). Tongans, of Polynesian descent, make up the bulk of the population. There are also relatively small minorities of other Pacific islanders and Europeans.

Language: Tongan is the official language, but all government documents are in both Tongan and English. English is also used in business correspondence and is taught in secondary schools.

Religion: Nearly all Tongans are Christians. The royal family, nobles, and less than one-third of the people belong to the Wesleyan Church. The Church of Jesus Christ of Latter-day Saints (Mormon) is second largest, with the Catholic Church, the Independence Church of Tonga and the Church of Tonga following. Rules of the Sabbath are quite strict and widely upheld in Tonga. Virtually everything is closed on Sunday, except for emergency facilities.

LIFESTYLE

The Family: Families are close knit and take care of each other in almost every situation. One's immediate family includes grandparents, uncles, aunts, cousins, and others. In many cases, all family members work together to plant, harvest, cook, and fish. It is common for children to marry and still live with the husband's parents and grandparents. The average family in Tonga has 6.9 members, the largest in Asia and Oceania and the second largest in the world (3.1 in U.S.).

Dating and Marriage: Young people meet at school, church, or village activities. The traditional practice of dating only inside the girl's home gives the young man a chance to get to know the girl, her parents, and her family. Displays of affection, such as kissing between couples, or even parents and children, is not appropriate in public.

Social and Economic Levels: Homes in modern Tonga vary from the traditional coconut leaf and timber *fale* in rural areas to the frame, tin, or cinderblock *fale* in wealthier areas. All families own their homes, but often 2 or 3 families will live within the same house. All land is leased by heirship allotment from the nobles and owned by the King. For all intents and purposes, however, the land is "owned" by the residents. The people in Tonga generally are very healthy; the Tongan death rate of 1.9 per 1000 people is the lowest in the world.

Diet: Tongans traditionally eat 2 meals a day, which may consist of yams, taros, sweet potatoes, cassava, fish, pork, and cooked taro leaves—often with coconut cream and corned beef. Many different varieties of tropical fruits are also available, according to the season. The European style of meals, with a light, early breakfast and with later meals at noon and in the evening, is becoming popular.

Recreation: Tongans are very sports-minded. Rugby is the national sport. Most villages compete in rugby, cricket, volleyball, basketball, and tennis. Movies and dances are also major forms of recreation in the large villages. Younger boys play with marbles and slingshots. Girls have many games, and often are expert at juggling. People often drink *kava* root juice and converse late into the night. Picnics on the beach are for special occasions. Men are proficient in building boats, canoes, and houses as well as in wood carving. Women weave mats and baskets and make dolls and special flower *leis*.

Holidays: Holidays include July 4, which is the King's birthday (King Taufa'ahau Tupou IV), Christmas, New Year's, Easter, and some public holidays of the United Kingdom, celebrated as part of the British Commonwealth.

THE NATION

Land and Climate: Tonga is composed of 169 islands stretching across 500 miles from north to south in the Pacific Ocean. The total ground area of the islands combined is approximately the same size as the city of Dallas, Texas. Only 36 of Tonga's coral and volcanic islands are inhabited. Approximately 77% of the land is arable, which is the highest percentage in the world. Although Tonga is located in the tropics, there are few extremes in heat, rain, or humidity. Hurricanes are somewhat common, hitting mainly in February or March. The rainy season lasts from December to May, and the dry season from June to November.

History and Government: Tonga's hereditary monarchs date at least from the 1000s A.D. The power of the Tonga monarchy stretched as far as Hawaii in the 13th century. The islands were first visited by the Dutch in 1616. Captain James Cook, who discovered the islands in 1773 and visited again in 1777, named Tonga the "Friendly Islands" because of the way he was treated by the inhabitants. British missionaries arrived in 1797. Civil wars ended in 1845 with the establishment of the Tupou dynasty. George Tupou I, a

Christian, became the first king. Tonga became a British protectorate in 1900. Seventy years later, on June 4, 1970, Tonga gained complete independence and became a member of the British Commonwealth of Nations. The government consists of a king, a prime minister, and a partly-elected legislative assembly. Tonga's royalty are held in high esteem by their subjects. Currently, the king is King Taufa'ahau Tupou IV, and the prime minister is Prince Fatafehi Tu'ipelehake, the King's younger brother.

Economy: Agriculture and fishing are the mainstays of the economy. Main agricultural products include coconuts, bananas, taros, yams, sweet potatoes, and breadfruit. Less than 4% of the people are employed in industry, the fourth lowest percentage in the world. Copra (dried coconut meat which yields coconut oil) is the main export. The major imports are textiles, food, iron, steel, and petroleum products. Average annual gross national product (GNP) per capita is about $520 ($14,300 in U.S.). The basic unit of currency in Tonga is the *pa'anga*.

Education: The government provides free and compulsory education for children ages 6 to 14. Tonga is among the highest in the world in school enrollment per capita. Approximately two-thirds of the secondary school students attend church-sponsored schools. The government Teacher's Training School is the only post-high school in Tonga. The literacy rate is 90%.

Transportation and Communication: Public buses and taxis serve the entire island of Tongatapu, but are limited on other islands. Ferries travel between the islands and air service is also available to the four main island groups. Most Tongan people listen to the daily broadcasts of the one radio station. Television stations receive broadcasts from New Zealand and Australia. Few telephones are available.

Health: For specific medical information, contact International Health Consultants, PO Box 34582, Bethesda, MD 20817.

For Further Information

Because space is so limited in this *Culturgram* and needs are so varied, no suggested readings are included. We recommend a visit to your local library or bookstore. Check *Books in Print* and various cataloging systems for country-specific titles. Review *Encyclopedia Britannica* or similar comprehensive summaries. The U.S. government publishes *Country Profiles* which many libraries subscribe to. Computer searches (DIALOG, SDC, BRS, ISI) are now available at most major libraries. Contact the Tonga Visitors Bureau, C/O TCI, 700 S. Flower St., Suite 1704, Los Angeles, CA 90017.

How to Use This Culturgram

Quickly read the whole text as an overview. Then circle or give priority numbers to specific questions you have or ideas you want to pursue. Use the *Culturgram* as a guide to check on regional differences and current situations.

Maps

Culturgram maps are meant only as simple geographical orientations. Boundary representations are not necessarily authoritative. Different sources also vary spelling, transliterations, and accents.

Rev. 1/88

CULTURGRAM*

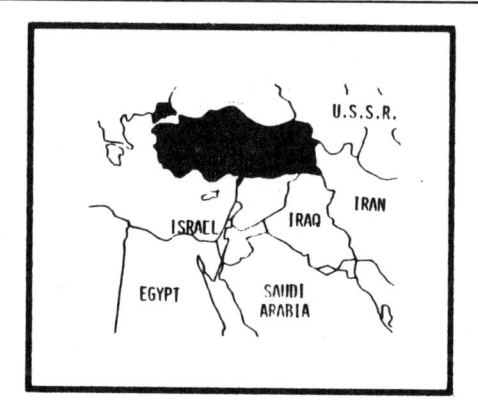

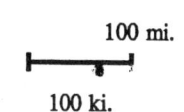

Republic of Turkey

CUSTOMS AND COURTESIES

Greetings: When greeting friends or strangers, one shakes hands and says *Merhaba* (Hello) or *nasilsiniz* (How are you?), to which the reply is *Iyiyim, teshekur ederim* (Fine, thanks!). When greeting a close friend of the same and sometimes the opposite sex, Turks clasp hands and kiss on both cheeks.

Clothing: In the major cities, Turks often judge people by their clothing. Accordingly, visitors should dress as well as they wish to be treated. Men should dress neatly; business suits are generally worn. Turks wear suits rather than slacks and sports coats. Casual dress should only be worn for informal occasions. Women generally wear skirts and dresses and do not bare their upper arms. Slacks are sometimes worn by the women. The rule is to dress modestly.

Visiting: Middle class Turks remove their shoes when entering a home. In most cases, guests should remove their shoes at the door and put on slippers. Hosts will probably say that it is not necessary, but it is best to insist on removing them. Visitors are supposed to bring a pleasant presence to a home; bad news or accounts of problems should be saved for other occasions. Avoid asking personal questions or bringing up controversial topics. Should such discussions

---

*Culturgrams are briefings to aid understanding of, feeling for, and communication with other people. Culturgrams are condensations of the best information available. Your insights will be appreciated. If you have refining suggestions, please contact Brigham Young University David M. Kennedy Center for International Studies, Publication Services, 280 HRCB, Provo, Utah 84602 (801) 378-6528. Copyright © 1986. All rights reserved. Printed in the USA.

arise, try to be sensitive to the Turkish point of view. Guests may wish to bring candy, fruit, or flowers to their host.

Gestures: Directing the sole of one's foot toward a Turk is an insult. It is considered rude for women to cross their legs if facing someone. Visitors should ask permission before smoking. However, Turks may insist that visitors be free to smoke even if they consider it improper. One should refrain from eating or smoking on the street.

THE PEOPLE

Population: An estimated 50 million (1984) people inhabit Turkey, a nation slightly larger than Texas. The capital city of Ankara in central Turkey has an estimated 2.5 million people. Turkey's largest and most famous city of Istanbul (historic Byzantium and Constantinople) has a population of approximately 5 million. It is the primary industrial, commercial, and intellectual center of the country. Located on both sides of the strait, Istanbul is the only city in the world to bridge two continents. About 50% of the nation's population reside in agricultural villages. Population growth is estimated at 2.2% (0.9% in U.S.).

Language: Turkish, which belongs to the Altaic language family (related to Mongolian and Manchu), is the principal language spoken by 90% of the population. Kurdish is spoken by about 7%. Arabic and Caucasian tongues comprise the remaining 3%. English, French, and German are the major foreign languages spoken.

Religion: The 1923 Turkish Constitution proclaimed Turkey a secular state. Approximately 90% of the people are Sunni Muslim. Non-Muslim groups have equal rights in Turkey but receive no governmental financial support. In 1924, the office of Caliph — the spiritual head of Islam — was abolished. Before the declaration of the Turkish republic, Turkey was the seat of the Caliph of the world's Muslim community. It is illegal for any religion to proselyte.

General: Turkey is often described as a bridge between East and West. The people have incorporated many European and Asian features into their thinking and lifestyle due to centuries of interaction with both. Despite this incorporation, the people are fiercely nationalistic — they are Turks, not Arabs. They are not semitic but descendants of various indigenous peoples and of Turkic tribes that moved into Anatolia in the 11th century A.D.

LIFESTYLE

Role Relationships: Turkey is a hierarchical society. Power flows from top to bottom. To accomplish more in less time, it is best to deal with the most powerful person in one's field. Dealing with lower personnel is often futile since they probably will not have the power to do what you need. Do not offer "bakhshish" (tips) in offices. If you recognize an obligation, trade favors rather than assume that they can be purchased.

Family, Marriage and Dating: The fundamental social unit in Turkey is the family. In the countryside, traditional values and practices still prevail. The Turkish household is an extended one, consisting of a husband and wife, their unmarried children, and in some cases married sons with their families until they are self-sufficient. It is uncommon for an individual to live alone, mostly for economic reasons. In 1927, Turkey adopted the Swiss civil code. Polygamy was ended in 1930; in 1934, women gained the right to divorce and civil marriage was introduced. Except on some university campuses, there is generally no dating as there is in the West. Young people tend to go out in groups. Still, there are major differences between the city and the country. In the city, people may date freely, while in the country they are closely chaperoned.

Social and Economic Levels: Turkey's economy varies greatly between the east and west. The west includes Istanbul, Izmir, and Ankara, and it is more advanced and industrialized. Factories and plants are numerous, agriculture is modernized and mechanized, and farms are richer and more productive. In addition, the west is more advanced culturally and has better roads, utilities, and services. As one travels east, society becomes more tribal and traditional. Agriculture is the major industry; traditional farming methods prevail.

Diet: Turkish cuisine is one of the best in the world. Bread is baked fresh daily everywhere, and lamb and rice are served with many dishes. On the coast, there is abundant seafood. Turkish coffee, a thick brew, was developed by the Ottomans. The largest meal is dinner, usually eaten in the late evening. Breakfast is light: tea, white cheese, bread, butter, jam or honey, and olives. Many hotels will serve a typical Western breakfast, except ham and bacon, of course, if asked. Practicing Muslims will not eat pork or drink alcohol. The favorite Turkish drink, however, is *raki* or *ouzo;* made from fermented grapes. Wine and beer are also readily available.

Work Schedule: Like Europe and the U.S., Turkey practices a Monday through Friday work week from 9 a.m. to 6 p.m. In the private sector, businesses will also work a full or half day on Saturday and frequently they will work later in the evening as well. Lunch is at noon, often lasting 1 or 2 hours.

Recreation: Most Turks are avid sports fans, and there are clubs for most every sport. Professional sports, such as soccer and basketball, are very popular. Turks have won many Olympic medals in wrestling, a traditional Turkish sport. August is when most people take vacations and head for the beaches. Picnics are popular, weather permitting.

Holidays: The ninth month of the Muslim lunar calendar is Ramazan (Ramadan in Arab countries), during which practicing Muslims fast from dawn to dusk. At the end of Ramazan there is a three-day holiday called *Seker Bayrami* (sugar holiday) during which sweets are eaten to celebrate the end of the feast. A second Muslim holiday is *Kurban Bayrami* (sacrifice holiday), which marks the season of pilgrimage to Mecca. It is celebrated by butchering an animal, frequently a sheep, and distributing the meat to the poor. Other official holidays include: New Year's, National Sovereignty Day (23 April), Ataturk's Memorial and Youth Day (19 May), Victory Day (30 August), which commemorates victory over the Greeks in the War of Independence, and Republic Day (29 October), which commemorates the founding of the Turkish Republic.

THE NATION

History: Modern Turkey is the most recent of a series of important states and empires that have inhabited the Anatolian peninsula since the beginning of history. The oldest known site of human urban habitation is located in central Turkey at Chatalhuyuk (6500 B.C.). The great Hittite Empire (2000–3000 B.C.) which dominated much of the Middle East was centered east of Ankara. Ancient Troy, the scene of much of Homer's Iliad, is located near the Dardanelles. Alexander the Great captured Anatolia in the fourth century B.C., and the Romans followed 3 centuries later, making important cities such as Ephesus and Antioch major provincial capitals. Christianity was brought to Anatolia by St. Paul, who addressed famous epistles to the Christians in Ephesus and Galatia (the area around modern Ankara). In 330 A.D., the Roman Emperor Constantine founded the city of Constantinople as the capital of the Eastern Roman Empire, subsequently the Christian Byzantine Empire. This great state dominated eastern Europe for 1,000 years. The Muslim Seljuk Turks entered Asia Minor in the 11th century and began the long process of Islamization and Turkization. In 1453, the successors of the Seljuks, the Ottoman Turks, captured Constantinople and went on to create a vast empire of their own which stretched beyond the bounds of the Byzantine Empire into the Balkans, the Middle East, and North Africa. The Ottoman Empire survived until World War I when it allied itself with the defeated Central Powers, at which point the empire was dismembered. Out of the ruins of the empire, Mustafa Kemal, a general in the Turkish army, fashioned the modern Republic of Turkey. Out of gratitude for Kemal's military and political genius, the Turkish parliament bestowed upon him the name of Ataturk (Father Turk). In 1952, Turkey joined NATO and has been a major base for U.S. military. In the past 3 decades, the country has gone through several cycles of political turmoil. In the late 1970s, serious economic problems and political upheaval which nurtured widespread domestic terrorism so paralyzed the government that the military was forced to seize control in 1980. After restoring stability to Turkey, the military called for new elections in 1983 and withdrew from power. The military commander, Kenan Evran, was subsequently elected president of Turkey.

Economy: Turkey's economy is primarily based on agriculture, which employs around 65% of the labor force. Turkey is self-sufficient in foodstuffs and also exports many products, primarily to other Middle Eastern countries. Agricultural goods comprise over half of Turkey's exports. Major agricultural products include cotton, tobacco, fruit, cereals, nuts, and opium for medicine. Textile and clothing production are Turkey's largest manufacturing industries, followed by ceramics, steel, and paper. The country produces a variety of mineral-based chemicals and metals. Turkey is one of the world's 3 largest producers of chromite. Remittances for more than a million Turks working abroad, most in Germany, are an important source of revenue. In 1987, inflation was about 40%. In 1983, GNP grew by 3.2% and per capita income was about $1,200. The nation is heavily indebted to outside creditors; the national debt is equal to almost 50% of the Turkish GNP.

Education: The government is highly concerned with educating the population but so far has been unable to meet all the needs of the people. There are great disparities between urban and rural facilities; overcrowding and shortages are common. Primary and secondary education is free and coeducational. These programs last until a student is 17 or 18. If the student wishes to proceed further, a state exam must be taken. Students are required to study either English, French, or German. There are 28 universities in Turkey, the oldest being Istanbul University, founded in 1453. There are more than 250 specialized colleges and institutions. The literacy rate is an estimated 65% in the cities, while the village rate is about half that.

Health: In rural areas, water, if cloudy, should be filtered and then boiled for 2 minutes. All tap water should be boiled for 2 minutes before drinking, however, excellent bottled water is available. Insure that all food is well cooked and served hot. Peel all fruit and vegetables before eating. Dairy products are of unreliable quality. Air pollution, especially in Ankara, is severe in winter. This can pose a problem for smokers and persons with chronic respiratory problems, allergies, etc. For further health and medical information, contact International Health Consultants, P.O. Box 34582, Bethesda, MD 20817.

For Further Information

Because space is so limited in this *Culturgram* and needs are so varied, no suggested readings are included. We recommend a visit to your local library or bookstore. Check *Books in Print* and various cataloging systems for country-specific titles. Review *Encyclopedia Britannica* or similar comprehensive summaries. The U.S. government publishes *Country Profiles* which many libraries subscribe to. Computer searches (DIALOG, SDC, BRS, ISI) are now available at most major libraries. Contact the Embassy of Turkey, 1606 23rd St., NW, Washington, DC 20008, or Turkish Tourism and Information, 821 United Nations Plaza, New York, NY 10017.

How to Use This Culturgram

Quickly read the whole text as an overview. Then circle or give priority numbers to specific questions you have or ideas you want to pursue. Use the *Culturgram* as a guide to check on regional differences and current situations.

Maps

Culturgram maps are meant only as simple geographical orientations. Boundary representations are not necessarily authoritative. Different sources also vary spelling, transliterations, and accents.

Rev. 1/88

CULTURGRAM*

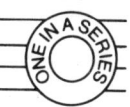

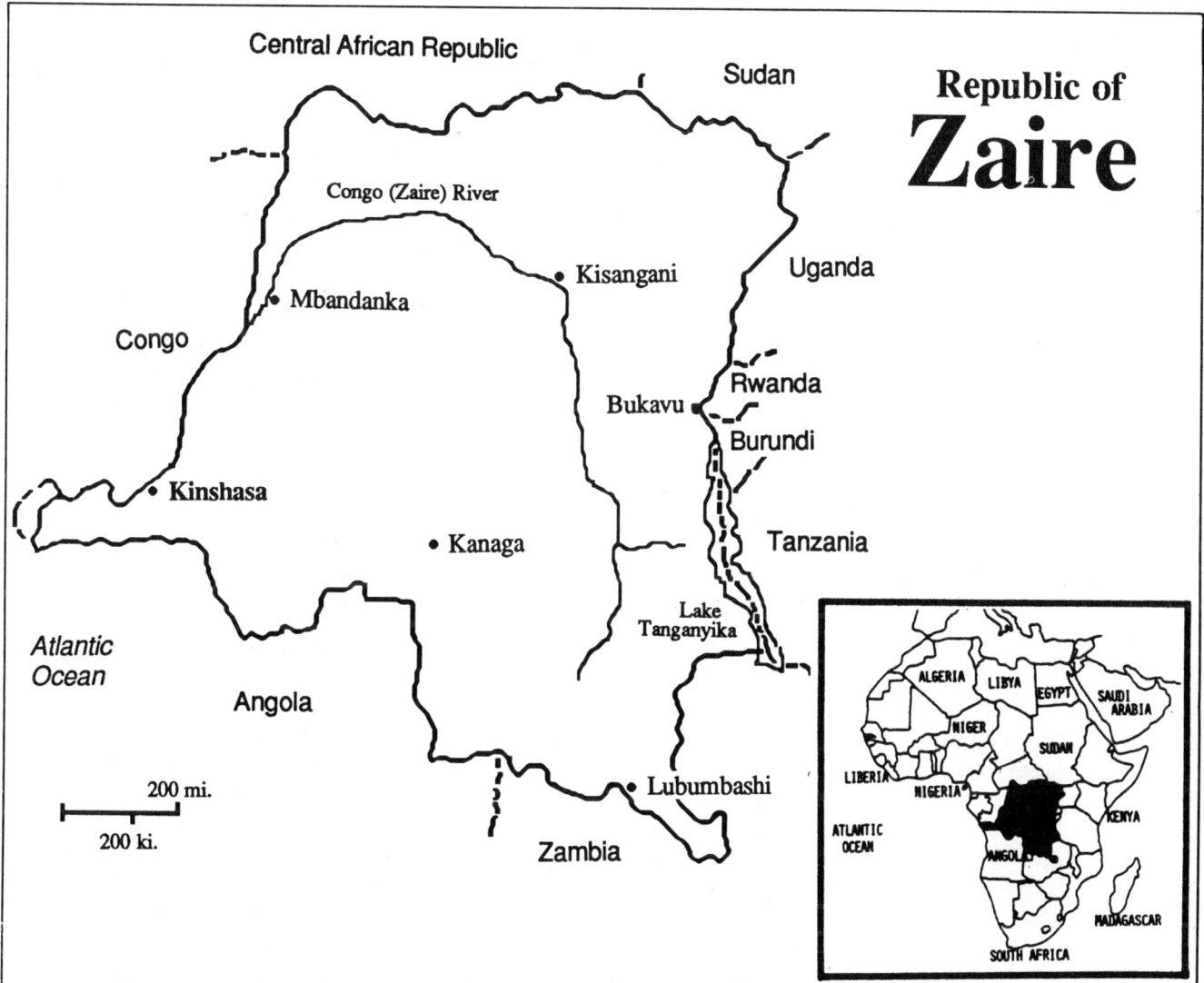

Republic of Zaire

CUSTOMS AND COURTESIES

Note: There are many differences in social customs and behavior in Zaire, reflecting the extremely large number of varying tribal cultures. Those described here are particularly appropriate for the Lingala-speaking population of western Zaire and the capital city of Kinshasa.

Greetings: In both urban and rural regions a handshake, a smile, and a *bon jour* are appropriate between members of the same sex. There is little public contact between men and women in Zaire.

Visiting: Gifts should be avoided when first visiting a Zairian urban home, but small gifts, such as food or an item for the house, may be given after a relationship is established. If a Zairian offers to share a meal, the visitor is expected to accept. If for any reason the guest is unable to eat, he should try some of the food as a gesture of goodwill. One should keep in mind that Zairians will judge the sincerity of their guests by the way they eat.

Eating: Except in the more westernized urban environments, meals are usually eaten using the fingers of the right hand only. Although it is rarely used, many families have western silverware and may bring it out to accommodate guests.

---

*Culturgrams are briefings to aid understanding of, feeling for, and communication with other people. Culturgrams are condensations of the best information available. Your insights will be appreciated. If you have refining suggestions, please contact Brigham Young University David M. Kennedy Center for International Studies, Publication Services, 280 HRCB, Provo, Utah 84602 (801) 378-6528. Copyright © 1986. All rights reserved. Printed in the USA.

Personal Appearance: Zairians wear a wide variety of clothing styles, including western, as well as traditional native dress. Visitors should wear conservative clothes. Shorts or immodest attire should not be worn in public.

THE PEOPLE

General Attitudes: The majority of the Zairian people are members of one of the many Bantu tribal groups. The majority of Bantu peoples share a common cultural heritage and set of behavioral traits. Most characteristic, perhaps, is the general politeness and genuine concern for the welfare of others. This politeness sometimes manifests itself as a gentle disposition and shyness with strangers, which visitors occasionally interpret as reticence. Although they may seem shy, Zairians will reciprocate open and sincere friendliness. Another characteristic of Zairian Bantu groups is abruptness in speech—requests may be made without a "please" and help accepted without a "thank you." This is not impolite, but simply a cultural habit: the words "please" and "thank you" are not native to the Bantu languages. Zairians appreciate personal efforts, but show their thanks through actions rather than words. The Zairian is always careful not to offend, and the desires of friends, family, and colleagues as well as maintaining the status quo are paramount forces controlling personal actions. Individualism is acceptable only if it does not conflict with group needs.

Population: Zaire has a population of approximately 33 million, with an annual growth rate of about 3%. Nearly half of the population is under the age of 15. Only 30% of the people are city dwellers. There are over 200 distinct tribal groups, with Bantu peoples accounting for the majority of the population. Minority groups include Pygmy, Nilo-Saharan, and Afro-Asiatic peoples who mainly inhabit the the northeastern part of the country. Although most groups increasingly identify themselves as Zairians, tribal affiliations remain strong. There are fewer than 1 million Europeans and Asians concentrated in urban areas. Kinshasa, the capital, has a population of approximately 3 million.

Language: With more than 700 different languages and dialects, Zaire has had to adopt a special language policy. Although French is the official language and is used in large business, education, and administration, it is spoken by only about 10% of the population. The majority of broadcasting, local business, and general daily communication occurs in 1 of 4 official regional languages (all Bantu). These are Lingala (largely in the west and in Kinshasa), Kikongo (in the west and southwest), Kiluba (central and southern Zaire), and Swahili (eastern Zaire). Most people speak their own tribal language as well as one or more of the regional languages. Lingala is the official language of the military, and is slowly emerging as the primary national language.

Religion: Approximately 90% of the population is nominally Christian (Roman Catholic 45%, Protestant 28%, indigenous Christian 17%), but there has been a great deal of mixing between Christianity and traditional animistic religions. There is a small Moslem minority (1%) primarily in the eastern sections of the country, and the remaining 9% practice native tribal religions.

LIFESTYLE

The Family: The family is the most important thing in life for the Zairian. Although family structure varies greatly from tribe to tribe, great emphasis is placed on group goals and overall family welfare. Extended families are the norm in Zaire, usually living under the same roof or in a group of closely joined homes. In western Zaire, families are mostly matriarchal, with the mother's brother as the the male with the greatest authority (not the husband). In other areas of the country, patriarchal, polygymous (multiple wives), and combinations of these family structures are common. Urban families, particularly among the more affluent, tend to become more outwardly patriarchal and include fewer relatives in the immediate family. The visitor is advised to remain very open-minded and understanding in contacts with Zairian families, for one may find patterns of behavior both alien and difficult to understand.

Dating and Marriage: Western-style dating occurs only among the affluent in large urban areas. Traditionally, marriage is a family affair and at least partly arranged by parents. In many parts of the country the preferred marriage partner is a cousin (one of the mother's brothers' children). That pattern is slowly changing, however, especially in urban areas.

Social Levels: There are relatively sharp socio-economic class distinctions in Zaire. The social ladder is largely unclimbable because one's social class is determined by birth. The upper class is politically, militarily, and economically dominant. It generally governs, however, in a benevolent manner.

Work and Recreation: Most people live in small villages and farm small plots of land or catch fish. In the cities, work is highly bureaucratic. Rural Zairians enjoy tribal gatherings with dancing and drum music. Many urban people spend their leisure time in bars, socializing, dancing, or listening to Zairian jazz. Soccer is the most popular sport.

Holidays: Zairian holidays include New Year Day, Commemoration of the Martyrs of Independence (January 4), Easter, Labor Day (May 1), MPR Day (May 20), Independence Day (June 30), Parents Day (August 1), Youth Day (October 14), Anniversary Day (October 27), Army Day (November 17), and Christmas.

THE NATION

Land and Climate: Zaire's land area (about the size of the U.S. east of the Mississippi River), is situated almost entirely within the equatorial zone. While the Mitumba mountain range in the far east is part of the Great Rift system, the bulk of Zaire lies within the vast, low-lying Congo (Zaire) River basin. The Congo is the world's fifth largest river, and is Zaire's major geographical feature. Most of the land is covered by lush tropical rain forest. The average annual temperature is 75°F. and the humidity is very high. Atlantic coastal temperatures and mountain temperature the far east are somewhat more moderate. Rainfall is frequent, except from April to October, and the average annual rainfall is approximately 62 inches.

History and Government: Long ago, Bantu peoples from western Africa penetrated the Congo basin. The powerful Bakongo people were in firm control of much of present Zaire when the Portuguese appeared in the late 1400s. Little European intervention, however, took place until the late 1800s, when Leopold II of Belgium formed an international trading company for purposes of exploiting the Congo region. The so-called Congo Free State, recognized by the Conference of Berlin in 1884, became in effect a feudal estate. In 1908, the area became part of Belgium, and was called the Belgian Congo. The harsh treatment of native peoples by the Belgian administration led to an independent Democratic Republic of the Congo in 1960. Soon after the first elections, the province of Katanga seceded, followed by general upheaval and unrest throughout the region. United Nations troops were called in to keep peace in the area. After years of bloody fighting, the revolts subsided in 1965. In 1971, the nation was renamed the Republic of Zaire, after the name originally given to the Congo River by the Portuguese. In an effort to create a sense of national identity, Zairians were asked to reject foreign models and to draw upon their own heritage in shaping their nation's future. As part of this national campaign, cities as well as individuals were required to replace their Christian or other foreign names with African names. The process of internal consolidation of the many variant tribal groups within Zaire has not yet been completed, and area loyalties have often shown themselves in difficult—and sometimes violent—confrontations with the Kinshasa government. Political stability seems to be gradually coming to the area, reflected in an increasingly solid, though still precarious, economic base. There is presently a single political party in Zaire (the Popular Movement of the Revolution or MPR), and the government is strongly centralized in the hands of the president, an advisory cabinet, and an elected 420-member National Legislative Council. The nation is divided into regions, each of which is further subdivided into smaller political jurisdictions.

Economy: Vast mineral deposits and other resources make Zaire potentially one of the richest nations in Africa, but this potential remains largely untapped. National per capita income is only

$110 ($14,300 in U.S.). The bulk of the labor force (75%) is involved in agriculture, and the country's main products are cassava, corn, palm oil, bananas, rice, and timber. Coffee is the major export crop. Zaire is the world's principal supplier of cobalt and industrial diamonds, and is a leading copper producer. Vast inland waterways and water resources give this country an estimated 13% of the world's hydroelectric potential, and a basic transportation infrastructure. As a former colony, Zaire's relations with Belgium remain important to both countries. Belgium is Zaire's principal trading partner and source of technical assistance.

Education: The literacy rate is approximately 40% for men and 15% for women. About 80% of school-age children are in school. The government is very much aware of the need for increased educational facilities. The Ministry of Education's budget is regularly one of the greatest governmental expenditures in the country, but lack of funds makes progress difficult. The National University of Zaire has several campuses, and there are 32 trade and professional schools.

Health: There are very few physicians (one for every 15,000 people) in Zaire at present. Boiled water must be used for ice cubes, brushing teeth, etc., and is provided by major hotels. Make sure all food is well cooked and served hot, and that all fruits and vegetables are peeled before eating. Medical help can be found in Kinshasa, but evacuation to South Africa is recommended for serious medical attention. Adequate health care is a major problem, particularly in rural areas. The Zairian government is acutely aware of this problem and is attempting to improve medical care. For further information contact International Health Consultants, PO Box 34582, Bethesda, MD 20817.

For Further Information

Because space is so limited in this *Culturgram* and needs are so varied, no suggested readings are included. We recommend a visit to your local library or bookstore. Check *Books in Print* and various cataloging systems for country-specific titles. Review *Encyclopedia Britannica* or similar comprehensive summaries. The U.S. government publishes *Country Profiles* which many libraries subscribe to. Computer searches (DIALOG, SDC, BRS, ISI) are now available at most major libraries. Contact the Embassy of Zaire, 1800 New Hampshire Ave., N.W., Washington, D.C. 20009 or the Zaire Tourist Office, P.O. Box 12348, Kinshasa, Zaire. The U.S. Embassy in Zaire is located at 310 Avenue des Aviateurs, Kinshasa, Zaire.

How to Use This Culturgram

Quickly read the whole text as an overview. Then circle or give priority numbers to specific questions you have or ideas you want to pursue. Use the *Culturgram* as a guide to check on regional differences and current situations.

Maps

Culturgram maps are meant only as simple geographical orientations. Boundary representations are not necessarily authoritative. Different sources also vary spelling, transliterations, and accents.

Rev. 1/88

CULTURGRAM*

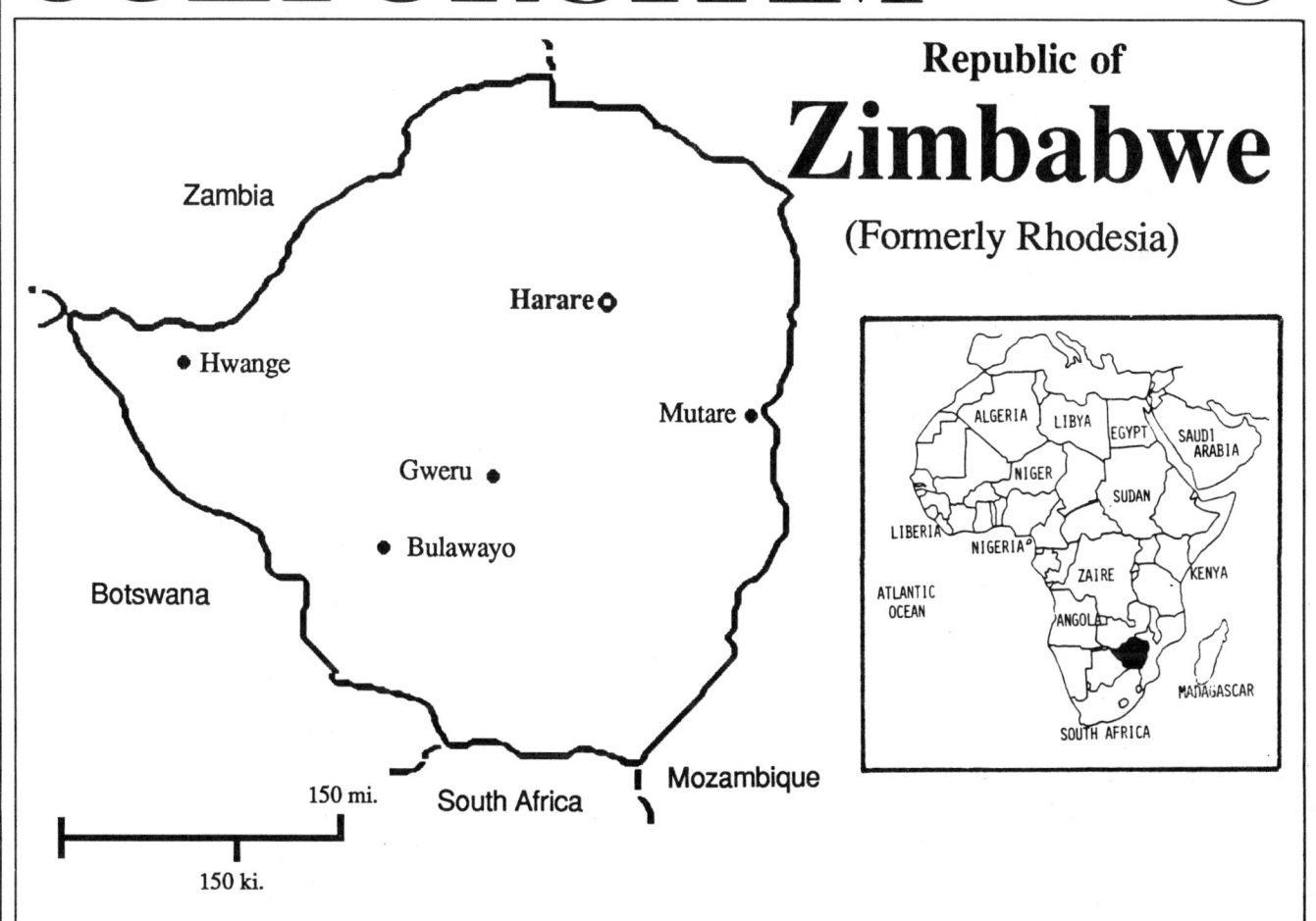

Republic of Zimbabwe
(Formerly Rhodesia)

CUSTOMS AND COURTESIES

Greetings: A handshake is commonly used in greeting. "Good morning, how are you?" is the usual greeting understood by all language groups. Traditionally, to pass a stranger without any word of greeting was considered bad manners, though this is no longer true in the cities.

Visiting: The pace of life is much slower in country villages, than in the cities. In the rural areas, one may either sit or stand without waiting for an invitation. In the more westernized urban areas, one should wait for an invitation to sit down. In the cities, one should also be more careful to be on time for appointments. Small gifts for both urban and rural families are appreciated but not necessary. Gifts for the children or useful gifts for the family are good choices. Visitors create a good impression if they listen carefully and attempt to understand their hosts' feelings. It is important to be both patient and polite in conversation. Zimbabweans are very conscious of sarcastic language and respond negatively to pomposity.

Gestures: Traditionally, a gift was given and accepted with both hands. This is still practiced, particularly in the rural areas. Clapping the hands is a gesture of thanks and politeness. Women and girls, particularly in the rural areas, often curtsy. Direct eye contact during conversation is viewed as rude, especially in the rural areas. Although more westernized people may tolerate direct eye contact, it is advisable to avoid it.

---

*Culturgrams are briefings to aid understanding of, feeling for, and communication with other people. Culturgrams are condensations of the best information available. Your insights will be appreciated. If you have refining suggestions, please contact Brigham Young University David M. Kennedy Center for International Studies, Publication Services, 280 HRCB, Provo, Utah 84602 (801) 378-6528. Copyright © 1986. All rights reserved. Printed in the USA.

Personal Appearance: Generally speaking, Zimbabweans dress in western-style clothes. Smartness in dress is more important than it is in the U.S. For men, a suit is the preferred attire for conducting business. Formal clothing is common during the week, especially during business hours. Some social gathering places require a jacket and tie. Young girls sometimes wear shorts, but generally women wear long and short cotton dresses, in both modern and traditional styles.

THE PEOPLE

General Attitudes: Zimbabwe has an interesting variety of customs. It is in many ways a very modern and developed country. In an urban environment, one can expect to find the cosmopolitan habits that prevail in the cities of the western world. Hotels are plentiful and well run. The food is excellent and the water is safe to drink. In the remote rural districts, the food and customs are more traditional. To avoid social mistakes one should follow the host's example (e.g., washing hands, eating with fingers, etc.). Zimbabweans are generally very friendly, cheerful, and courteous people. However, they dislike sarcasm and loud, showy behavior; humility is highly esteemed. Because of many years of colonial subjection and racial discrimination, black Zimbabweans are sensitive to racism.

Population: The population of Zimbabwe is more than 8.6 million and is growing at a rate of 3.3% annually, one of the highest growth rates in Africa and the world. Ninety-six percent of the people are black—77% Shona and 19% Ndebele. There are also about 200,000 whites, including those of British descent and a small population of Greeks. There are also some small minorities of coloureds (mixed race) and Asians. Only 19% of the population lives in urban areas (78% in U.S.). The population density is only 40 people per square mile (58 in U.S.).

Language: English is the official language and is spoken by all whites and most educated blacks. In the rural areas, however, most of the people do not understand English and converse in their native tongues. The Shona language is spoken by about 85% of the people and Ndebele is used mainly in the west. It is quite common to hear people mix several languages in daily usage.

Religion: There are many established Christian churches and missions, and a few religious minorities (Judaism, Hinduism, and Islam). Traditional African religions, in which respect for ancestors plays an important role, are still widely practiced in rural areas. Many of the people practice a mixture of Christian and traditional faiths.

LIFESTYLE

The Family: The father is usually the leader of the family unit, but the mother also exercises considerable influence in the home. Two different types of family life are to be found in Zimbabwe. The traditional, extended family unit is strongly evident in the rural areas. However, in many urban areas, the tendency is toward the nuclear family unit.

Dating and Marriage: In the past, marriages were often arranged by families and affection was never shown in public. However, these practices are being replaced by modern social patterns. Marriage customs usually follow family tradition. When a couple signifies that they want to marry, many customary visits and gifts are exchanged between the groom's representative and the bride's family. A bridal token, known as *roora* (or *lobola*) is paid to the bride's parents. A wedding ceremony in church for a Christian couple is often one of many ceremonies that mark the marriage.

Social and Economic Levels: A wide gap still exists between the urban and rural populace. Electricity and piped water are not yet available in most villages, but some conveniences are available. Televisions are available in the towns, and many people also have telephones and refrigerators. Cars are still considered more of a luxury. Only the people living in urban areas are able to enjoy a relatively high standard of living. The government is currently making strenuous efforts to improve the standard of living, especially among the poor.

Work: In cities, businesses and shops are open Monday through Friday, from 8:00 or 8:30 a.m. to 5:00 or 5:30 p.m. Shops remain open until 12 noon on Saturday. Small shops, where necessities and perishables are sold, are open longer and on Sundays. Shops in the rural areas keep more flexible hours.

Diet: *Sadza*, a stiff porridge made from maize meal, is the staple food of most Zimbabweans. It is garnished with various local vegetables, or meat when available. In the cities, people tend to eat a more western diet, with more meat, and potatoes or rice instead of *sadza*. Fine cuisine is served in hotels in metropolitan areas. Locally grown fruits, such as mangoes, bananas, melons, guavas, and paw-paws (papaya) are enjoyed at various times of the year. Tea is a very popular drink and is frequently served at office visits or social calls.

Recreation: Soccer is the favorite sport, but tennis, boxing, rugby, cricket, polo, bowling, squash, golf, and horse-racing are enthusiastically pursued by various sections of the population. Swimming in open-air pools is a favorite pastime, but swimming in rivers and dams is dangerous because of *bilharzia* (a disease of the liver carried in African rivers since ancient times).

Holidays: The following holidays are celebrated in Zimbabwe: New Year's Day (January 1), Good Friday (date varies), Easter Monday (date varies), Independence Day (April 18), Worker's Day (May 1), Africa Day (May 25), Heroes' Day (August 11 and 12), and Christmas (December 25).

THE NATION

Land and Climate: Zimbabwe is slightly larger than the state of Montana. It is an inland country, but the pleasant climate of the high grasslands 5,000 feet above sea level makes up for the lack of a seaboard. Although Zimbabwe is in the tropics, the altitude ensures cool, sunny winter months (May to August) and summers that are not unbearably hot (September to April). The rains during these summer months can be heavy, but are rarely continuous. Rivers, lakes, mountainous areas, game-parks, wide expanses of open country, and pleasant towns and cities, with their white buildings and colorful flowering trees, are characteristic of Zimbabwe.

History and Government: Between the 9th and 13th centuries A.D., a group of people who had established trading contacts with commercial centers on Africa's southeastern coast lived in this area. In the 15th century, the Karanga people (ancestors of the Shona) established a major trading empire at Great Zimbabwe (near present-day Masvingo). The empire lasted until the end of the 17th century, when it came under Portuguese domination. In 1830 the Ndebele people entered the area and conquered the Karanga. In the 1890s, white people began to trek north from South Africa hoping to discover new gold fields. The countries of Matabeland (home of the Ndebele) and Mashonaland (home of the Shona) were claimed by Cecil John Rhodes for England, under the terms of a Royal Charter from Queen Victoria, and became known as Rhodesia. In 1965 the white minority government, led by Prime Minister Ian Smith, issued a declaration of independence from the United Kingdom. However, it took pressure from foreign countries (particularly Britain and the United States) and several years of civil war before Zimbabwe regained its independence in 1980 and set up a government based on the black majority. Zimbabwe's constitution provides for a figurehead president, a prime minister who is the head of the government, and a parliament composed of a Senate and a House of Assembly. Currently Canaan Banana is president and Robert G. Mugabe is prime minister. Zimbabwe is a member of the U.N., the Non-Aligned Movement, the O.A.U. (Organization of African Unity), and S.A.D.C.C. (Southern African Development Co-Ordination Conference). Political strife continues to afflict the country.

Economy: The gross national product (GNP) per capita in Zimbabwe is $870 annually ($14,300 in U.S.). The economy is growing at a rate of 2% annually (0.9% in U.S.), one of the highest growth rates in Africa. Before the declaration of independence in 1965, Rhodesia was, along with South Africa, the most economically developed country in sub-Sahara Africa. But the U.N. economic sanctions and the cost of anti-guerrilla operations took a heavy toll. Today, agriculture, mining, and manufacturing are the most important aspects of the economy. The principal crops are maize, sugar, wheat, cotton, tobacco (Zimbabwe is Africa's leading producer of tobacco), groundnuts, sorghum, *munga* (cereal) and *rapoko* (cereal). Minerals mined are gold (Zimbabwe is the world's 5th largest producer of gold), asbestos, chrome, coal, copper, and nickel. Manufacturing includes foodstuffs, textiles, clothing, footwear, furniture, paper, chemical and petroleum products, nonmetallic mineral products, metals, and metal products. The inflation rate is typically higher than in the U.S. The currency is the Zimbabwe dollar, divided into 100 cents.

Education: The literacy rate in Zimbabwe is approximately 50%. The government is working towards free, compulsory education for all. There are many primary and secondary schools owned by the government or by church-sponsored missions. Some private, high-status, schools requiring tuition still exist. There are also several teacher-training colleges, and one university in Harare. There is a Polytechnic in Harare and one in Bulawayo, where technical and commercial training is offered. Private educational institutions are located only in the major cities.

Transportation: Nearly 3% of the people own cars, which, though low by western standards, is quite high by African standards. Buses are the principal means of transportation in the rural areas. They do not always run on schedule. Buses in the towns are more reliable, but may not run frequently. Many urban dwellers own cars, some of which are used as "pirate" taxis. Taxis are readily available in the cities and larger towns. Bicycles are common, especially among school children. A railway connects the main cities. Because Zimbabwe is landlocked, it is highly dependent on ports in South Africa and Mozambique.

Health: The towns and cities are clean, with high standards for plumbing, water, and sanitation. The rural areas present a very different picture, and great efforts are being made to improve the quality of life in rural areas. The malarial mosquito has been almost eradicated in the towns, although it is still advisable to take a malaria treatment if living or traveling in the rural, low-lying areas. Swimming in rivers should be avoided. For further medical information contact International Health Consultants, PO Box 34582, Bethesda, MD 20817.

For Further Information

Because space is so limited in this *Culturgram* and needs are so varied, no suggested readings are included. We recommend a visit to your local library or bookstore. Check *Books in Print* and various cataloging systems for country-specific titles. Review *Encyclopedia Britannica* or similar comprehensive summaries. The U.S. government publishes *Country Profiles* which many libraries subscribe to. Computer searches (DIALOG, SDC, BRS, ISI) are now available at most major libraries. Contact the Embassy of Zimbabwe, 2852 McGill Terrace, N.W., Washington, D.C. 20008, or the Zimbabwe National Tourist Board, 525 Fifth Ave., New York, NY 10017. The U.S. Embassy in Zimbabwe is located at 172 Rhodes Ave., (P.O. Box 3340), Harare, Zimbabwe.

How to Use This Culturgram

Quickly read the whole text as an overview. Then circle or give priority numbers to specific questions you have or ideas you want to pursue. Use the *Culturgram* as a guide to check on regional differences and current situations.

Maps

Culturgram maps are meant only as simple geographical orientations. Boundary representations are not necessarily authoritative. Different sources also vary spelling, transliterations, and accents.

Rev. 1/88